P9-AGA-327

THE HEALTH OF NEWCOMERS

The Health of Newcomers

Immigration, Health Policy, and the Case for Global Solidarity

Patricia Illingworth and Wendy E. Parmet

NEW YORK UNIVERSITY PRESS

New York

NEW YORK UNIVERSITY PRESS
New York
www.nyupress.org

References to Internet websites (URLs) were accurate at the time of writing. Neither the author nor New York University Press is responsible for URLs that may have expired or changed since the manuscript was prepared.

ISBN: 978-0-8147-8921-6

For Library of Congress Cataloging-in-Publication data, please contact the Library of Congress.

New York University Press books are printed on acid-free paper, and their binding materials are chosen for strength and durability. We strive to use environmentally responsible suppliers and materials to the greatest extent possible in publishing our books.

Manufactured in the United States of America

10 9 8 7 6 5 4 3 2 1

Also available as an ebook

For

Joan Illingworth (1928–2015)

and

Ron Lanoue

CONTENTS

ACKNOWLEDGMENTS

This book would not have been possible without the inspiration, guidance, and assistance of many practitioners, scholars, and students. We are deeply grateful to Lorianne Sainsbury-Wong for helping to introduce us to the plight of immigrants who are denied access to health care, and also to Matt Selig, Steve Rosenfeld, and the rest of the legal team behind the *Finch* case for teaching us about the legal rights of immigrants.

We also want to thank Deans Emily Spieler and Jeremy Paul of Northeastern University School of Law for supporting this book and Deans Uta Poiger and Laura Frader from the College of Social Sciences and Humanities for their support. Susan Setta and Ronald Sandler, chair of the Department of Philosophy and Religion, were also supportive, and we are grateful to them.

Many students at Northeastern University have assisted in the research for this book. Special thanks are owed to Maureen Nothnagle, Karim Sabbidine, Alissa Brill, Adam Cernea Clark, Ashley Jones-Pierce, Brett Watson, Anne Sheldon, Caitlin Perry, Frank Vitale, Isabelle Lew, Jennifer Huer, Julie Lum, Julie Gharagouzloo, Kristi Marcinik, Lindsey Cei, Meredith Lever, Michelle Virshup, Michael Spera, Natalie Higgins, Tristan Sullivan-Wilson, Christine Sunnerberg, and Stephanie Parker. Ben Flickner, Jan McNew, and Keith Wise provided excellent administrative support. Law librarian Scott Akehurst-Moore provided invaluable assistance, especially with international materials. We are also enormously grateful to Henry Shull for his outstanding research and for helping to bring the final manuscript to press.

Introduction

Natives and Newcomers, Partners in Health

Over 200 million of us are newcomers, travelers, and migrants living outside our nation of birth. Newcomers and natives alike live, work, play, and die together, a fact that became increasingly evident in 2015, as a rapid surge in migration from the Middle and Near East and North Africa led to more than a million newcomers arriving in Europe.

Across the globe, the increasing presence of newcomers has sparked intense backlashes. Buffeted by years of economic austerity, as well as fears of terrorism, epidemics, and a changing way of life, many natives have turned against newcomers and have demanded that their nations take bold and even punitive steps to stop the flow of migrants. But 2015's rapid rise in migration, including many forced migrants, also prompted expressions of generosity and solidarity, as doctors and nurses working for NGOs cared for the refugees as they arrived in Europe, and communities across the West opened their doors and hearts to new neighbors. Both reactions, the generous and the fearful, illustrate the complex and intense reactions that migration invites, as well as the increasing interdependency of newcomer and native.

The recent increase in human migration has coincided with a renewed awareness of the risks of microbial migration, and the interdependency of human health. In 2014, the world witnessed the worst Ebola epidemic to date, with more than 11,000 people dying of the disease in West Africa. Although the disease did not spread widely outside that region, with only a few cases occurring in the United States and Europe, Ebola underscored the interdependency of human health across the globe. The resources and efforts that the international community eventually invested to combat the epidemic, albeit late in coming, also demonstrated a recognition that in our global age, the health of people in one part of the globe affects the health of people living far away. Or, as we shall argue, health is at least partially a global public good.

In this book we explore the connections and implications of these two insights—the interdependency of newcomer and native, and the public good aspect of health, arguing that the latter has important normative implications for how nations ought to respond to the health threats posed by as well as the needs presented by newcomers.

In so doing, we seek not only to demonstrate why it is rational and moral for nations to treat the health interests of natives and newcomers alike, but also to dispel myths about newcomers, that have undermined the willingness of natives to promote the health interests of newcomers as they would those of family and compatriots. For example, we show that contrary to the widely held belief that newcomers are especially unhealthy, newcomers are healthier in general than natives. We also argue that contrary to the belief that poor countries are responsible for their own health problems, the global economic structure, often instituted at the behest of wealthy countries, has contributed to the ill health of many of those who live in many poor countries. In addition, one of the key social determinants for health is inequality, both globally and nationally. Inequality hurts health. Although one might expect that inequality would hurt the health of the poor because they cannot afford food, shelter, medications, and top medical care, it hurts not only the poor, but all people, including affluent natives in wealthy countries.

Our goal in dispelling myths about migration and health is to unpack the many ways in which these myths have infiltrated public policy at the intersections of immigration and health. As we show, far too many policies that relate to immigrants and health undermine public health rather than securing it. Many of these policies are also, we argue, morally indefensible. Our hope is that once weaned from false beliefs about both newcomers and health, nations will tear down old policies relating to the health of newcomers and replace them with new approaches that are more effective in protecting the health of both natives and newcomers and more respectful of the rights of newcomers.

Plan of This Book

We begin in chapter 1 by offering some illustrations, in all-too-human terms, of the harms caused when health policies are infected by anti-immigration sentiment. We then survey the state of global migration today, a survey that illuminates both the diversity of newcomers, and the falsity of many commonly held beliefs about them. Chapter 1 concludes with a brief analysis of what we mean by health, and the factors that help shape human health. This relatively brief discussion lays the foundation for a thorough treatment of health as a public good later in the book.

Having introduced migration and health, we turn in the next four chapters to a review and critique of some of the laws and policies, both in the United States and across the globe, that lie at the nexus of health and migration. These chapters reveal the often-subtle ways in which myths about immigrants undermine health policy, and how misunderstandings about the nature of health have complicated immigration law. They also provide the policy backdrop for the normative arguments we develop in subsequent chapters. In effect, chapters 2 through 5 lay out and analyze the current policy climate, which is subjected to a normative challenge in later chapters.

Chapter 2, "Keep Out!: Immigration Control as Public Health Protection," focuses on health-based immigration exclusions. As we demonstrate, human beings have long blamed people who appear to be different, including minorities and members of already stigmatized populations, for disease, especially for new and fearsome diseases. Immigrants have borne the brunt of this scapegoating, which has led nations to impose a range of health and disability-based limitations on immigration. For the most part, these exclusions are ineffective from a public health perspective. Rather than protecting the health of natives, they divert resources from effective public health interventions. They also reinforce the misimpression that nations can be free of disease and disability if only the "other" is kept out. By so doing, these policies not only add to the stigma experienced by newcomers but also exacerbate the stigma laid upon natives who live with the excluded conditions.

While chapter 2 examines how a false association between immigrants and disease drives immigration policy, chapter 3 considers the impact of public health policies that pertain to newcomers once they are in their new nations. We begin by noting that nations have a duty both normatively and under international law to protect the health of their populations. But far too often, states attempt to do so by restricting the liberties of immigrants. In effect, public health policies become meshed with, and offer a rationale for, punitive, anti-immigration measures.

We first illustrate the troubling association between public health protection and anti-immigrant policies by reviewing the history of the battles in the late nineteenth and early twentieth centuries between health authorities in San Francisco and that city's Chinese community, a struggle that helped establish the constitutional limits of state authority over non-citizens in the United States. Next we turn to an examination of public policies regarding tuberculosis. In many ways tuberculosis offers the strongest case for the disparate use of public health legal powers against immigrants. Tuberculosis is today the one significant communicable disease found more frequently in immigrant than native populations. Still, we argue, the threat of TB posed by newcomers is overstated. Moreover, the disparate use of highly coercive legal restraints such as isolation and quarantine on immigrants can never be justified. Both domestic and international human rights law sanction the use of significant restraints of liberty in the name of public health only when they are the least-restrictive means necessary for protecting public health. If less-restrictive means are available to natives, they must be used on newcomers. Moreover, we contend, at least in the case of tuberculosis, highly restrictive policies, such as enforced isolation, are likely to be ineffective for a number of reasons, including the fact that they deter people from seeking treatment. When it comes to public health, access to culturally competent health care is far more apt to be effective than policies that look "tough" on immigrants.

In chapters 4 and 5 we turn to policies affecting immigrants' access to health care, focusing in particular on access to the insurance that is so often necessary to pay for health care. Chapter 4 looks at the issue within the United States. Although the United States, unique among developed nations, does not ensure that all of its citizens have access to health care, it has established a complex patchwork of federal and state health insurance programs to cover large numbers of citizens. Some classes of immigrants are eligible for some of these programs. But many newcomers, especially those who are undocumented, are left without insurance.

Indeed, after the implementation of the Affordable Care Act, widely known as Obamacare, the uninsurance problem in the United States has become, to a large degree, an immigration problem.

But it is too simple to assert that the United States denies immigrants access to health care. The actual situation is far more nuanced, and more perplexing. Our survey of US policies pertaining to immigrants' access to care shows a tangle of inconsistent and conflicting policies, some opening the door to immigrants, others shutting the door. This morass, we contend, reveals deep conflicts in our attitudes toward the health of immigrants. At times we understand that newcomers are part of our communities, and that we cannot for both normative and pragmatic reasons ignore their health care needs. At other times, we seek to deny their participation in our health care system, often based on the false belief that including them will draw them to our borders.

The result of these inconsistent policies, we show in chapter 4, is a system that is far more complex and confused than it should be. Thus the complexity and fragmentation for which the US health care system is infamous is made worse by the inconsistent and incoherent policies that relate to newcomers. But even more problematic is the fact that the exclusions and inconsistencies are bad for the health of both newcomers and natives. As chapter 4 shows, because natives live among newcomers, and use the same health care institutions, they are affected when the diseases of newcomers are left untreated, or their providers are left unpaid.

Chapter 5 continues the exploration of immigrants' access to health care by looking at the situation in nations that purport to respect a human right to health, especially Canada and the nations within the European Union. As we explain, international human rights law establishes a right to health that demands that nations, subject to resource limitations, assure the means for accessing necessary health care services. There are strong reasons to conclude that that right to health applies in full force to newcomers, including those who are undocumented. However, caveats and limitations included in many international legal documents offer some support for a more limited conclusion: that nations must provide undocumented immigrants only with emergency care.

In fact, as our survey demonstrates, many nations, including some proclaiming respect for the right to health, provide less than full participation in their national health care programs for noncitizen newcomers.

Indeed, several nations provide only the bare minimum to undocumented newcomers. Many other nations impose a range of limitations and barriers that make it difficult for newcomers, sometimes even those with quasi-legal status, from attaining care. In short, once we focus on the health of newcomers it becomes all too apparent that even so-called universal health care systems are not really universal. And in these nations, as in the United States, the erection of barriers to care has had a deleterious impact on the health of both newcomers, and potentially natives.

After discussing in chapters 2 through 5 the myriad and problematic ways in which immigration and health policy intersect, and how myths about newcomers undermine nations' attempts to protect health, we turn in chapters 6 through 8 to a fuller discussion of the public and global nature of health. This analysis provides the foundation for the moral argument and policy recommendations that appear in chapters 9 and 10.

In chapter 6, "Health as a Global Public Good," we argue that health has global public good dimensions. In this respect we depart from the standard view, which generally holds that health is a private good. Understanding health as a global public good underscores the fact that when it comes to health we are all in this together. This means that we are likely to cause more harm in general if we treat health as a private good, and create more good when we recognize health's public good dimensions.

This conclusion would certainly resonate with utilitarians. Attending to the health needs of newcomers and citizens alike will produce better health for both, a conclusion that we demonstrated empirically in prior chapters and support conceptually in chapter 6. For example, in a context in which natives and newcomers dwell together, often intimately, if we only treat the health needs of natives and ignore those of newcomers, the health of both will be compromised. If newcomers are left untreated, their illness will have consequences for both natives and newcomers. In a world in which natives and newcomers live side by side, ignoring the health of the latter is at the health peril of the former.

The insight that health is a global public good does double duty in this volume. It grounds practical and self-interested reasons for treating newcomers and natives in the same way, and provides a utilitarian foundation for doing so. In subsequent chapters we provide additional moral reasons for equal treatment.

In chapter 7 we explain that our obligation to treat the health needs of newcomers is not solely based on the good outcomes that will follow. Instead, we show that receiving nations have strict moral duties to newcomers, based on the harms that they have caused to the global poor. In other words, following philosopher Thomas Pogge and others, we argue that people in affluent countries have strict moral duties to people in poor countries because of the role affluent countries have played with respect to poverty and, in turn, health. Given this, the duty to fulfill the health rights of newcomers is morally demanding. It is not only that it would be good and charitable for us to recognize newcomers' health rights, we are morally obligated to do so because of the harms we have caused, and the attending moral responsibility to address them.

Taken together, chapters 6 and 7 show that it is in the interest of receiving countries to attend to the health of newcomers because health is a global public good, and that because affluent nations have compromised the health of the global poor, they have duties to address those harms.

The global nature of health, as well as the claim that receiving nations have duties to newcomers, are further developed in chapter 8. In "Strangers for the Sake of Health," we introduce three ways in which health is treated as a global resource by people in affluent nations, and in some cases people from the same nations that draw migrants to their shores. First, and significantly for both sending and receiving nations, many health care workers migrate from poor countries, overburdened with disease, to affluent nations. Unfortunately, this practice often leaves poor sending countries without enough health workers to meet their own needs, even when they have subsidized the training and education of health workers. Second, we discuss the example of medical tourism, the growing practice of people from wealthy countries traveling to other countries, often very poor countries, in order to purchase health care, ranging from knee and hip surgery to cosmetic surgery. Typically, patients travel to other nations for medical care because it is less expensive than what is available in their home country. Medical tourism can have harmful consequences for the health of people in the poor nations where care is received. Medical tourists can be a lucrative source of income for medical workers—shifting their interest and expertise from local patients and their needs to the needs of international patients. Finally, we consider the example of international transplantation in which people travel to another country to both purchase an organ and to have the transplantation done. Again, this can have an adverse impact on the health of natives.

These examples of health's global dimension illustrate two points. First, they show that health is a global undertaking in some significant ways, and that affluent nations have made substantial use of the health resources of poor countries. Morally, this raises concerns about reciprocity and fairness. For our purposes, it shows that although natives express fear and sometimes hysteria about the health of newcomers and the diseases they carry, the natives of wealthy countries also are eager to use the health resources of the very nations from which the newcomers migrate. It would not be surprising to find, for example, that a migrant nurse from Africa is not only the object of fear that he might bring a loathsome disease, putting natives at risk, but also the very same person caring for patients in a hospital in Canada. Rather than consider what this might demonstrate about the bias against newcomers, especially when it comes to redistribution of wealth to "strangers," we think it demonstrates reason for optimism—namely, that when it comes to strangers, whether next door, or across the ocean, people from affluent countries are able to trust those in poor countries. The ability to trust strangers is important not only for health reasons. It also speaks to the possibility of natives acting in solidarity with newcomers for the sake of newcomers' health.

In chapter 9, we develop this point and argue that solidarity need not be tied to citizenship and that it is indeed possible for natives to act in solidarity with migrants, for the sake of the health of newcomers. Not only is it possible for trust and solidarity to exist among diverse people, but we argue, using Iris Young's notion of structural injustice, that it is morally indicated. For Young, duties of solidarity are triggered in part by our connection to a harm and ability to effectively change the injustice. There is an enormous amount of injustice in the world, and people in affluent nations are tied to much of it, whether by recruiting scarce migrant workers or buying inexpensive clothes made in factories that exploit workers. Arguably, it would be difficult, if not, impossible to redress all the injustice with which we are implicated. Using Young's parameters, we argue that the health of newcomers has priority both because our ties are close, but also because the health infrastructure is in place to effect the change.

In the final chapter, "Natives and Newcomers: Moving Forward Together," we employ the 2014 Ebola outbreak as a case study to show the continuing relevance of the fear of strangers and resulting irrational health policy. But we also look at how international actors galvanized in the end to help the people of West Africa.

We note that the willingness of nations and international agents from around the globe to come to the aid of the people of West Africa, at some cost to themselves, should give rise to a sense of optimism about the future. Norms about our obligation to help strangers seem to be in the midst of radical change: mainstream *Time* magazine honored the international Ebola workforce as its Person of the Year in 2014. Leadership is critical to norm change. In December 2015, Justin Trudeau, prime minister of Canada, welcomed Syrian refugees to Canada with the words, "You are home. . . . You're safe at home now." Newcomers were then given health insurance cards, demonstrating solidarity with them. This example, we believe, offers the hope that respect for the health of others can create a virtuous cycle that is able to override our bias, find shared humanity, and create trust and solidarity that will spill over to other domains.

1

Health and Migration

A Combustible Mix

In 2006 Johnson Aziga, an immigrant from Uganda, became the first person in Canada to be convicted of murder because he had infected his sexual partner with HIV.[1] Aziga's conviction followed the 2003 conviction in Great Britain of Mohammed Dica, a Somali asylum seeker, who became the first person convicted in Britain for recklessly transmitting HIV.[2]

On September 9, 2009, in Washington, DC, a Republican congressman from South Carolina, Joe Wilson, shattered decorum by shouting "You lie!" to President Barack Obama as Obama promised Congress that his health care reform bill would not provide any health care to undocumented immigrants.[3]

In October 2015, Poland's right-wing Law and Justice Party came out on top in parliamentary elections after its leader, former prime minister Jarosław Kaczyński, warned that migrants entering Europe could bring "diseases that are highly dangerous and have not been seen in Europe for a long time: cholera on the Greek islands, dysentery in Vienna." He added, "there are some differences related to geography, various parasites, protozoa that are common and are not dangerous in the bodies of these people, [but] may be dangerous here. Which doesn't mean there is need to discriminate anyone [sic], but you need to check."[4] As Kaczyński spoke, thousands of migrants from the Middle East languished in detention camps in Hungary and other parts of Europe. According to reports by Human Rights Watch, detainees experienced "heart attacks, insulin shock or seizures" and newborns had suffered from "serious fevers and vomiting" without receiving any medical assistance.[5]

These very different incidents, from different corners of the globe, illustrate the pain, passion, and complexity that arise when immigration and health policy collide. On their own, both immigration and health are increasingly salient and ever more contentious. Questions of health policy—what care to offer, to whom, and how to reduce its cost, as well as how to prevent the spread of both communicable and noncommunicable diseases—have a unique and personal impact on people's lives. They influence how long we live as well as the quality of our lives. They touch upon our deepest cultural, religious and moral beliefs, as debates about reproductive and sexual health, and the "right to die" attest. They also have an enormous impact on the economy of persons, nations, and the globe. Individuals, families, and governments can and do go bankrupt trying to pay for health care, and in the absence of a healthy population, the prospect of economic progress is dim.

Politics and rhetoric also run hot when it comes to immigration. As globalization, war, civic unrest, and economic deprivation have led to steep increases in migration to the West from the Middle East and less developed regions of the world, many residents of wealthy countries have worried about migration's impact on their own security, jobs, communities, culture, and very way of life. Terrorist attacks in Paris and California in the autumn of 2015 only added to these concerns, fueling fierce anti-immigrant sentiment in many parts of the West. Even in Germany, the European nation that has been most welcoming to the recent wave of migrants, the anti-immigrant Pegida group organized ten thousand people to march in Dresden in autumn 2015.[6] Earlier that summer, Hungary closed its borders to Middle Eastern refugees. In the United States, thirty-one governors claimed that they would not accept Syrian refugees in their states,[7] and Donald Trump, then the front-runner for the Republican Party's nomination for the presidency, called for banning the entry of Muslims into the United States.[8]

Complex and contentious in their own right, questions about health and immigration often provoke even more intense reactions when they intersect. In a time of economic insecurity, nations understandably wonder what health benefits they can afford to offer, and whether noncitizens, or at least those who lack legal residency, are deserving of the benefits provided. Likewise, in an era in which both health officials and the media repeatedly warn of the next global pandemic, residents of highly developed nations worry that immigrants from less developed countries will transmit fearsome germs, a concern clearly on display during the Ebola outbreak of 2014. In such an atmosphere, reasoned analysis and effective policy can be hard to find.

In this book we offer that analysis and provide principles for developing policy that is both effective and ethically sound. Looking beyond the overblown rhetoric and partisanship to review the nexus of health and immigration, we show that the relationship between the two is deeper and far more complex than is acknowledged, and that many laws and policies are often counterproductive and unethical, reflecting widely shared misperceptions about immigrants' health and the burdens they impose on their new homelands.

In the chapters that follow, we explore many widely held misperceptions about the relationship between immigration and health. In this chapter we note four misperceptions that have been especially influential. The first is that migration and migrants pose a unique and significant threat to public health. To be sure, throughout history infectious diseases such as bubonic plague, influenza, and smallpox have followed travelers across the globe. Such epidemics, however, were more likely to follow the movement of armies, commerce, or even casual travel than migration. Indeed, with rare exceptions, newcomers—a term we use to refer to all nonnative residents, regardless of their citizenship or immigration status—are generally healthier than natives. With some exceptions that we will discuss in chapter 2, they are no more likely today to spread novel and fearsome diseases than others who cross borders, or those who live within them. Still, media reports in developed nations continue to stress the supposed high risks of disease-bearing immigrants with headlines such as "'Potential for a Public Health Disaster': Illegal Immigrant Surge Leaves Officials With 'No Idea' Which Diseases Are Coming Across."[9] Reflecting such fears, nations across the globe screen immigrants for a range of diseases and bar entry to those who are thought to pose a health risk. Such exclusions, we demonstrate, misuse public health resources, offering a false illusion of safety instead of effective infectious disease control. Such policies also reinforce the false perception that immigrants are the source of disease.

A second misperception is that newcomers are sicker than natives due primarily to their own irresponsible ways. This was evident in warnings by Alabama congressman Mo Brooks about the role of "illegal aliens" in a recent measles outbreak in the United States. Representative Brooks reportedly stated:

> I don't think there is any health care professional who has examined the facts who could honestly say that Americans have not died because the diseases brought into America by illegal aliens who are not properly health care screened, as lawful immigrants are. . . . [U]nfortunately our kids just aren't prepared for a lot of the diseases that come in and are borne by illegal aliens.[10]

Reflecting such sentiment, public authorities often target newcomers such as Johnson Aziga and Mohammed Dica for highly coercive and punitive public health controls on the assumption that they pose a unique public health threat. The refusal by many states to provide state-supported health care to immigrants has likewise been justified on the claim that the health care needs of immigrants result from their own unhealthy ways. In reality, for the most part, newcomers are healthier and use fewer health care resources than natives. Although their lesser use of health services may be due in part to policies that make it hard for them to obtain health care, there simply is no evidence supporting the widespread belief that newcomers are more likely than natives to engage in unhealthy lifestyles. To the contrary, for many newcomers, the risk to health arises not from adhering to their traditional culture but from assimilating. The longer newcomers reside in their new countries, the more their health patterns begin to converge with that of natives.

A third false perception is that newcomers engage widely in what is sometimes called "health tourism," migrating precisely in order to take advantage of Western health care systems. Although as we shall discuss in chapter 8, there is a robust global market in medical tourism, most of that travel is from wealthy countries to less developed nations. In other words, natives of highly developed countries tend to go to poorer nations for (usually cheaper) health care. The flow does not go the other way. Migrants do not come, in any significant numbers, to wealthy countries for health care. They do, however, move to wealthier countries to provide health care services, creating a brain drain in poor countries, as their most educated health professionals emigrate for better employment opportunities.

The final fiction is that medical services for immigrants place an inordinate strain on taxpayers. In a 2004 survey, more than 60 percent of Americans agreed that taxpayers have to pay too much to support services such as education and health care for undocumented immigrants,[11] and a 2013 survey found that over 40 percent of the US population believed that immigrants (both documented and undocumented) placed a burden on the country.[12] More than 60 percent of Australians hold a similar belief, as do majorities in many European Union countries.[13] In reality, although the provision of services to immigrants can at times strain the budgets of local communities with large numbers of refugees or undocumented immigrants, as occurred in parts of Europe during the migration crisis of 2015, immigration as a whole provides economic benefits to receiving countries.[14] Moreover, as noted earlier, immigrants as a group use fewer health care resources than do natives. Indeed, newcomers often pay taxes to support health care services they are barred from receiving. Thus they subsidize the health care of people far wealthier than they are.

In the chapters that follow we explore the impact of these misperceptions and analyze the laws, policies, and norms that lie at the juncture between immigration and health. Throughout, our focus remains on the nexus of migration and health. We do not, except where necessary to examine health policies relating to immigration, address other contentious issues related to immigration, such as whether nations should be more or less open to refugees, or create a path to citizenship for undocumented newcomers. We also do not consider what type of health care system would best serve any nation. Rather, we ask, how should immigration and health policies intersect? How should nations respond to the health of newcomers?

We begin in this chapter by looking more closely at migration and migrants in the twenty-first century. This examination reveals that immigration is more varied and nuanced than is commonly appreciated. We then consider the relationship among health, individuals, nations, and the global community, looking first at how fear about immigrants spreading disease has influenced immigration law, sanctioning health and disability-based discrimination that would be viewed as deeply troubling in other contexts. We next consider how domestic public health policies and hence public health are adversely affected by the punitive policies that result from the misperceptions of the health risks posed by immigrants. We then turn to a discussion of access to health care and demonstrate that nations throughout the globe erect a multitude of barriers to newcomers' access to care. In effect, once immigration is considered, it becomes clear that no nation's health care system is truly universal. Newcomers, or at least some classes of them, are often excluded from their receiving nation's health care system. This exclusion, based largely on false beliefs, hampers efforts to create high-quality, cost-effective health care systems.

We then more fully explore the global dimensions of health, explaining why many current policies are unethical as well as ineffective. We begin by noting the obvious: health is an essential human good. Every developed country attempts to protect the health of its population, and all regulate both the provision of health care, as well as industries and practices that can threaten health (such as the sale of tobacco). In addition, all developed countries spend a large portion of their budgets on financing health care for many of their residents. In effect, the nations of the world act as if health were a public, rather than a private, matter.

Still, we tend to think of nations' obligations for health in national terms, as if a nation's duties were limited to its own citizens, or perhaps its own legal residents. This is not to say that nations don't target health in their foreign aid policies, but such aid is viewed as supererogatory. This widely shared assumption overlooks the fact that both the benefits and threats to health cannot be confined to any one nation's citizens or legal residents. Rather, an individual's health, we will show, is determined at a far broader population level, influenced by a host of factors, often called the social determinants of health. These social and environmental factors influence the health of both citizens and newcomers, as well as populations across the globe, creating an interdependency of health that transcends both immigration status and national boundaries. Indeed, as we will urge, health is a global public good, meaning that its consumption by one does not diminish the health of another, nor can its benefits be confined to an individual or group. As our discussion of medical tourism and the medical brain drain will show, the flow of health care needs and services is more complex and multidirectional than is acknowledged. The homelands of newcomers often provide significant health benefits to those in receiving countries. Sending countries also bear many of the health consequences of policies that emerge from wealthier countries. The medical brain drain is a good example. When it comes to health, the costs and benefits, duties and obligations, are widely dispersed around the globe.

These characteristics of health, we explain, are not simply descriptive. They have important normative implications. The global public good dimensions of health create duties with respect to health. While some of these duties may extend to all persons, regardless of residency, other factors that have moral weight, including proximity, solidarity, cost, and even the depth of interdependency among all people mean that policies that discriminate against newcomers in either the provision of care or the enforcement of public health policies are especially problematic. None of the oft-cited arguments for the disparate treatment of newcomers with respect to health can survive careful analysis. Or to put it another way, when it comes to health, neither country of origin nor citizenship is of moral consequence.

The Diversity of Newcomers

For twelve years Maridel Sagum worked as a nanny in Paris. In 1998, after paying a recruiter $3,600 for a one-month visa to France, she left her eight-year-old twin daughters so that she could provide for their basic necessities and a college education. Only too familiar with the irony of the situation, Maridel, now forty-seven, commented, "I've looked after other people's children to give my own children a better future. . . . It was the hardest thing I ever did, but it was the right thing."[15] Like many undocumented workers, Maridel works six days a week and sends remittances to her native country to care for her children. She rarely sees them other than by Skype. Before Skype, Maridel could only call them once a month, and she worried that her daughters would forget the sound of her voice. She mailed her daughters recordings of her voice to remind them of her. Maridel, who has three older children in addition to the twins, paid for five professional degrees, a fish pond, and rice paddies for her husband.[16] She also paid a very high emotional price for her twelve-year absence; not only did she miss her children and husband, but she also missed the birth of her grandchildren and her father's funeral. She now suffers from debilitating arthritis.

Another woman, whom we shall call Maria, was found on the banks of the Rio Grande by a local constable. She had paid $1,000 to make the arduous trip to the United States, travelling first by bus from Honduras, then by raft across the river. Her nine-year-old son accompanied her, his arm in a cast. She told the constable that he needed an eye operation and that she had been told that she would be able to work in the United States long enough to save money to pay for the surgery. Border Patrol took her and her son off to an overcrowded station. Crying, Maria informed the agent, "We can stay temporarily, and get money, and if we have to go, we go."[17]

Mohammad Bakkar fled worn-torn Syria in 2015 with his pregnant wife, Samiya, and his young son, Husam. When the train he was on was halted in Hungary, he was told by authorities that he and his family would be separated. Desperate he pulled his wife and child onto railway tracks, hoping they would be killed: "I felt that death would be better—or in death we would find peace."[18]

Migrants are a diverse group. At the time of writing, the world's population was over 7 billion. In 2013, there were 232 million people living outside their country of origin. In 2000 there were 175 million and in 1990, 154 million people. These numbers reflect a trend toward increased migration over the last thirty years.[19] The increase became more dramatic in 2015 when more than a million migrants entered Europe, the largest flow seen since the end of World War II.[20] Most of these new migrants were asylum seekers from Syria, Afghanistan, and other countries experiencing unrest in the Middle and Near East. They reached Europe mostly by sea, sailing in often unseaworthy vessels to Greece or Italy.[21] Tens of thousands, however, came by land via Turkey. Many sought asylum in Germany, but Hungary experienced the largest number of asylum seekers in proportion to its population.[22]

Although Europe saw the most dramatic rise in migration in 2015, immigration is a global phenomenon. Overall the United States is home to the largest number of migrants (45.8 million), but most migrants live in Europe and Asia. In 2015, the Russian Federation was home to 11 million; Germany, 9.8 million; Saudi Arabia, 9.1 million; the United Arab Emirates, 7.8 million; the UK, 7.8 million; France, 7.4 million; Canada, 7.3 million; and Australia and Spain, 6.5 million each.[23] In some of the Gulf Cooperation Council nations, such as the United Arab Emirates, Qatar, and Kuwait, newcomers make up over 50 percent of the population.[24] In the United States more migrants come from Mexico than any other country. Newcomers also migrate from India, China, the Philippines, El Salvador, and Guatemala. The Soviet Union has also been a source of immigrants.[25] Canada receives newcomers from China, the Philippines, India, Pakistan, the United States, France, and Iran, among other places.[26]

People migrate for a number of reasons. In 2015 the large influx of migrants to Europe was spawned in large measure by the civil war in Syria. Other people migrate to reunite with family or escape persecution, conflict, or natural disasters.[27] Between 2013 and 2015, for example, more than 77,000 unaccompanied minors from Mexico and Central America migrated into the United States across the Mexican border.[28] These children fled their homes to escape violence, extreme poverty, or to be reunited with families who had immigrated previously. Many others immigrate to pursue a better life for themselves and send money home to family as Maridel Sagum did. These cash flows are called remittances.

Immigrants tend to be younger than the general population of receiving countries and often have children in their new countries. In the United States, 24 percent of births are to immigrant mothers.[29] Twenty-two percent of the children living in the United States are the children of immigrants.[30] In addition, immigrants constitute 15 percent of the labor force. Immigrants make up 21 percent of low-wage workers and 45 percent of lower-skilled workers.[31] Many of these jobs put their health at increased risk.

The diversity among newcomers is also reflected in their legal status, which is far more varied and complex than is reflected in popular discourse about "legal" and "illegal" immigrants. Many, but not all, newcomers become citizens of their new countries. In the United States, over 40 percent of nonnatives are naturalized citizens.[32] In Canada, 79 percent of immigrants who arrived in 2000 had attained citizenship by 2014, though only 26 percent of those arriving in 2008 became citizens within six years in the country.[33] Fewer newcomers become citizens in countries such as Germany in part because some countries make it harder for newcomers to attain that status.

Some noncitizens are lawful permanent residents who have many but not all of the rights of citizens. Others, such as international students and temporary guest workers, are in the receiving country lawfully, but for a limited period of time, and may not intend to resettle permanently. In effect, they are migrants, but not immigrants.

Other newcomers are refugees. Under US law, to be a refugee an individual must demonstrate a well-founded fear of persecution on the basis of race, religion, nationality, political opinion, or membership in a special group prior to entering the country. Asylum seekers, or asylees, in contrast, are individuals who raise a claim of a well-founded fear of prosecution on similar grounds once they are within the country. Many immigrants, including some who may ultimately be found to have a valid claim for asylum, enter their new country without any lawful status. They have a right, however, to continue to reside in their new country while their claim is being settled. Other undocumented immigrants may be permitted to stay pursuant to a government policy allowing them to remain. This is what happened to young immigrants who came to the United States as children when President Obama issued an executive order blocking their deportation and permitting them to work.

Others newcomers, of course, come and remain without any legal status, some hoping to resettle, others hoping to find work. Some later return to their country, a practice that is known as circular migration. Noncitizens, whatever their formal legal status, reside in the gray zones of the law, granted some, but not all, of the legal rights of citizens, participating in, but partially excluded from, their new temporary or permanent polity.

Some of the controversies around immigration concern the fear that immigrants cause crime and terrorism. Worries about the former were stoked in June 2015 when GOP front-runner Donald Trump stated that Mexico was sending to the United States "people that have lots of problems, and they're bringing those problems with us. They're bringing drugs. They're bringing crime. They're rapists. And some, I assume, are good people."[34] In fact, immigrants have lower crime rates than native-born Americans.[35]

As for terrorism, the 2015 terrorist attacks in Paris and San Bernardino demonstrated that immigrants may be terrorists and that terrorists may at times enter a country alongside refugees. The same attacks, however, also demonstrated that native-born citizens may commit acts of terrorism. Indeed, most terrorist acts within the United States since 9/11 have been committed by native-born Americans,[36] although rates of terrorism, while extremely low, may be higher among immigrant populations than native-born populations. In the discussion that follows we do not explore the complex and controversial questions that pertain to antiterrorism policies, as our focus remains on health.

Another widely held belief is that immigrants take jobs from natives. This belief is founded in part on the idea that immigrants have next to no skills, and thus have nothing to contribute to a new country. When immigrants are skilled, the assumption is that they will take jobs from citizens who are equally, if not better, skilled. The arguments and assumptions at the heart of these beliefs are complex, and we do not attempt to address them here. There are certainly many low-skilled immigrants, including those involved in domestic work of one kind or another, child care, house cleaning, and farming. But this is only part of the story.

The immigrant population includes both those who are low skilled (lacking a high school diploma) and those who are high skilled (those with one or more college degrees). Since 1980, among working-age immigrants in the United States, the number of high-skilled immigrants has exceeded those who fall into the low-skilled category. During 2010, high-skilled working-aged immigrants constituted 30 percent of the immigration population and low skilled 28 percent.[37] High-skilled workers are in demand in the changing US economy. The H-1B visa for specialty occupations has also fostered an increase in skilled workers. Typical caps for this visa are exempt with respect to institutions of higher learning, nonprofits, and government research organizations. The number of international students also increased from 250,000 in 1978–79 to more than 880,000 in 2013–14.[38] Some portion of these students will become residents and, later, citizens. In the United States, low-skilled workers are concentrated along the border states of California, Arizona, New Mexico, and Texas, while high-skilled workers can be found along the coasts, Seattle, San Francisco, and Washington, DC. In addition, college towns such as Columbus, Knoxville, and Madison draw high-skilled workers.[39]

The story of immigrants is not only a story about the factors that "push" people to leave their native countries. Immigrants are pulled to host countries by the opportunities these countries offer. Sometimes they (international health care workers, for example) are aggressively recruited by host countries to meet needs. Newcomers make up a significant portion of the working population. Frequently, they work in less than ideal conditions while earning far less than citizens doing the same job. But there is clearly a demand for their work.

Immigrants are not only a source of cheap labor. Many highly skilled immigrants are innovators who create new technology and foster globe-spanning networks and economic growth both in the United States and their home countries. In an important study of California's high-tech community, AnnaLee Saxenian found that immigrants, especially from China and India, were making important contributions to the California economy not only because of labor supply and wage effects but also because they stimulated trade between California and their home countries and increased investment flows.[40] In a more recent study, Vivek Wadhwa, Saxenian, and F. Daniel Siciliano found that from 2006 to 2012, 24.3 percent of new engineering and technology firms in the United States had an immigrant founder. The most common countries of origin for high-tech immigrant entrepreneurs were India (33.2 percent) and China (8.1 percent). The results were even more striking in Silicon Valley, where 43.9 percent of tech firms had at least one foreign-born founder.[41] Highly skilled immigrants forge networks with their home countries that enhance information and capital flows that are to the benefit of both sending and receiving countries.[42]

This trend is not restricted to California. About ten years after Saxenian's study, researchers found that her observation that immigrants were at the helm of innovation and new job creation was a nationwide phenomenon.[43] Microsoft's CEO, Satya Nadella, born in Hyderabad, India, is a good example. He came to the United States to secure an MS in computer science, then went on to receive an MBA at the University of Chicago Booth School of Business. In February 2014, he became the CEO of Microsoft.[44] The top five nations from which innovative leaders such as Nadella come are India, the United Kingdom, China, Taiwan, and Japan.

In addition to California, New Jersey, Michigan, Georgia, Virginia, Massachusetts, and several other states draw immigrant entrepreneurs. More than 50 percent of immigrant entrepreneurs came to the United States to study, and about 40 percent for a job opportunity. Typically they have a stronger background in the STEM-related fields than US-born founders (75 percent versus 46.5 percent).[45] About one-fourth of all companies in engineering and technology in the United States have at least one immigrant founder, and the immigrant entrepreneurs are contributing to both wealth and job creation.

Immigrant entrepreneurs are a dynamic group who have created successful social and professional networks. In Silicon Valley, professional associations such as the Indus Entrepreneur and Silicon Valley Chinese Engineers Association support ethnic groups and provide professional mentoring. They help members advance professionally by both developing ties within the ethnic community and facilitating integration into "mainstream technology and business networks."[46] The professional and social networks cultivated through these organizations foster transnational entrepreneurship and the process enhances global markets. According to Saxenian, "For every 1 percent increase in the number of first-generation immigrants from a given country, for example, California's exports to that country go up nearly 0.5 percent. The effect is especially pronounced in the Asia-Pacific where, all other things being equal, California exports nearly four times more than it exports to comparable countries elsewhere in the world."[47] The benefits of "brain circulation" extend to both sending and receiving countries as they also develop opportunities in less advanced regions of the world.[48] Thus, far from taking jobs from citizens, many immigrants create jobs for citizens both in their adopted countries and in their native countries.

The Health of Migrants

One of the critical misperceptions that has informed conversation about providing health care to immigrants is the view that immigrants form an especially unhealthy population that would draw excessively on expensive health care resources. Connected to this assumption is the view that receiving countries cannot afford to pay for the health care of immigrants. The other cost-related concern is that paying for the health needs of immigrants would incentivize people to immigrate precisely in order to secure health care.

Before reviewing this argument, it is worth keeping in mind that given the nature of illness, the failure to treat newcomers who are sick and in need of health care threatens not only their health and well-being but also that of natives. Moreover, there is good evidence that immigrants are for the most part healthier than their native-born counterparts. One study, done in 2004, found that male immigrants had a 3.4-year longer life expectancy than US-born men, while female immigrants had a 2.5-year longer life expectancy. More specifically, black and Hispanic immigrant men lived 9.4 and 4.3 years longer respectively than their US counterparts while black and Hispanic women had 7.8 and 3.0 years longer life expectancy. In contrast, Chinese, Japanese, and Filipino immigrants had lower life expectancies than their US counterparts. In addition, immigrants had an 18 percent lower risk of low birth weight and 27 percent lower infant mortality rates between 1998 and 2000 than US natives. Chinese and Koreans had the lowest rates compared to their US counterparts. Recent studies support that immigrants have better overall health.[49] The healthy-immigrant effect has been observed in newcomers in the United States, Canada, the United Kingdom, and Australia.[50] Refugees and asylum seekers who flee violence, however, are more apt to have chronic health problems, especially mental health conditions that may result from their experiences in their native country and on their journeys to safety.[51]

Newcomers often have healthier lifestyles than their native counterparts, as shown by recent studies in the United States and in Canada. They may have healthier diets, and drink and smoke less.[52] Immigrants appear also to have better social support systems, and increased social capital is associated with better health.[53]

Thus, contrary to what many may assume, immigrants appear for the most part healthier than the native born when they arrive, and especially so in their early years as newcomers. Unfortunately, there is also evidence that the health advantage of immigrants does not persist. Acculturation, a process through which immigrants adopt the habits, values, and practices of their adoptive countries, contributes to diminishing their health advantage.[54]

There is also evidence that the close communities of immigrants have a protective effect on their health. One study found that the odds of perpetrating violence were 85 percent higher for blacks than they were for whites, while Latino violence was 10 percent lower. Researchers found that the level of violence is lower for recent immigrants. They speculate that one reason whites have lower violence levels than blacks is that the percentage of whites and Latinos who are recent immigrants is much higher than the percentage of blacks who are recent immigrants.[55] Incidentally, some of the protective effects of immigrant communities may extend to natives.[56] Ironically, it seems that immigrants who remain in ethnic communities in their adopted countries may fare better, at least healthwise, than those who assimilate. Once immigrants assimilate and acculturate they appear to lose the protective advantage of living within more insular communities. Thus assimilation can put their health at risk.

Others have suggested that one reason that immigrants who assimilate fare worse than those who remain in ethnic community is that those who try to assimilate are exposed to increased discrimination, which itself has an adverse impact on health. Ironically, the policies that receiving countries subject newcomers to in the name of protecting citizens from newcomers, whether from their diseases or the cost of caring for newcomers, may harm the health of newcomers.

The relatively good health of immigrants is put at increased risk as they settle into their new countries. This is obviously detrimental to newcomers who are sick. But it is not only newcomers who are harmed by their decline in health. Newcomers represent a significant portion of the working population and have an impact on growth and the economy. This is true not only for highly skilled immigrants but also, and in a different way, for lower-skilled immigrants. In addition, the relative youth of immigrants means that they subsidize social security for many older citizens.[57] When the health of immigrants suffers, the well-being of citizens will also suffer in myriad ways. But sick immigrants may also be less able to send remittances to their home countries. This, in turn, could increase the need for foreign aid, which lags behind remittance money.

Ethics and Law Colliding

As we consider the policy status quo with respect to immigrants and their health, it is important that we not be intellectually complacent. For example, it is tempting to take the position that because the law maintains that newcomers who are in a country illegally should not benefit from breaking the law, they should not receive health care. This is problematic for a few reasons.

First, it is a mistake to assume that just because something is lawful it is morally sound. Not all law is ethical. Most would agree that laws that sanctioned slavery in the United States, or apartheid in South Africa, were unethical. Most would also accept that compulsory sterilization laws, which were adopted by many US states and some Canadian provinces, were unethical. Today there continue to be a number of laws in the health field that may be challenged on moral grounds. One lens from which to view our project is as an effort to evaluate health law and policy regarding newcomers from an ethical perspective. Certainly, the fact that there is a universal right to health, according to which *all* people are entitled to some health care, should make us think critically about any law that denies health care to newcomers.[58] Sometimes, the law gets it wrong. As we argue, this has been the case for many laws relating to the health of newcomers.

2

Keep Out!

Immigration Control as Public Health Protection

After President Jean-Bertrand Aristide of Haiti was ousted in a military coup in 1991, twenty-six-year-old Joel Saintil, like thousands of his countrymen, fled to the United States by boat, only to be interdicted at sea by the US Coast Guard, which transported him to a military camp in Guantanamo Bay, Cuba. While there, Saintil was found to have a possible claim for asylum, but he was denied entry to the United States because he was infected with human immunodeficiency virus (HIV), the virus that causes AIDS.[1] For fourteen months he was kept behind razor wire at the camp at Guantanamo, even as his health deteriorated.[2] Despite pleas by refugee advocates, US officials denied Saintil and others who shared his plight entry into the United States until their health demanded special care. Two weeks before his death, Saintil was flown to Florida, where he was reunited with his parents.[3]

Saintil died in 1993. A year later, Richard Preston's *The Hot Zone: A Terrifying True Story*, climbed to the top of bestseller lists. *The Hot Zone* told the story of Charles Monet, a French expatriate living in Africa, who contracted the deadly Marburg virus after visiting a cave in Kenya. In a "true story" that reads like a novel, Monet becomes violently ill while on a plane to Nairobi Hospital, exposing fellow travelers to the loathsome and lethal infection. The lesson of *The Hot Zone* and many similar books and movies that followed it was clear and seemed to support Saintil's confinement: no matter how harsh the judgment might seeem, travelers from the developing world pose a terrifying danger to the health of the developed world.

Preston's book and the fear that motivated Saintil's confinement exemplify what Priscilla Wald has called "the outbreak narrative."[4] This narrative, which is found widely in popular culture, as well as public policy, portrays migrants and travelers as sources of contagion who carry the dangerous diseases of the developing world to the West. The narrative resonates strongly because it summons ancient and deeply rooted associations among disease, death, and foreignness, as well as modern anxieties about globalization, migration, and the erosion of cultural and racial homogeneity.[5]

Without question, the outbreak narrative is grounded in part on actual experience: throughout history travel and migration have played an important role in spreading disease.[6] During the Middle Ages, the Black Death traveled across Eurasia along trade routes. Later, the Spanish conquistadors brought smallpox to the Americas, and in the process decimated indigenous civilizations. In the nineteenth century, cholera followed travelers and merchants around the globe. In the twenty-first century, the growth of global travel has increased the incidence of so-called traveling diseases. For example, in 2003, travelers from China brought Severe Acute Respiratory Syndrome (SARS) to Vietnam, Canada, and Europe. In 2014, travelers spread Ebola across four West African countries, as well as to the United States and Europe. A few months later, travelers carried Middle Eastern Respiratory Syndrome (MERS) from the Middle East to Korea and China.

Most of these outbreaks were spread by travelers, not by migrants. Indeed, immigrants to developed nations are generally healthier than native populations. Still, they often come from regions with higher rates of many infectious diseases, such as tuberculosis (TB), and have been known to spread such diseases to native populations.[7] Migration, like travel, has carried and can carry disease.

Nevertheless, migration's impact on the spread of disease is often exaggerated. In the twenty-first century, most of the diseases prevalent among migrants, with the exception of TB, do not pose a significant risk to native populations, and as will be discussed in chapter 3, the risk of TB spreading as a result of migration is overstated.[8] Even the rapid mass migration of refugees from war-torn Syria to Europe does not pose a significant threat of spreading novel infectious diseases in the West. Although many refugees have untreated illnesses, Zsuzsanna Jakab, regional director of the World Health Organization in Europe, explained that there is no "systematic association" between infectious disease and migration, and that the risk of exotic infectious agents such as MERS and Ebola is higher from regular travelers and traveling health care workers than from migrants.[9] That has not stopped anti-immigrant advocates from demanding that borders be closed to keep out fearsome diseases. Nor has it kept receiving nations from restricting immigration in the name of public health.

To understand why nations limit immigration in an attempt to prevent the spread of disease it is important to understand that disease, or at least the perception of it, is not simply a biological phenomenon. It is also a socially constructed one. Societies perceive the risk of disease, and react to it, in multiple, complex ways that often have little to do with an illness's lethality, incidence, or even its mode of transmission. Instead, reactions to a disease have much to do with the social meanings that are attached to it and the way in which societies perceive those who are stricken.

Some diseases are especially likely to incite fear and finger pointing. For example, diseases that are new and novel are generally feared more than those that are endemic and accepted as part of the landscape.[10] For this reason, relatively rare infections such as Ebola or SARS generate far more terror than do relatively common causes of death, such as diabetes or motor vehicle accidents. Likewise, diseases that kill their victims quickly cause more apprehension than those that kill slowly.[11] And diseases such as Hansen's disease (leprosy) that cause visible and putrid symptoms provoke special loathing. The media's coverage of a disease also reflects and reinforces these social perceptions. Illnesses and outbreaks that receive significant attention in the media, including social media, are viewed as more prevalent and more dangerous than commonplace hazards that receive scant attention.

Contagious diseases that have the capacity to travel tend to elicit especially negative reactions. They are terrifying in part because they undermine the false but comforting belief that one's home is safe and secure. Traveling diseases also expose the permeability of borders and shine light on the risks of global interdependence.[12] In the developed West, these diseases evoke deeply seated fears dating from the colonial period of less developed parts of the world. Such fears may underlie much of the unease about globalization and migration, and perhaps help to explain why anxiety about traveling diseases reached a fever pitch in the 1990s, along with the rise of globalization. Best-selling author Laurie Garrett may have captured the public mood of that decade the best when she warned that a plague was "coming"—from a crowded city in Asia or Africa, because the world was "out of balance."[13]

Scholars have debated whether reactions to so-called emerging infectious diseases such as Ebola or MERS qualify as full moral panics, or should be thought of as mere "hot crises."[14] Regardless of the classification, reactions to emerging, traveling diseases often bear the hallmark of a full panic.[15] The discovery of a new traveling disease, or of an old disease transported to new locales, frequently receives heightened attention from both public officials and the media, both of which have a tendency to fall back upon on stereotypical presentations of "dangerous foreigners," who are quickly cast as scapegoats. The tendency to blame "the other" for disease seems to be a common one, as those who are different, perhaps because of their race, religion, or cultural ways, are perceived as unclean and dangerous, a bias that may arise from evolutionary forces that favored groups that treated outsiders, who might have sought to harm the group, with suspicion.[16] Thus in the Middle Ages Christians blamed the Jews for the Black Death; in the nineteenth and twentieth centuries, nativist Americans blamed the Irish for cholera, the Italians for polio, the Chinese for plague, and Mexicans for tuberculosis and typhus.[17] Such scapegoating continues today. In the twenty-first century, television anchor Lou Dobbs blamed undocumented immigrants for causing seven thousand cases of leprosy in the United States.[18] In 2014, Congressmen Todd Rokita and Phil Gingrey separately suggested that undocumented immigrants from Mexico and South America might spread Ebola within the United States, even though there were no cases in either Mexico or South America.[19] More recently, anti-immigrant politicians and activists have pointed to the supposed dangers of disease in arguing that Europe should close its borders to refugees from the Middle East.[20]

The usually erroneous belief that foreigners cause disease often leads people to assume that their own health can be protected by keeping foreigners out. In ancient and medieval times, lepers were ordered not to enter cities. When the Black Death struck, Italian city-states closed their ports and made ships wait forty days before docking, giving rise to the term *quarantine*, based on the Latin word for "forty days." In the seventeenth and eighteenth centuries, cities and colonies in North America quarantined both travelers and immigrants arriving by ship in an often-futile effort to keep out smallpox.[21] And in the nineteenth century, ports quarantined ships to try to stop the spread of cholera and yellow fever.

In the modern era, quarantines and the closing of borders continue to be employed to keep diseases out. In 2003 quarantines were widely used (to questionable effect) to stem the spread of SARS.[22] Quarantines have also been used to contain outbreaks of Ebola.

Quarantines that are applied to people who have possibly been exposed to a disease should be distinguished from the more common, and usually more effective, practice of isolation, which is applied to someone who actually has a contagious disease. In the case of SARS, it was the strict isolation of sick patients, as well as the careful use of infection-control procedures in hospitals, that proved decisive. Likewise the isolation of patients with strict infection controls was critical to containing Ebola in 2014. In contrast, quarantines, which reach more broadly and limit the freedom of movement of people who may not be infectious, are often far less effective.[23] They can also backfire by undermining a community's trust in public health officials, as happened during the Ebola outbreak in Sierra Leone, when residents of Monrovia's West Point District rioted in response to a quarantine.[24]

Policies that attempt to deny entry into a country to protect health are also of questionable efficacy. They are seldom capable of identifying and keeping out disease, and by discouraging travel, they can undermine efforts to provide medical resources to regions experiencing an outbreak, as occurred during the 2014 Ebola epidemic. Perhaps most troubling, however, are immigration-based border controls. Although nations frequently try to keep out diseases by keeping out nonnatives, germs do not comply. They don't care about nationality or passports. Nevertheless, nations continue to screen and bar nonnationals for communicable diseases for which they do not test their native travelers.

Health-Related Immigration Controls

The history of health-related immigration controls in the United States demonstrates the ways in which xenophobia, eugenics, and the need for labor have collided to create ineffective and discriminatory health policies in Western countries. In the nineteenth century, natives believed that immigrants to the United States and other Western countries

presented a significant public health threat.[25] Over time, as the demo-
graphics of immigrant populations changed from Northern Europeans
to Southern and Eastern Europeans, and then Asians, Latinos, and Africans, different ethnic groups, often perceived as distinct racial groups,
bore the brunt of immigration's association with disease as public health
protection combined with nativism and racism in toxic ways.[26] But
the association between immigration and disease, and the stigma that
attached to that relationship, remained constant. So did the misguided
belief that the nation's health depended upon controlling immigrants at
the border.

Initially, the states within the United States led the way in restricting the entry of newcomers.[27] Early in the eighteenth century, Supreme
Court Chief Justice John Marshall explained that under the Constitution, the states retained all of the powers not delegated to the federal
government.[28] These so-called police powers included, "[i]nspection
laws, quarantine laws, [and] health laws of every description."[29] A few
years later, while upholding a New York law requiring ship captains to
submit reports on their passengers, the Supreme Court described the
breadth of the states' police power while also expressing the linkage between immigration and disease. Writing for the Court, Justice Barbour
remarked: "We think it as competent and as necessary for a state to provide precautionary measures against the moral pestilence of paupers,
vagabonds, and possibly convicts; as it is to guard against the physical
pestilence, which may arise from unsound and infections [sic] articles
imported, or from a ship, the crew of which may be laboring under an
infectious disease."[30] Although the Supreme Court later recognized important limits on the states' power over immigration, courts continued
to uphold the states' authority over so-called dangerous immigrants.[31]

Throughout the nineteenth century, the states exercised their police powers by enforcing a wide range of measures designed to prevent
travelers, often both native and foreign-born, from importing disease.
For example, until Congress in 1893 enacted legislation establishing national quarantine standards and inviting the states to transfer quarantine
functions to federal authorities,[32] coastal states routinely required ships,
travelers, and cargo to be held for a period of time and often inspected
to insure that they were not a threat to public health.[33] The specifics of
the quarantines and the strictness with which they were enforced varied

greatly depending upon the perceived severity of the threat, but captains and passengers who evaded quarantines were subject to criminal
sanctions.[34] States also enacted a variety of other laws designed to deal
with the danger of travelers introducing disease. For example, in 1797
New York imposed a tax on ships' crews and passengers, designed to
defray the cost of caring for patients being treated in isolation hospitals.[35] This law was eventually struck down as unconstitutional.[36] More
than a hundred years later, Louisiana authorized the prohibition of all
immigrants in parts of the state in which there was disease. As Supreme
Court Justice Brown stated in a dissent to an opinion upholding the law,
the state surmised that healthy immigrants would somehow add "fuel to
the flame" of an epidemic.[37]

As the nineteenth century progressed and immigration from southern and eastern Europe as well as Asia increased, the federal government asserted greater authority over both quarantines and immigration.
For example, in 1879 Congress established the National Board of Health,
which was charged with advising state and local authorities, but also had
authority to erect quarantines when the states did not do so.[38] Although
the board expired in 1883, a decade later Congress enacted the Federal
Quarantine Law of 1893, which required state and local quarantine stations to be approved by the Marine Health Services.[39] The act also authorized the Marine Hospital Service to establish interstate quarantines
in cooperation with state and local authorities.[40]

During this same period, Congress also began to impose new controls
over immigration. These laws shifted the focus away from measures ap-
plicable to all travelers (native and foreign-born) and toward restrictions
that were aimed primarily at nonnationals. In effect, immigrants, rather
than specific diseases, became the focus of public health measures. Indeed, the idea that control of immigration was needed to protect public
health was stated in one of the Supreme Court's earliest immigration
cases, upholding Congress's power to restrict immigration.[41] The Court
stated:

> The exclusion of paupers, criminals and persons afflicted with incur-
> able diseases, for which statutes have been passed, is only an applica-
> tion of the same power to particular classes of persons, whose presence
> is deemed injurious or a source of danger to the country. As applied to

them, there has never been any question as to the power to exclude them. The power is constantly exercised; its existence is involved in the right of self-preservation.[42]

Congress quickly took advantage of its newly affirmed power to restrict immigration by enacting the Immigration Act of 1891, which imposed the first federal health-based prohibition upon entry. That Act excluded from admission into the United States aliens who were "idiots, insane persons, paupers or persons likely to become a public charge," as well as "persons suffering from a loathsome or a dangerous contagious disease."[43] It also required steamship companies to inspect, examine, and certify the health status of passengers before embarkation.[44] Passengers found to have prohibited illnesses upon arrival in the United States were to be returned at the expense of the steamship company.

In 1893 Congress tightened the health-based restrictions on immigration. The Federal Quarantine Law of 1893 authorized federal officers to conduct medical inspections overseas, leading to the placement of inspectors in Italy, China, and Japan.[45] According to Amy L. Fairchild, "inspectors working abroad sometimes rejected staggering percentages of immigrants."[46] For example, in 1906, inspectors in Italy rejected more than 25,000 immigrants for medical reasons; in 1907 more than 35,000 immigrants were rejected. In 1912 the Marine Hospital Service's successor, the US Public Health Service, was established and commanded to prevent contagious diseases from entering the country.[47]

Immigrants who made it across the ocean faced the much-feared medical examination at ports of entry. Although the Statue of Liberty claimed to beckon the tired and poor, the "huddled masses yearning to breathe free," the medical examinations at Ellis Island in New York's harbor and at Angel Island in San Francisco Bay offered a very different sort of welcome as inspectors gazed at the lines of immigrants who arrived by steerage—first and second class passengers were inspected in a more respectful manner on ship—deciding who to mark for further medical inspection. Those who were marked were then subjected to frightening and often humiliating examinations, sometimes being asked to partially disrobe in public.[48] Amy L. Fairchild quotes an Irish immigrant, Manny Steen, recounting his memory of the dreaded inspection: "doctors were seated at a long table with a basin full of potassium chloride and you had to stand in front of them, follow me, and they'd ask you to reveal yourself. . . . Right there in front of everyone!"[49]

In the early years of the twentieth century, inspectors enforced the Immigration Act of 1903, which created classes excludable on the basis of health.[50] Class A consisted of "dangerous contagious diseases," and Class B included "all diseases and deformities which are likely to render a person unable to earn a living."[51] According to the *Book of Instructions for Medical Inspection for Immigrants*, conditions warranting Class A certification included trachoma, pulmonary tuberculosis, and "loathsome diseases," including favus, syphilis, gonorrhea, leprosy, and insanity.[52] Reflecting the prejudice against immigrants, the instruction manual warned inspectors about misdiagnosing insanity, noting that "[i]n the case of immigrants, particularly the ignorant representatives of emotional races, due allowance should be made for temporary demonstrations of excitement, fear, or grief, and reliance chiefly placed upon absolute assurance of the existence of delusions or persistent refusal to talk or continued abstinence from eating."[53]

Although the medical examinations at Ellis Island and other inspection stations were often traumatizing, few immigrants were found to have a Class A loathsome or contagious disease. Between 1890 and 1924, the percentage of immigrants returned for a disease (including Class A and Class B conditions) never exceeded 3 percent.[54] However, a majority of the people who were excluded were kept out for health-based reasons,[55] demonstrating the important role that health policies played in shaping immigration. Interestingly, throughout the period, trachoma, a chronic infection of the eye caused by *Chlamydia trachomatis*, was the most frequently diagnosed disease resulting in exclusion. In fiscal year 1911, for example, 85.6 percent of those excluded for having a physical or mental defect were excluded as a result of trachoma.[56] As new diagnostic approaches were developed for syphilis and tuberculosis, more people were excluded for these conditions.[57]

Historians have debated both the forces that led to the medical inspections and their impact. Without question, the inspections followed and built upon the historical practice of quarantining travelers, as well as the then widely held belief that some ethnic groups had greater susceptibility to certain communicable diseases than did northern Europeans. Perhaps most important, the medical examinations offered the imprimatur of science to the contested process of accepting and assimilating immigrants. In effect, the examinations served more to reassure the public that the immigrants who were admitted were "safe" than to exclude.[58] In a time when growing industries desperately needed laborers, this reassurance may have been vital to maintaining economic growth.

The medical inspectors' search for disease via examinations conducted openly and symbolically also provided a distinct and powerful way of highlighting immigrants' tenuous status in their new country. The examinations warned all newcomers who came by steerage that they were perceived as unhealthy and dangerous. In addition, as Amy L. Fairchild has argued, the medical examinations, conducted on a mass scale in an open and humiliating manner, helped to acculturate newcomers to their future role as laborers in an industrialized workforce.[59]

The one thing that medical examinations were not well suited for was preventing the spread of the most dangerous diseases. Although TB and, later, influenza were the most prevalent and lethal infections of the era,[60] the medical examiners focused on less-lethal threats, such as trachoma.[61] At the time, officials claimed that the medical inspections helped to reduce trachoma's spread, but this is questionable, as the infection was most prevalent in parts of the nation, including Appalachia, other parts of the South, and Native American reservations that saw little immigration.[62]

Rather than protecting public health, the medical examinations and the immigration laws that authorized them led to the exclusion of immigrants who were thought lacking in the ability to labor. Thus immigration law authorized the exclusion of those who were thought "likely to become a public charge," a term that was applied to anyone deemed likely to require public support as a result of poverty, insanity, "idiocy," criminal conviction, or disease.[63] As Amy L. Fairchild explains, even immigrants with contagious diseases such as trachoma and tuberculosis were excluded more because of the fear that they would become a public charge than because of worries about the communicability of their diseases.[64] Immigrants who had disabilities, such as epilepsy, or were simply presumed to have a different disability because of their appearance, were also vulnerable to exclusion.[65]

The determination of whether or not an immigrant was feeble-minded, insane, or likely to become a public charge was highly influenced by the racial prejudices and eugenic beliefs of the period.[66] In 1910 the Public Health Service asked Dr. H. H. Goddard, director of research at the Vineland Institutes for Feebleminded Girls and Boys, to determine whether he could identify immigrants who would cause social problems. As Kraut reports, after administering the Binet-Simon intelligence test, Goddard declared that 83 percent of Jews, 87 percent of Russians, 79 percent of Italians, and 80 percent of Hungarians were "feebleminded or below the age of twelve."[67] Opponents of immigration warned about the "'intergenerational contagion'" spread by these immigrants.

The medical examinations and the exclusion of immigrants on the basis of contagion, disability, disease, and the likelihood of becoming a public charge continued throughout the early years of the twentieth century, even affecting immigrants who had already been admitted into the country. Under a policy known as "delayed exclusion," immigrants were deported if officials determined that they had had an excludable condition that was overlooked at the time of entry. As Polly J. Price explains, this policy allowed state officials to effectively "engineer the deportation of any non-citizen who had become a public charge or who had spent even a small amount of time in a mental institution."[68] Although the legal authority for delayed exclusion remains in place, the federal government no longer engages in the practice. Nevertheless, the close association between immigration law and health policy remains. Current law continues to exclude immigrants on the basis of health conditions, intertwining immigration and health in ways that are problematic not only for the rights of newcomers but also for the health of citizens.

HIV-Based Exclusions

In 1981 a new disease—Acquired Immunodeficiency Syndrome (AIDS)—began killing young gay men in the United States. Within a few years, both a global pandemic and a full-fledged germ panic were unleashed. High-risk groups—gay men, Haitians, hemophiliacs, and users of IV drugs—were identified by public health authorities and blamed by a fearful public. Children with hemophilia were cast out of school, gay men were evicted from their apartments, and immigrants were denied entry.

Although US immigration law continued to bar the entry of individuals with a "communicable disease of public health significance,"[69] the ancient practice of quarantine had fallen into disuse in the years since the discovery of antibiotics. Indeed, after World War II, communicable disease control had ceased being a major focus of immigration restrictions. AIDS and later HIV, which was identified as its cause, changed that, reviving the ancient linkage between immigration and communicable disease policies.

In 1986 the US Department of Health and Human Services (HHS) proposed adding AIDS to the list of excludable contagious diseases of "public health significance."[70] Congress was not content, however, with relying on administrative action. In 1987, it mandated that HHS add HIV to the list.[71] Doing so made little sense from a public health perspective. At the time, health authorities estimated that more than 1 to 1.5 million Americans were infected with HIV.[72] Thus the entry ban could not have kept the United States free from the HIV virus; it was already well established in the United States. Moreover, as the President's Commission on the Human Immunodeficiency Virus Epidemic explained in 1988, border screening for HIV would require an unjustified, immense diversion of resources from other critical programs of education, protection of the blood supply, and care. At best, border screening programs would only retard the spread of HIV briefly.[73]

The HIV exclusion undermined public health efforts to reduce fear, stigma, and discrimination, forces that the commission concluded impeded efforts to educate people about how to prevent the spread of the disease.[74] The ban also diminished the United States's standing in the HIV research and prevention community by barring many would-be participants from attending the Sixth International AIDS Conference in San Francisco. Until the ban was lifted in 2008, the International Conference was not held again in the United States.[75]

Although the entry ban applied to all foreign nationals traveling to the United States, immigrants were hit the hardest. As in the early years of the twentieth century, a medical exclusion of newcomers ostensibly aimed at stopping the spread of a communicable disease was implemented to prevent disfavored groups from immigrating. Haitian immigrants suffered the worst.

After a military coup overthrew Haitian President Jean-Bertrand Aristide in 1991, tens of thousands of Haitians fled by boat to the United States. Because of a court order that temporarily suspended forced repatriations at sea,[76] the US Coast Guard sent Haitians who were interdicted to the US military base at Guantanamo Bay, Cuba, where they were forced to live in prison-like camps. Once at Guantanamo, the Haitians were screened to determine if they had a credible fear of return. Those who were found to have a credible fear were then eligible for transfer to the United States for a determination of their asylum claim. The others were repatriated to Haiti.

In the fall of 1991 the Immigration and Naturalization Service (INS) began testing Haitians who were found to have a credible claim of fear of return for HIV. Those who tested positive were interviewed again and required to establish their eligibility for asylum by demonstrating a well-founded fear of prosecution in order to be transferred to the United States. Many did not meet that standard and were kept at the camp for nearly two years. Life there was very harsh. In 1993 a federal court noted:

[T]here are approximately 200 'screened in' HIV+ Haitians remaining at Guantanamo. They live in camps surrounded by razor barbed wire. They tie plastic garbage bags to the sides of the building to keep the rain out. They sleep on cots and hang sheets to create some semblance of privacy. They are guarded by the military and are not permitted to leave the camp, except under military escort. The Haitian detainees have been subjected to pre-dawn military sweeps as they sleep by as many as 400 soldiers dressed in full riot gear. They are confined like prisoners and are subject to detention in the brig without a hearing for camp rule infractions.[77]

Medical care was inadequate. The court found that "the unfortunate victims of a fatal disease" were treated like "spies and murderers."[78]

The INS eventually freed the Haitians, but only after the court declared their detention unconstitutional in a decision that was vacated following a settlement.[79] The United States, however, continued to list HIV as an excludable disease of public health significance for almost another fifteen years, long after scientists had learned how to control HIV with antiretroviral therapy and long after the international community had agreed to eliminate all forms of discrimination against persons who are HIV positive.[80] Not until 2008 did Congress repeal the statutory ban; and only in 2009 did the federal government remove HIV from the list of excludable communicable diseases of public health significance.[81]

The United States was not the only country that denied entry to newcomers infected with HIV. According to UNAIDS, as of January 2013, forty-four countries continued to have some form of HIV travel restriction. As of 2013, five other countries, all in the Middle East, Asia, or North Africa, imposed a complete ban on the entry or stay of people infected with HIV. Five more countries prohibited travelers and migrants from staying for short periods (ten to ninety days) if they were HIV positive. Nineteen countries including Russia, Singapore, and many Middle Eastern states deported nonnationals who were found to be HIV positive. Many other countries imposed limits on those seeking residence or work visas.[82]

HIV-specific restrictions are especially common and harsh in the Middle East and North Africa. In Saudi Arabia, for example, HIV testing is required for those seeking initial work permits or extensions of their permits.[83] Migrants who have tested positive have been confined, sometimes in extremely harsh conditions, for months prior to deportation.[84] According to a 2008 US State Department report, the United Arab Emirates deported 1,518 HIV-positive noncitizens in a single year.[85]

Both human rights advocates and public health leaders strongly decry the continuation of HIV-based exclusions. Human rights advocates argue that these restrictions violate international norms against discrimination and non-refoulment, the principle that rejects the return of refugees to where they face harm.[86] A 2008 report by UNAIDS noted that there was no reason to believe that nonnationals posed any greater risk of spreading HIV than nationals.[87] Moreover, HIV-based travel restrictions might actually harm public health. The report explained that travel restrictions might

(a) misdirect resources into intimidating screening and enforcement activities versus using these resources to expand voluntary HIV counseling and testing, prevention, treatment and care; (b) drive HIV prevention and care issues, as well as those living with HIV, underground, with negative outcomes for both individual and public health; and (c) pressure

HIV-positive people to leave their medicines behind when traveling, with the result that they become ill and/or develop drug resistance.[88]

Despite these risks to health, the restrictions remain in many parts of the world, a troubling testament to the continued association of immigration, disease, discrimination, and fear.

Public Health Preparedness and the Epidemic of Fear

Although most developed nations have lifted their travel restrictions for individuals infected with HIV, health-based immigration and travel restrictions continue to play a prominent role in what has become known as public health preparedness. In the wake of the 9/11 terrorist attacks and the 2003 SARS outbreak, the United States and many other developed nations turned increasingly to efforts to prepare for and respond to a major public health disaster, as might be caused by a bioterrorist attack or a highly lethal emerging infection, such as pandemic influenza.[89] Many of these efforts, including those aimed at increasing research on vaccines and treatments, improving the regulation of laboratories working with dangerous pathogens, and strengthening the public health infrastructure, helped improve the capacity of health agencies to respond to a public health threat, regardless of its source. Nevertheless, during the early years of the twenty-first century, public health was increasingly conflated with national security. In this atmosphere, "control of the border" emerged as a critical imperative for keeping the homeland safe from the twin evils of "invasion and contagion."[90] The result was a renewed focus on screening and barring travelers and migrants.

The 2003 SARS outbreak occurred in this climate. Emerging in Guangdong, China, the virus followed travelers around the world. In response, the World Health Organization (WHO) issued a travel advisory, suggesting that people postpone travel to affected areas, including parts of Asia and Canada.[91] Taiwan went further, barring travelers from affected regions. Although some health experts credited these measures with helping to control the outbreak, later studies suggested that the isolation of sick patients in hospitals played a more important role in ending the epidemic. Nevertheless, the travel bans reinforced the association between the disease and affected regions, an association that helped to incite discrimination against Chinese immigrants and their descendants in many parts of the world.[92]

In 2005, responding to the SARS outbreak, the World Health Assembly, the WHO's legislative body, approved new regulations designed to enhance the global response to dangerous infectious diseases. The International Health Regulations (IHR) authorize states to conduct medical examinations on international travelers and to bar their entry to prevent the spread of disease.[93] Travelers, however, must be treated without discrimination and "with respect for their dignity, human rights and fundamental freedoms and [states must] minimize any discomfort or distress associated" with health-based restrictions.[94] Despite this recognition of the dignity and human rights of travelers, the IHR reinforce the highly problematic belief that nations can be remain free of disease if they keep their borders secure, offering the imprimatur of both international law and the world's leading public health authority for the misplaced belief that travelers and migrants pose a major threat to public health.

Since the issuance of the IHR, travel restrictions have been central to public health preparedness. For example, in 2005 health authorities became increasingly alarmed about the H5N1 strain of avian influenza as it spread across the globe. Although relatively few people had died, and the virus did not appear to be easily transmitted among people, a characteristic that would be necessary for a pandemic to begin, health authorities warned that H5N1 could easily evolve into the next global influenza pandemic, which, if it matched the 1918 outbreak, could kill tens of millions of people. In response, President George W. Bush told reporters that the military might have to enforce quarantines within the United States, and his Homeland Security Council issued the "National Strategy for Pandemic Influenza."[95] While noting that influenza does not respect borders, the strategy emphasized the need to contain an epidemic beyond the United States's border.[96] Around the same time, the Centers for Disease Control and Prevention (CDC) published proposed revisions of the nation's quarantine regulations that would have significantly expanded the CDC's authority to detain travelers, both at the border and within the nation.[97]

The enhanced quarantine regulations were never promulgated; nor did H5N1 spark a pandemic. But in 2009 another influenza virus, H1N1, did become pandemic. Although this strain proved to be no more lethal than ordinary "seasonal flu," it initially incited great fear. As was predictable given the human tendency to blame contagion on those who are viewed as outsiders, much of the anxiety in the United States turned on nonnational travelers, especially from Mexico, where the virus was first widely reported. In the United States, talk show hosts blamed Mexican immigrants and suggested the border should be closed,[98] something that the Obama administration refused to do.[99] In China, Mexican travelers and US nationals were quarantined.[100] Australia quarantined passengers on a cruise ship.[101]

The panic over the H1N1 epidemic was short-lived. Health authorities quickly recognized that the disease was not especially dangerous. But there was little reason to believe that the travel restrictions made any difference, or that they could have.[102] Although some research suggests that quarantines imposed by isolated localities within the United States provided some protection against the very deadly 1918 influenza pandemic,[103] there is no reason to believe that border screenings or restrictions will prove effective against influenza today. Given the interdependence of the global economy, closing all borders would be economically disastrous, not to mention unenforceable, especially given the many immigrants who cross borders illegally. Studies, however, have found that anything short of a total border closing would fail to keep pandemic flu out for more than a very brief period.[104]

Health experts also counseled against imposing travel restrictions during the 2014 Ebola outbreak that struck West Africa, fearing that restrictions might deter health workers from providing desperately needed care in the affected countries. Yet as panic erupted in the autumn of 2014, many in the West demanded that their nations' borders be closed and that quarantines be imposed. In response, both Canada and Australia closed their borders to West Africans.[105] Although the United States did not follow suit, it required all travelers from affected nations in West Africa to land in one of five designated airports and undergo screening. The federal Centers for Disease Control and Prevention (CDC) also recommended that states actively monitor and restrict the activities of returning health care workers who had had contact with Ebola patients even though asymptomatic individuals could not transmit Ebola.[106] Many states went further, requiring returning health care workers, even if they were asymptomatic and therefore not infectious, to undergo a twenty-one-day quarantine.[107]

Travel bans such as those imposed for HIV and Ebola may hinder more effective public health policies. Border screening programs are expensive and divert resources from other public health programs that may save more lives. In addition, by stigmatizing those who are ill, travel bans may discourage people from seeking treatment if they are ill. It can also, as in the case of Ebola, dissuade health care workers from fighting outbreaks where they start. Travel bans may also motivate some people to travel early in an effort to "beat the ban," or to change their itinerary in order to evade controls. For all of these reasons, some studies using mathematical models of influenza transmission have predicted that travel bans may actually increase the incidence of pandemic influenza.[108]

Perhaps most critically, travel bans erect a false façade of security. They offer comfort by suggesting that the disease may be contained abroad, but by doing so they may discourage nations from investing in vaccines, medicines, and the public health infrastructure that is needed when a public health disaster strikes. In short, except in very limited cases, travel bans imposed in the name of public health preparedness may do little to protect public health. And bans that focus on nonnationals and immigrants can never keep disease out.

Discriminating against Disability

In 2011, Robert and Pauline Crowe hoped to move from England to Calgary, Canada. Robert's seventeen-year-old son, Lewis, lived in England with his mother, Robert's ex-wife. Even though he was not planning to move to Canada, Canadian authorities required Lewis to have a medical assessment as a "non-migrating dependent." The assessment determined that Lewis had autism and that he "might reasonably be expected to cause excessive demand on the health or social services."[109] As a result, Canadian immigration authorities denied the Crowes' application for permanent residence in Canada.

As in the days of Ellis Island, nations today continue to screen and ban immigrants—and sometimes, as in the Crowes' case, their dependents—for a variety of infectious and noninfectious conditions and practices. Frequently, these restrictions aim to keep out not only those with communicable diseases, such as TB, but also people with mental illness or cognitive disabilities. If such screenings were applied outside the context of immigration, they would almost certainly be viewed as unlawful discrimination on the basis of disability. In the context of immigration, however, these screenings are defended as an exercise of a sovereign nation's right to exclude those it believes will or might impose a fiscal burden on taxpayers.

Although the United States no longer bans gay men and lesbians (they were barred as sexual deviants until 1990),[110] federal law continues to give immigration authorities broad discretion to restrict those who are deemed undesirable. For example, current law excludes aliens who have a "physical or mental disorder and behavior associated with the disorder that may pose, or has posed, a threat to the property, safety or welfare of the alien or others," as well as those who have a history of such behavior and it is "likely to recur or to lead to other harmful behavior."[111] Drug abusers or addicts are also inadmissible.[112] So are immigrants other than refugees who are found "likely at any time to become a public charge."[113] In determining whether an applicant is likely to become a public charge, officials are directed to consider the applicant's health, as well as age, family status, assets, and education and skills.[114]

For the most part, these exclusions are enforced only against would-be immigrants and visa seekers, not short-term travelers. But sometimes travelers are caught in their web. For example, in 2013 the *New York Times* reported on the plight of Ellen Richardson, a Canadian who sought to travel to New York, where she intended to board a cruise to the Caribbean. Richardson's request to enter the United States was barred by the Department of Homeland Security because she had been hospitalized in 2012 for depression. Even though she only sought to travel through the United States for a short period, she was told she could not enter the country unless one of three doctors approved by the department gave her a "medical clearance."[115]

Although the United States no longer requires immigrants to stand in long lines and undress as health officials gaze down at them, it enforces health-based immigration restrictions by requiring all aliens applying for a visa at an embassy or consulate abroad to have a medical examination.[116] Immigrants who are already in the country and want to have their visa adjusted are also examined.[117] These examinations are sometimes defended not only as a way of detecting excludable communicable diseases such as active TB but also as a way of informing health officials of the medical needs of immigrants so that they can be treated before migration, or provided with appropriate care once they settle in their new home. With respect to many communicable diseases, such as influenza or even active TB, the medical examinations are unlikely to prevent infections given that they don't apply to the vast majority of people crossing the border, as citizens, permanent residents, short-term travelers, and undocumented immigrants.[118] In addition, the requirement that immigrants be screened when they seek a change in visa status makes little sense from an infection-control perspective, as such immigrants are already within the country and their need for health screening has little to do with their decision to seek a change of visa.

In some cases, medical screenings can pave the way for better care for immigrants. For example, federal officials have worked with partners overseas to provide refugees with vaccines and treatment prior to departure to the United States.[119] In addition, on the basis of pre-arrival screenings, the CDC notifies local health departments of the arrival of immigrants with serious health conditions and asks the departments to provide follow-up. Under the Refugee Act of 1980, state and local health agencies may receive grants for providing follow-up care for refugees resettled in their jurisdiction.[120] Nevertheless, most of the time the screenings are not followed by the provision of needed medical care for the immigrants. Rather, they are simply used to bar entry.

The United States is not alone in screening immigrants and denying entry to nonnationals who have a wide range of diseases and disabilities. Many nations deny residence visas to persons with cognitive disabilities, or, as in the Crowe case, to those who have family members with such disabilities. Countries also screen would-be newcomers to determine whether they will be self-supporting or will use significant health resources. For example, the medical examination required of immigrants by Canada includes a physical examination, mental examination, laboratory and diagnostic tests, and medical assessment of the applicant's records.[121] Applicants may be found inadmissible if they are determined to be a danger to public health or safety; applicants other than refugees or their family members may also be barred if they are found likely to cause excessive demand on health or social services.[122] According to the regulations, a would-be immigrant poses an excessive demand on health or social services if the anticipated costs would likely exceed the costs for the average Canadian resident, would add to existing wait lists, or would increase the rate of morbidity or mortality in Canada by denying or delaying services to citizens or permanent residents.[123] Likewise, the United Kingdom requires an examination of anyone who intends to stay for more than six months. Immigrants who have a conduct disorder (such as alcoholism or serious sexual aberration) are rejected, as are those with active pulmonary tuberculosis. Individuals with a medical illness that may interfere with their ability to support themselves or their dependents may also be rejected.[124]

Australia similarly screens not only for diseases that may threaten the public's health,[125] such as tuberculosis, but also for conditions that would result in significant costs or "prejudice the access" of Australian citizens or permanent residents to health services,[126] a policy aimed at safeguarding scarce resources such as organs for transplant, blood, and radiotherapy. In deciding admissibility, Australia traditionally applied a "one fails, all fails" rule that denied entry to an entire family if any member of the family was found to have a health condition that would burden community services. Under this policy in 2012, Peter Threlfall, a British citizen, was denied a visa to work in Australia because his twenty-five-year-old stepdaughter was autistic.[127] Threlfall's case was not an isolated one; in fiscal year 2008–2009, 282 visa applications were denied due to the policy.[128] Although in response to criticism the government later abolished the "one fails, all fail" policy, it continues to apply the health and resource related exclusions.[129]

Many critics of immigration argue that nations are justified in denying entry to newcomers who are likely to require expensive medical care or would be unable to support themselves due to their disability. Allowing such persons to enter, critics claim, would harm the receiving nation's economy, posing enormous strains on public budgets. The health and disability criteria thus serve to safeguard a nation's own resources for its own citizens.

The actual economic impact of the health and disability-based exclusions, however, may be modest. Most people do not immigrate in order to receive health care. They come to join their family, work to improve their lives, or send remittances home to families. Moreover, given the difficulties of migrating, it seems doubtful that many persons with significant disabilities would migrate if the exclusions were lifted. Indeed, data suggest that the health exclusions bar relatively few people. For example, the Australian Department of Immigration and Citizenship reported to a parliamentary committee studying the issue that only 1,586 persons were denied visas or entry on health grounds in 2008–2009.[130] The department further found that these exclusions had saved the country AUD 70 million. This estimate, however, did not take into account the economic benefits that excluded newcomers, and their families, might have brought to Australia.

Even if the bans do keep public costs down, they remain troubling. In subsequent chapters we argue that receiving nations have a moral responsibility to provide health care to the immigrants who reside within them. Whatever the ethics of restricting immigration overall, doing so simply to prevent immigrants from using health care is troubling for much of the same reason: it breaches receiving nations' moral responsibility for the health of those beyond their boarders, ignoring the substantial economic benefits that immigrants bring to their new home, as well as receiving countries' role in causing some of the health problems and disabilities experienced by newcomers. In short, as we discuss in chapter 6, the exclusions ignore the fact that health is a global public good, and that receiving nations have moral duties to immigrants. Enjoying the benefits newcomers offer while refusing to provide for their health care needs is morally unsettling.

For present purposes, however, several additional points warrant discussion. The first is that the common practice of denying entry to persons with cognitive or mental disabilities violates the principles of respect for diversity and equality for persons with disabilities that are articulated in the United Nations Convention on the Rights of Persons with Disabilities (CRPD).[131] Indeed, Article 18 of the Convention states that persons with disabilities have the right to "liberty of movement, to freedom to choose their residence and to a nationality, on an equal basis with others." States must assure that individuals have "the right to acquire and change a nationality and are not deprived of their nationality arbitrarily or on the basis of disability."[132] The widespread practice of screening for and denying entry on the basis of physical, mental, and cognitive disabilities disregards these rights, denying individuals with disabilities and their families the same basic rights of migration enjoyed by others, often on little more than the ill-founded assumption that individuals with disabilities contribute less to society than the so-called able-bodied, and that the costs associated with disability are costs nations need not bear.

To be sure, international law does offer some sanction for the common practice of examining and barring would-be immigrants on the basis of health conditions. For one thing, not all countries have ratified the CRPD. Although the United States signed the Convention, it did not ratify it. And Australia, which ratified the CRPD, did so subject to the explicit reservation that the Convention "does not create a right for a person to enter or remain in a country of which he or she is not a national, nor impact on Australia's health requirements for non-nationals seeking to enter or remain in Australia, where these requirements are based on legitimate, objective and reasonable criteria."[133]

More broadly, the IHR allows nations to require medical examinations as a "condition of entry for any travelers seeking temporary or permanent residence."[134] In theory, such examinations are justified as a way of preventing the spread of dangerous communicable diseases, such as tuberculosis, SARS, or pandemic influenza. But as we have seen, in practice these screenings more often serve to keep out people with certain disabilities—and others who are viewed as undesirable—than to keep out dangerous pathogens. Thus even if they are at times legal in a technical sense, the restrictions make little public health sense. They also violate the very principles of nondiscrimination and inclusivity that are enshrined in the CRPD, as well as domestic antidiscrimination laws such as the Americans with Disabilities Act.[135]

Most importantly, health-based immigration restrictions place the "blame" or cost for disabilities and health problems—from HIV to autism, from TB to depression—on the individuals who have those conditions. Echoing the worst of the eugenicists, health-based immigration restrictions assume that illness, impairment, and disability reside within individuals and can be kept out of the broader society by isolating those individuals. Thus rather than attempting to address the social causes of disease and disability, or accommodating those who have impairments, health-related immigration exclusions attempt to keep away those who have the disfavored conditions. While the restrictions are for the most part aimed only at immigrants (and sometimes travelers) who are associated with the disfavored illnesses, they inevitably tell citizens with disabilities that they too are a burden on society. As the Canadian Council on Disabilities noted, "Canadians with disabilities realize that if they had not been born here they could never become a Canadian for the simple reason they have a disability."[136]

There is another equally significant problem with health and disability-based restrictions: they are bad for public health. There is little reason to believe that except in very rare and limited cases, health-based immigration restrictions protect the public's health. In any case, entry restrictions can only be effective if they are based on actual or probable exposure to a pathogen: restrictions based on nationality or immigration status simply make no sense from a public health perspective. Germs don't care about passports and visas.

The belief that borders can be hermetically sealed from either germs or disabilities, that diseases and health problems can be kept offshore and national health can be maintained by keeping newcomers out, is not simply foolish; it's also dangerous. It distracts attention and diverts resources from both domestic and global public health strategies that are far more likely to be effective. As in the case of HIV, health and disability restrictions encourage stigmatization and discrimination that may discourage individuals with excludable diseases and conditions from coming forward, getting treatment, and working with health authorities.[137] It also turns our gaze away from the underlying social, political, environmental, and economic conditions, the so-called social determinants of health, that help to foster the very diseases and disabilities, such as HIV and mental health issues, that immigration restrictions target. Indeed, it blinds us to the reality that we are best protected from health threats external to our borders by addressing the root causes of disease and disability within the regions from which people migrate. In effect, it lulls us into thinking that the health problems of other nations, in particular of low-income nations, need not be *our* problem.

Under international law, nations have both the right and the responsibility to implement policies to protect the health of their residents. Health and disability-based immigration restrictions do not fulfill that duty. Even if they save money (and we don't know that they do), they do not protect the health of citizens, and they do not stop the spread of disease or disability. The restrictions cannot, therefore, be justified on moral grounds, nor can they be justified instrumentally as necessary for the protection of health. Rather than preventing the spread of disease or the prevalence of disability, immigration-based restrictions offer only the illusion of security. They give false comfort to citizens who want to be reassured that dangerous or expensive conditions can be kept at bay. They can't be. In our highly interconnected globe, no nation can seal itself off from either human or microbial migration. Only when nations recognize that and disentangle immigration control from health policy, can they begin to develop effective approaches to public health protection.

3

Blaming the Victim

Public Health Protection and the Scapegoating of Newcomers

Typhoid Mary. The very name evokes an image frightening in its mundane malevolence. But Mary Mallon, who was better known as Typhoid Mary, was no monster. She was a middle-aged Irish immigrant, supporting herself as a cook in early-twentieth-century New York when health authorities discovered that she carried typhoid. Vilified in the press as a source of disease and death, health officials quarantined her on an island in the East River. She was released after a few years on the condition that she refrain from practicing her trade, but authorities provided her with no means of support or training for another vocation. Lacking another source of income, Mary eventually returned to the only profession she knew: cooking. Once again she spread typhoid. When health officials discovered this, they returned her to quarantine, this time for the rest of her life, a fate that that was not imposed on other so-called recalcitrant typhoid carriers.[1]

Mary Mallon's story illuminates the close and troubling relationship between public health protection and immigration. At first blush, Mary's detention appears to be a justifiable response to a public health threat. By continuing to cook, Mary without doubt endangered others: all told she infected forty-seven people, three of whom died of typhoid.[2] In detaining Mary, the City of New York had acted to stop an epidemic and save lives.

In quarantining Mary, the city was exercising its so-called police powers. These are the legal powers that all sovereigns have to safeguard the health and safety of their citizens. These powers, which in the United States belong to the states, are both fundamental and obligatory, at least in a moral sense. Indeed, they help to justify and define sovereignty. As the early-twentieth-century legal scholar James Tobey proclaimed: "Government is, in fact, organized for the expressed purpose, among others, of conserving the public health and can not divest itself of this important duty."[3]

Contemporary international law concurs, recognizing public health protection as a human right that governments are obligated to respect. For example, Article 12 of the International Covenant on Economic, Social and Cultural Rights (ICESCR), which the United States signed but did not ratify, requires nations to progressively realize, to the extent possible given available resources, "the right of everyone to the enjoyment of the highest attainable standard of physical and mental health."[4] To fulfill that obligation, the ICESCR requires states, among other things, to undertake the "prevention, treatment and control of epidemic, endemic, occupational and other diseases."[5] Although the scope of that obligation is both contested and contextual, depending upon a wide range of circumstances including the material conditions of a society, the rationale for the right to public health is self-evident: left to their own accord, individuals cannot protect themselves against a wide range of health threats. Only concerted action, often reinforced by law, can reduce many health threats. This is most obvious in the case of an infectious epidemic such as typhoid. Mary's victims had no way of knowing the risk she posed and could not protect themselves from the disease she spread. Only government action could save them.

The same rationale applies, albeit less obviously, to a wide range of other health threats. Consider the dangers posed by bad drivers or polluters. In each case, the risks are collective. The costs created by bad drivers or polluters are externalized onto others. In such situations, individuals can do little on their own to reduce the risks they face. Although nongovernmental community-based efforts to change norms can often help reduce risky behaviors, as occurred when organizations such as Mothers Against Drunk Driving helped to change public attitudes about drunk driving, laws can help create or reinforce those norms. And, sometimes, laws are needed when individual or private sector responses aren't up to the task. For example, it simply isn't practical for everyone downwind of an industrial polluter to negotiate with the polluter to reduce emissions. Only a legal requirement to reduce emissions, supported with reinforcing social and moral norms, can do the trick. Likewise, in the absence of a law requiring vaccination, it is rational for individuals to forego vaccination and rely on the herd (group) immunity that arises when there are no longer a sufficient number of people in a community susceptible to a disease to maintain its presence in the population. The problem, of course, is that if too many people opt for that rational choice, not enough will be vaccinated in order for the herd immunity to be sustained. In such cases, public health demands legal action. In other cases, legal action may not be essential but is still the most efficient mechanism for solving a public health problem. Thus, although individuals can theoretically test their own food for its wholesomeness, it is far more efficient for the state to pass food safety laws.

In these cases, and many others, public health laws serve both as social determinants of health that help to shape the environment in which health risks arise and as tools for public health protection. Research has shown that in many cases public health laws can be powerful tools that significantly reduce the risks that populations face.[6] Public health laws, for example, have played a major role in reducing a wide range of health risks, such as motor vehicular accidents, occupational hazards, and vaccine-preventable illnesses.[7]

Public health laws, however, often impose significant restraints on the liberty of individuals or enterprises. These restraints may at times be justified as necessary for preventing harm to the community. This was the view expressed by the Supreme Court of the United States in the seminal case of *Jacobson v. Massachusetts*, which upheld the conviction of an immigrant preacher who violated a city law by refusing to be vaccinated during a smallpox epidemic:

> There are manifold restraints to which every person is necessarily subject for the common good. . . .
> . . . Upon the principle of self-defense, of paramount necessity, a community has the right to protect itself against an epidemic of disease which threats the safety of its members.[8]

Similar sentiments are recognized today in international law, which allows states, subject to conditions, to derogate civil and political liberties when necessary to protect public health.[9]

Although the protection of public health may at times justify restrictions on individual liberty, Mary Mallon's detention demonstrates the risks that arise when public health protection confronts immigration.

As discussed in chapter 2, societies have long viewed newcomers as a source of disease; they have likewise tended to fear the diseases associated with newcomers more than those that are endemic among native populations. In response, public health efforts often target newcomers. Thus nations restrict immigration in an often-futile effort to keep diseases out. Nations also deport immigrants they fear will spread disease. These efforts, we have seen, offer the illusion but not the reality of safety. Such policies can also reinforce the misperception that newcomers pose a public health menace.

That misperception can also influence the way nations treat immigrants once they have crossed the border and settled in their new land. The same socially constructed associations between illness and newcomers that lead to entry restrictions often prompt health and immigration officials to exercise their police powers both disparately and punitively toward immigrants, treating them more as vectors of disease than as part of the public whose health should be protected. This anti-immigrant approach to public health protection was very prominent in the United States during the nineteenth and early twentieth centuries, when health officials were quick to attribute the health problems of immigrants to their poor hygiene and other habits, often neglecting the role that poverty, dangerous labor conditions, and poor housing had in undermining immigrants' health.[10]

Believing that immigrants were responsible for their own ill health, and that their health problems posed a threat to the native population, American health authorities used their broad legal powers to target immigrants in highly coercive and punitive ways, as was done with Mary Mallon, who was treated far more harshly than native men who also spread typhoid.[11] Indeed, when it came to protecting the public from typhoid, officials viewed Mary as the problem, rather than as a victim of the disease. Thus, rather than try to help her find a way to support herself without endangering others, they locked her away, as if she were not a part of the "public" they were charged with protecting.

In the United States, the most chronicled example of the coercive application of public health powers against immigrants comes from the treatment of the Chinese American community by public health officials on the West Coast, particularly in San Francisco. Throughout the late nineteenth and early twentieth centuries, health officials routinely viewed the Chinese American population, including those born within the United States, as unclean and responsible for a wide range of illnesses, including smallpox and leprosy.[12] In response, officials imposed many laws that targeted the Chinese American community and the industries, especially the laundries, in which they worked.[13] These restrictive ordinances set the stage for a series of court battles that explored the breadth of the state's power to protect public health, and its unequal application to immigrants.

One of the earliest cases, *Barbier v. Connolly*, challenged a San Francisco ordinance prohibiting the washing and ironing of clothes in public laundries and washhouses within certain areas of the city, from 10 p.m. to 6 a.m.[14] In upholding the ordinance as a reasonable effort to protect the public from fires sparked by laundries, the United States Supreme Court, in an opinion by Justice Field, explained that the Constitution's newly enacted Fourteenth Amendment which guaranteed Equal Protection and Due Process was not "designed to interfere with the power of the state, sometimes termed its police power, to prescribe regulations to promote the health, peace, morals, education, and good order of the people."[15] Rather, the Amendment prohibited only "[c]lass legislation, discriminating against some and favoring others," but not laws, such as the laundry ordinance, that affect "alike all persons similarly situated."[16] In rendering this decision, the Court did not consider the fact that the Chinese American population was disparately employed in the laundry business. Nor did the Court note the anti-immigrant rhetoric that was used to support the passage of the legislation. Rather, the Court asserted that "[t]here is no invidious discrimination against any one within the prescribed limits by such regulations."[17] As a result, the police regulation stood.

A year later, in *Soon Hing v. Crowley*,[18] the Supreme Court reached the same conclusion as to an almost identical San Francisco ordinance. This time, however, the challengers specifically alleged that the ordinance stemmed from hatred of the Chinese community. In effect, the challengers claimed that the ordinance was not genuinely aimed at protecting the city from fire; rather, it was simply designed to disadvantage Chinese American residents.[19]

To the Supreme Court, this allegation of blatant discrimination made no difference to the law's constitutionality because there was nothing "in the language of the ordinance, or in the record of its enactment, which in any respect tends to sustain this allegation."[20] The Court added that courts could not consider a legislature's motives for enacting a law. As long as a law did not discriminate against a class, like Chinese Americans, on its face, it did not violate the Equal Protection Clause of the Fourteenth Amendment.[21] That meant that as long as an act appeared to be a public health regulation and did not single out a racial or ethnic group in its text, it would be upheld, even if it was motivated by the desire to harm minorities. In effect, as long as a police regulation, ostensibly designed to protect the public, was neutral on the face of its text with respect to race, it was constitutional, even if it was motivated by racial antipathy.

Despite the Supreme Court's strong endorsement of San Francisco's laundry ordinances, the Chinese immigrant community continued to challenge them in court. In 1886 in *Yick Wo v. Hopkins*, the community finally won an important victory.[22] The ordinance at issue in *Yick Wo* prohibited anyone from operating a laundry in any building other than one made from brick or stone without first obtaining the consent of the city's board of supervisors. Importantly, this ordinance provided no criteria for the board to apply in granting or denying consent. Perhaps not surprisingly, all two hundred Chinese American applicants who sought the board's consent were denied it; eighty other applicants, who were not of Chinese descent, received the consent.[23] Faced with this extreme disparity, the Supreme Court was forced to recognize the discriminatory nature of the provision, and struck it down. In so doing, the Court first articulated the principle that non-citizens, regardless of their race or national origin, are recognized as persons entitled to equality under the Constitution.[24] As to the ordinance before it, the Court distinguished it from those upheld in *Barbier* and *Soon Hing* on the ground that the ordinances in those cases were simply exercises of the state's police power that barred washing and ironing of clothes during a set time period. The ordinance in *Yick Wo*, in contrast, delegated total discretion to the board of supervisors to determine who could and who could not operate a laundry. This broad delegation, which allowed the board "room for the play and action of purely personal and arbitrary power," fell outside the "domain of law."[25] Moreover, the risk of such discretion, the Court noted, was not simply hypothetical, it had come to pass. The facts showed that the ordinance had been "applied and administered by public authority with an evil eye and an unequal hand, so as practically to make unjust and illegal discriminations between persons in similar circumstances."[26] The Court therefore concluded that the city's enforcement of the ordinance was unconstitutional.

The Court's decision in *Yick Wo* made clear that state laws that arbitrarily discriminated against noncitizens could be found to violate the Constitution's guarantee of equal protection of the laws. In turn-of-the-century San Francisco, however, the Court's decision did not dissuade health officials from blaming or targeting immigrants when health problems surfaced, as became evident when bubonic plague appeared in the city in 1900. In March of that year, a forty-one-year-old Chinese American man died of what was thought to be bubonic plague.[27] In response to the arrival of the fearsome disease, city officials focused on Chinatown, viewing its crowded and unsanitary conditions as the source of a scourge that threatened not only the health but also the economic standing of the city. Rather than working with the Chinese immigrant community to ameliorate the overcrowded and unhealthy living conditions in Chinatown, city officials, with the support of federal health authorities, instituted a punitive program of "fumigation, disinfection, and quarantine" aimed squarely at the Chinese community.[28] This was the standard approach, but it was applied to a greater than usual extent and severity.[29] First, Chinatown was disinfected and quarantined. Then local health officials began a program of mass inoculation with a controversial and unproven vaccine known as the Haffkine prophylactic.[30] Chinese residents and others of Asian descent were barred from leaving the city without proof of vaccination. This municipal order was bolstered by an order from J. J. Kinyoun, the acting quarantine officer of the United States, forbidding common carriers from transporting "Asiatics or other races particularly liable to the disease."[31]

A Chinese immigrant named Wong Wai challenged the orders as unconstitutional in federal court. A federal appeals court in an opinion written by Judge Morrow agreed, finding that they aimed at Asian Americans and made little sense as health policy.[32] The court stated:

> There is no pretense that previous residence, habits, exposure to disease,
> method of living, or physical condition has anything to do with their clas-

sification as subject to the regulations. They are denied the privilege of traveling home from one place to another, except upon conditions not enforced against any other class of people.[33]

The court's ruling was not the end of the story. The city responded by reinstating a quarantine in Chinatown, drawing the map to exempt houses belonging to whites. Once again the city's actions were challenged in federal court by another Chinese immigrant, Jew Ho. Once again the court found the quarantine unconstitutional.[34] After noting the breadth of the police power, Judge Morrow concluded that the court had the authority to determine "whether or not the quarantine established by the defendants in this case is reasonable, and whether it is necessary, under the circumstances of this case."[35] Turning to the facts, the court reviewed the quarantine map, focusing on the fact that it was gerrymandered to include the homes of Chinese Americans and exclude the homes of white residents. Relying on *Yick Wo*, the court found that with the lines drawn in this manner, the quarantine was "unreasonable, unjust, and oppressive," and beyond the purview of the police power.[36]

The courts' decisions in *Yick Wo, Wong Wai*, and *Jew Ho*, marked important victories for San Francisco's Chinese American community. The decisions also helped to establish the critical principle that public health protection does not justify blatant discrimination against immigrants or racial minorities. In the decades that followed, that principle would be extended by the Supreme Court to demand that most state laws that discriminate against lawful immigrants would be subject to so-called strict scrutiny.[37] This means that such laws will be found unconstitutional unless they can be shown to be necessary to further a compelling state interest. Discriminatory laws can rarely meet that standard. State laws that discriminate against noncitizens may also be struck down if they are found to be inconsistent with federal immigration laws.[38]

Perhaps more important for present purposes, cases such as *Yick Wo, Wong Wai*, and *Jew Ho* demonstrated that immigration-focused public health laws could be arbitrary and unreasonable. As the courts concluded in each of the cases, the discriminatory approach taken by the city could not be defended as benefiting public health or safety; hence the measures were not legitimate exercises of the police power. With the quarantines blocked by the court, the city slowly adopted a new, more effective approach, one that worked with rather than in opposition to the Chinese American community.[39]

For other immigrants subjected to harsh public health regulations, however, the San Francisco court decisions were limited in their reach, prohibiting only measures that flagrantly discriminated against individuals on the basis of race. The decisions did not question the city's ability to target the industries and communities associated with the Chinese American community. Nor did the courts question what Nayan Shah aptly calls the "epidemic logic," the belief that the presence of an epidemic demands "extraordinary intervention."[40] Rather the decisions reaffirmed the breadth of the police power, and the states' ability to impose otherwise unthinkable restrictions on individual liberty in the name of public health.

Indeed, the limitations of the San Francisco decisions became readily apparent a mere five years later when smallpox struck the East Coast of the United States. Once again the epidemic logic prevailed, and health officials undertook extraordinary measures, imposing quarantines and forcibly vaccinating, sometimes at the point of police batons, those who were unvaccinated.[41] Not surprisingly, these highly coercive measures were disproportionately employed against those who were most vulnerable, especially African Americans and immigrants. In Boston, for example, public health doctors were accompanied by guards as they went to the railroad yards to forcibly vaccinate, in the words of the *Boston Herald*, "Italians, negroes [sic] and other employees."[42] Similar shows of force against immigrant and African communities occurred in many other communities.[43]

Once again, the battle between the public health officials' coercive use of their police powers and civil liberties was taken to the courts, most famously by Henning Jacobson, an immigrant preacher from Sweden who refused to be vaccinated despite a law imposing a five-dollar penalty on anyone who could not show proof of vaccination. Jacobson's resistance against Massachusetts's vaccination law gave rise to the Supreme Court's most famous public health law case, *Jacobson v. Massachusetts*.[44] In *Jacobson* the defendant's immigration status was never placed before the Court; nor was the common practice of disparately applying the state's police powers against immigrants. Rather, in contrast to *Yick Wo*, in *Jacobson* the Court only considered the state's right to demand vaccination in the face of an epidemic, not the discriminatory manner in which the police power was applied. So framed, the Court extolled the state's right to protect the public against disease, stating that "upon the principle of self-defense, of paramount necessity, a community has the right to protect itself against an epidemic of disease which threatens the safety of its members."[45] At the same time, the Court recognized that there were limits to the police power, noting that a community might exercise its power "to protect itself against an epidemic threatening the safety of all . . . in particular circumstances, and in reference to particular persons in such an arbitrary, unreasonable manner, or might go so far beyond what was reasonably required for the safety of the public"[46] and that "[e]xtreme cases can be readily suggested."[47] Nevertheless, in the absence of such arbitrary or extreme cases, the Court made clear that the logic of the epidemic would prevail. For newcomers, this meant that except when discrimination was as blatant as it was in *Yick Wo*, *Wong Wai*, and *Jew Ho*, states would continue to wield broad and largely unrestrained authority to coerce immigrants in the name of public health.

Immigrants and Tuberculosis

In 2006, Robert Daniels, a Russian immigrant to the United States, was diagnosed with pulmonary tuberculosis after returning to Arizona from his native Russia, where he likely contracted the disease. A "drifter," Daniels was placed in a residence for homeless TB patients and ordered to take antibiotics and wear a mask when going out in public.[48] Like Mary Mallon, he failed to comply with the health department's orders. When he was diagnosed (erroneously) with the very dangerous extensively drug-resistant form of the disease known as XDR-TB, health officials ordered him to be detained by the Maricopa County Sheriff Joe Arpaio, who is notorious for his harsh treatment of inmates and immigrants.[49]

For ten months Daniels was kept in solitary confinement in a jail unit in a county hospital, without access to a window, reading materials, or exercise.[50] Only after the American Civil Liberties Union (ACLU) took his case was Daniels escorted to another hospital for treatment, where it was discovered that he was not actually infected with XDR-TB. Nevertheless, when Daniels was released from the hospital, Sheriff Arpaio threatened to prosecute him for defying the earlier court order. In response, Daniels decided to leave Maricopa County, opting to return to Russia.[51]

Although Daniels's treatment was especially harsh, his story illustrates the continued contemporary association between immigrants and the logic of the epidemic. As in Mary Mallon's day, the risks are real, the questions difficult. States have a legitimate need, indeed a solemn duty, to protect the health of their populations from infectious disease. Moreover, both domestic and international law allow states to use coercive police powers when doing so is the "least restrictive alternative."[52] Yet, as in Mary's day, when the logic of the epidemic is combined with anti-immigrant sentiment, it can undermine effective infectious disease control policies.

Pulmonary tuberculosis, the disease plaguing Robert Daniels, is the illness most closely connected with immigration today. Tuberculosis is an airborne infection that can be transmitted when someone who is actively infected with *Mycobacterium tuberculosis* coughs, sneezes, or otherwise speaks, or spits. According to the World Health Organization (WHO), 9.6 million people developed the active and infectious form of the disease in 2014.[53] Although tuberculosis is treatable, there were an estimated 450,000 new cases of so-called multidrug-resistant tuberculosis (MDR-TB) in 2014.[54] This form of the disease is far more difficult and expensive to treat. It can develop when patients such as Daniels fail to continue to take their medications as prescribed. Patients who develop drug resistance because of their lack of adherence to treatment can spread MDR-TB to others. The WHO estimates that 190,000 people died from MDR-TB in 2014.[55]

Extensively drug-resistant tuberculosis (XDR-TB), the form of the disease that Robert Daniels was erroneously thought to have, occurs when patients are resistant to several additional drugs beyond those for which an MDR-TB patient is resistant. XDR-TB is even more dangerous and more difficult to treat. With intensive and specialized care, only about 50 percent of patients can be successfully treated. As of 2015, there was at least one case of XDR-TB in 105 countries.[56]

The incidence of tuberculosis is far higher in many developing countries with high rates of emigration than in most high-income receiving countries. For example, in 2014, 28 percent of new TB cases worldwide were in Africa.[57] Indeed several countries in Africa have extremely high incidence rates; the WHO estimates that in South Africa and Swaziland one out of every one hundred people develop TB each year.[58] In contrast, only ten out of one hundred thousand people develop TB each year in Western Europe, the United States, Japan, Australia, and Canada.[59]

Most high-income countries screen some groups of immigrants for so-called active TB. Such screenings undoubtedly prevent some people with TB from immigrating. The Centers for Disease Control and Prevention (CDC) identified over one thousand cases of TB, and fourteen cases of multidrug-resistant tuberculosis that were kept out of the United States in 2012 due to screening. According to the CDC, this saved US health departments over $15 million that would have been spent on treating those immigrants.[60] Nevertheless, TB screenings cannot keep out all cases of TB among immigrants. In part this is because the screening methods used—most nations use a chest X-ray—are imperfect and fail to detect many cases.[61] In addition, many nations screen only some classes of immigrants, such as those seeking to work in certain fields, such as health care.[62] And of course, no nation can screen undocumented migrants. As a result, many immigrants are never screened.

Screenings are also limited in their ability to prevent TB from spreading within receiving countries because most nations, including the United States,[63] do not screen for so-called latent cases of TB. In latent cases, individuals are infected by the bacteria that causes the disease but their immune systems are able to keep the bacteria in check. Latent infections are neither symptomatic nor contagious. Yet 5 to 10 percent of latent infections will later turn into active infections, through a process known as reactivation.[64] By only screening for active TB, nations fail to detect latent cases that can reactivate and become infectious within their borders.

Because screening cannot prevent all cases of TB among immigrants, in most high-income nations immigrants have higher rates of active TB than does the native-born population. For example, in Canada some immigrant populations have a five hundred times greater risk of TB than do nonaboriginal native populations.[65] In the United States the incidence of TB among foreign-born persons is thirteen times that of the native-born population, and a majority of new cases reported are among foreign-born persons. [66] Rates are also higher among the immigrant populations than the native populations in Australia and New

Zealand.[67] Recent refugees from Syria may also have a higher prevalence of TB as TB control efforts have broken down in that country during the civil war.[68]

Given the limitations of screening and the process of reactivation, it isn't surprising that immigration from high-incidence countries is related to increases in overall incidence of disease in receiving nations. In 2008 R. L. Gilbert and colleagues reported on a study analyzing immigration and tuberculosis rates in Europe. During the period of study, from 1996 to 2005, TB incidence rates declined in most European countries, but not in the United Kingdom, Norway, and Sweden, where they went up.[69] The study noted that the United Kingdom was the only country in Europe with large numbers of immigrants from countries with TB rates of over five hundred per one hundred thousand and concluded, "The degree to which immigration affects TB rates in a particular country is related to the proportion of cases that occur in the foreign-born population. Increases in the number of migrants from highly endemic countries will potentially have a larger impact on overall TB rates in countries such as the United Kingdom, where a high proportion of cases occur in the foreign-born population, than in other European countries where a higher proportion of cases occurs in the indigenous population."[70] Likewise, a 2010 study by E. Svensson and colleagues in the journal *Clinical Microbiology and Infection* found that immigration from countries with high incidence rates of TB affected the epidemiology of TB in Sweden, a low-incidence country. In addition, the researchers noted that foreign-born patients were more likely than native-born patients to be infected with drug-resistant strains of the disease.[71]

Despite the association between immigration from high-incidence countries with overall incidence rates and the increased presence of drug-resistant strains among immigrant populations, migration does not necessarily pose as grave a TB threat to the indigenous population as one might think. Indeed, perhaps up to 80 percent of the TB cases among immigrants in high-income countries result from reactivation of latent cases, rather than infections spread and acquired in the receiving country.[72] This means the vast majority of TB cases among newcomers do not result from transmission within their new country. Even the population most at risk of infections spread by immigrants—others within their own community with whom they are in close contact—do not seem to face a very high risk of contracting TB from their fellow immigrants. Natives face an even lower risk. Indeed, infection of the native-born population by immigrants—especially those who are not closely related to immigrants[73]—is surprisingly rare. For example, a 1997 study found that tuberculosis infection in immigrants did not cause detectable levels of infection to native-born Canadians who attended school or were employed with immigrants.[74] After systematically reviewing epidemiological studies of TB transmission in EU countries in 2013, researchers concluded that although foreign-born cases of TB can infect natives, there was no evidence to support the belief that immigration significantly affected the TB rates of natives.[75]

Nevertheless, the higher incidence of TB among immigrants can increase the overall costs associated with treating TB in wealthy countries that have low rates of the disease. Moreover, although the occurrences are rare, immigrants can and sometimes do infect the native-born.[76] As a result, some have argued for more effective immigration screening programs. But, as discussed previously, even the best screening programs will inevitably miss many active cases because of both the limitations of the screening tests and the reality of undocumented migration. Moreover, most screening programs don't identify latent cases that can reactivate and become infectious, and programs that screen for latent infections face a host of problems. First, the tuberculin skin test, which is often used to screen for latent TB, gives false positives, especially in individuals who have received the bacilli Calmette-Guérin vaccine, which is used in many countries to prevent TB infection.[77] Second, the overwhelming majority of people with latent TB will never go on to develop active disease. Thus, if nations bar all immigrants with latent disease, they will end up excluding many immigrants who could contribute to their economy and would never have become infectious. A different approach, advocated by some TB control experts, would be to treat everyone who was found to have a latent infection. Theoretically this could prevent them from ever becoming sick and posing an infection risk to others. The problem with that is that treatment for latent cases is expensive, and adherence rates are poor.[78]

Once we recognize that the risk of transmission from immigrants to natives cannot be eliminated, the question arises: How should nations respond to the risk? Should low-incidence nations act as Arizona did in the Robert Daniels case, and use the full force of their police powers to ensure that newcomers with TB adhere to the prescribed treatment? Should receiving countries respond, as Australia has at times, and deport immigrants who develop TB on the grounds that they entered the country erroneously?[79] Or should nations adopt a less coercive approach?

To answer these questions, it is critical to understand that the treatment of tuberculosis, both for active and even for latent cases, is notoriously long and difficult. Patients need to take their medications for many months, even after they stop feeling ill or, in latent cases, even in the absence of any symptoms or any reason to believe that disease would develop in the absence of treatment. TB treatment can also be unpleasant. Many patients experience unpleasant side effects. Many people also have trouble avoiding alcohol, which is strongly contraindicated, given the potential liver damage that can result from TB medications.

Perhaps not surprisingly, many patients have trouble adhering to TB treatment, thereby increasing the possibility that they will develop and transmit drug-resistant forms of tuberculosis.[80] Although nonadherence occurs among all classes of patients, including those who are native-born, some patients, such as those who are homeless, have substance abuse or mental health problems, or lack a usual source of health care, may face particular challenges in adhering to a long and difficult medication regimen.[81]

As a result of the difficulty that patients have in taking their medications, TB control programs often rely on what is known as directly observed therapy (DOT), in which "a health care worker or other designated individual watches the patient swallow every dose of the prescribed drugs."[82] Although one recent meta-analysis by Jotam G. Pasipanodya and Tawanda Gumob found that DOT does not result in lower rates of drug resistance than when medication is self-administered,[83] DOT remains the "gold standard" in TB treatment and is recommended by the WHO and other global health authorities.

Nonetheless, the WHO recognizes that DOT is insufficient to control TB. In addition to DOT, the WHO's current Stop TB Strategy calls for addressing the needs of poor and vulnerable populations, strengthening health care systems, especially with respect to primary care, "empower[ing} people with TB, and communities through partnerships," and promoting the use of "The Patients' Charter for Tuberculosis Care."[84] This charter recognizes that TB patients have the "right to be treated with respect and dignity, including the delivery of services without stigma, prejudice, or discrimination by health providers and authorities."[85] But it does not acknowledge that TB patients have the right to choose whether to be treated, or the location of their treatment.

Although health officials recognize that coercive treatment alone cannot control TB, many jurisdictions continue to forcibly isolate some TB patients, especially those who fail to adhere to treatment regimens. For example in the 1990s New York City experienced a TB epidemic fueled by HIV, increases in the prison population, homelessness, and reduced funding for TB-control programs.[86] In response, the city amended its public health regulations to empower health officials to require patients to submit to DOT. Patients who failed to submit or adhere to DOT, or were otherwise noncompliant, could be forcibly held in isolation. Hundreds of patients were detained. [87] Many other jurisdictions have imposed similarly coercive approaches to TB control. For example, South Africa has detained large numbers of TB patients in prison-like hospitals, where they can be kept for up to two years.[88] Taiwan has also instituted a program of widespread isolation.[89]

Researchers have debated the efficacy, legality, and ethics, of imposing DOT involuntarily and detaining nonadherent TB patients. Supporters cite the decline in TB rates in New York in the 1990s as evidence that the aggressive use of DOT plus detention can work to lower TB rates.[90] In particular, supporters note that most patients placed on mandatory DOT remained adherent and were not detained.[91] Other researchers point out that detention was applied disproportionately to the homeless and substance abusers, raising concerns that coercion was applied disparately against already marginalized groups.[92] Moreover, critics suggest that the reduction in TB rates in New York was due less to the use of highly coercive public health powers than to the increase in resources for surveillance, prevention, and treatment that accompanied the policy of forced isolation.[93]

Although forced detention can limit the risk of transmission from the specific individual who is detained, by itself it cannot and does not address the broader array of social factors—poverty, homelessness, poor housing, poor nutrition, substance abuse, incarceration, and HIV infection—that support reactivation and the spread of TB. Nor does the establishment of a detention program assure increased funding for the public health infrastructure that is needed to detect cases, provide treatment, and implement DOT. On the contrary, the significant resources that are required for prolonged detention may diminish those available for the other components of an effective TB-control program.

Despite the uncertainty of the benefits of compulsory DOT and detention, health authorities and scholars endorse their application in limited circumstances. Lawrence O. Gostin, for example, has argued for a "nuanced" approach that balances the individual and public interests.[94] Although recognizing that coercive public health powers can infringe upon an individual's liberty's and dignity, he concludes that compulsory DOT (presumably enforced by the threat of detention for noncompliance), can be justified when individuals have previously failed to follow the prescribed treatment.[95] The WHO agrees, stating that detention must be used only as a "last resort," which can be "justified only after all voluntary measures to isolate such a patient have failed."[96] The few published court decisions in the United States on enforced detention for TB would seem to concur, holding that detention of nonadherent TB patients is constitutional only when it is the least restrictive alternative.[97]

Although limiting the use of detention to cases in which it is a last resort, or the least restrictive alternative, would seem to safeguard both individual interests and public health, drawing a careful balance in the face of a difficult dilemma, there is reason to question whether these limitations can safeguard either the liberty or the dignity of immigrants who are detained or the public's health. For one thing, although protective of individual interests in theory, in practice terms like "last resort," or "least restrictive alternative," grant health officials extraordinarily broad discretion to decide which patients who fail to take all of their medication can be detained. After all, there's no way to know for sure that any patient, especially one who has previously failed to take his or her medication, will not once again fail to do so and end up developing a drug-resistant form of the disease. As a result, detention can always be viewed as the necessary and least restrictive way of eliminating the risk that a given patient will transmit a dangerous disease—drug-resistant TB. Perhaps for this reason, there are no published decisions in the United States in the modern period finding the detention of a nonadherent TB patient to be inappropriate. (Courts have questioned the due process provided or the place of confinement, but not the appropriateness of detention).[98] In other words, confronted by the uncertainty of the risk and the danger of the disease, courts usually defer to health officials' decisions to detain an infectious patient.

Such broad discretion, however, invariably invites discrimination against immigrants and other marginalized groups who are blamed for health problems. Although studies have not shown that isolation is applied disproportionately to immigrants, given the higher prevalence of TB in immigrant communities, as well the common conflation of immigration and infection, there is a significant risk that health officials will wield their discretion disproportionately and inappropriately against immigrants. High rates of poverty in immigrant communities, as well as cultural and language barriers, may aggravate the risk of excessive coercion.

This risk of such unequal treatment is troubling for many reasons. Most obviously it recalls the "evil eye and unequal hand" at play in *Yick Wo*. Although nations have a right to protect their population's health, that right does not justify using public health laws as a pretext for targeting disliked minorities. Nor does it allow a state to treat noncitizens more harshly than it treats its own citizens. Indeed, if a noncitizen is subject to a highly coercive public health measure such as compulsory DOT or is detained simply because of his or her immigration status, the use of coercion would not be the least restrictive alternative; as the less restrictive measures would be those used on citizens. In other words, if the state can achieve its public health goal in a less coercive manner when citizens are infected, the principle that coercion is justified only when the measure is the least restrictive one demands that the less onerous approach that is applied to citizens be applied to non-citizens.

The fact that nations have a legal right to control their borders, and perhaps even to distribute some public benefits unequally to noncitizens, should not change the analysis. As the Supreme Court recognized long ago in *Yick Wo*, citizenship status and nationality are irrelevant when it comes to the application of public health laws. The only plausible justification for compulsory treatment and isolation due to infection is the protection of the public's health. And that justification does not warrant treating immigrant patients more harshly than natives who are similarly infected and nonadherent.

Perhaps most important is the fact that the disparate use of coercive public health is counterproductive. For one thing, the application of highly coercive measures against immigrants can distract public health efforts from more focused and more effective strategies. Thus as long as officials think they can "solve" the TB problem by detaining immigrants, they will not feel the need to do the hard work required to control the disease. In addition, highly coercive public health measures, especially when they are applied in a discriminatory manner, often backfire, as the individuals who are targeted by such measures become even more resistant and less willing to comply with official advice. Indeed, the literature is rife with cases, such as that of Robert Daniels, of immigrants who have run away from treatment after being detained.[99] For example, after a Chinese national in Australia on a student visa failed to take his TB medications, he was arrested and placed in a quarantine room in a hospital with twenty-four-hour guard. Unhappy with his situation, he escaped.[100] A patient in Germany, this one with XDR-TB, returned to Georgia after being kept for a considerable period of time in a locked facility.[101]

Coercive measures against some immigrants can also cause other immigrants to avoid and resist health authorities. For example, after immigrants with TB were deported from Oman, others went into hiding and abandoned treatment.[102] More generally, fears of deportation are associated with delays in diagnosis and thereby treatment, enhancing the risk of contagion.

The real risk of conflating public health and immigration in a punitive way is that it undermines trust between affected communities and public health. Public health works best when communities at risk have good relations with health officials and trust that they are acting in the interests of the community.[103] When there are high levels of trust, most members of a community voluntarily comply with the advice of public health officials—whether it is to take their TB medications, stay home during a flu outbreak, or even exercise. They want, after all, to be healthy and keep their loved ones healthy also. And the community itself, through its own norms and social controls, will help keep those who would be noncompliant in line. In the absence of trust, however, communities are less apt to follow health advice, and they may run, hide, or even riot in the face of highly coercive health measures. Thus, people under quarantine for SARS rioted in China in 2003, and those under quarantine for Ebola rioted in Liberia in 2014.[104]

Precisely because newcomers are at greater risk than native populations of contracting TB, either through reactivation or through infection with close contacts, they are the communities that most need to trust health officials with respect to TB. Yet by acting with too heavy a hand, by detaining and deporting nonadherent immigrants and conflating immigration control with public health protections, officials weaken trust and therefore are less likely to attain the compliance they seek.

The creation and maintenance of trust, however, requires more than the mere absence of a heavy hand. Lack of active discrimination is not enough. States must also actively engage with communities at risk, understand the hurdles they face, and work with them to reduce the barriers that help infections to spread. With respect to TB, immigrant populations experience some particular challenges that public health officials need to address. As will be discussed in chapters 4 and 5, in many nations, newcomers are denied access to public health insurance programs, making it hard for them to gain access to health care in the absence of an emergency. That means that their illnesses, including TB, are less likely to be diagnosed and treated in a timely manner. In addition, the clinics that treat immigrants are often overcrowded, inaccessible, and viewed by many patients as inferior to the facilities that serve natives, making newcomers less willing to continue seeking care. Language barriers, low levels of education, and lack of awareness about latent infections, drug resistance, and the need to continue taking medications even when feeling well, can also impede adherence. The fear that diagnosis can lead to deportation or forced isolation only compounds these problems, making immigrants reluctant to seek treatment or interact with health authorities.

For infection-control efforts, the challenge is to move past the perception that newcomers are the problem, the cause of the disease, rather than a population needing help to be kept safe from the disease. Rather than emphasizing the dangers posed by the noncompliant patients, health officials should work with affected communities—especially immigrant communities—to develop trust, and institute culturally sensitive, community-based interventions that protect rather than target TB patients, as well as those who are at greatest risk of getting TB. (We look more closely at the need for culturally competent care in chapter 10.) Such approaches may include voluntary screening and treatment for latent infection, but, most importantly, they should treat patients—whether they are natives or newcomers—as persons in need of care rather than as vectors of risk.

Ultimately, infectious diseases such as TB demonstrate the inescapable interdependency of human health. TB remains a risk in high-income nations not because of nonadherent patients, or even because of immigration. TB remains a danger to the wealthy nations of the world because its incidence is so high in lower-income nations. Only by lowering the disease's prevalence in low- and middle-income countries can developed nations truly be safe from TB.

In the early years of the twenty-first century, the world community came to appreciate the global nature of the TB epidemic and the importance of lowering TB rates in high-prevalence countries. Between 2002 and 2013, donor funding for TB, much of it through the Global Fund to Fight AIDS, Tuberculosis, and Malaria increased from $0.2 billion to $0.8 billion.[105] Nevertheless, the WHO estimates that at least $1.6 billion more is needed to address the global problem.

Of course, money alone cannot solve the TB problem in low- and middle-income countries. Resources need to be deployed effectively, and scalable systems need to be developed and implemented in high-prevalence countries. As is the case with TB control in high-income countries, interventions need to be community based, and health officials must earn the trust of affected communities. Without question, as the 2014 Ebola outbreak showed so clearly, this can be challenging where governments are weak, health care systems are fragile and impoverished, civil wars rage, and corruption is rampant. Still the only way to reduce the risk of infectious diseases such as TB, malaria, HIV/AIDS, or even Ebola to the populations of the developed world is to address the problems facing populations in low-income countries. There is no other effective way.

The good news is that with respect to TB, many strides have been taken and much progress has been made. The illusion that TB can be controlled by containing "the immigrant menace" undermines those efforts, destroying the fragile trust upon which public health depends and distracting us from the expensive and painstaking work of ensuring that all communities are safe from TB.

4

A Nation of Uninsured Immigrants

In 2008, thirty-four-year-old Sonia del Cid Iscoa, a legal immigrant living with her family in Phoenix, Arizona, went into premature labor. Doctors at St. Joseph's Hospital rushed her into surgery for an emergency C-section and a hysterectomy. While in surgery, something went horribly wrong. Sonia fell into a coma; later her kidneys began shutting down. After treating her for less than a month, hospital staff told her family that they were sending her to Hospital Escuela in Tegucigalpa, Honduras, a facility with only four ICU beds and no dialysis unit.[1] Her family found a lawyer who was able to convince the hospital not to move her. Eventually she recovered.[2] Her story is not unique.

The United States of America has often been called a nation of immigrants. Forged by successive waves of immigrants, newcomers have been crucial to the nation's economy and identity. As of 2014, more than 13 percent of the population was foreign-born. Over 47 percent of these newcomers were naturalized citizens.[3] In addition, unlike many countries, the United States recognizes so-called birthright citizenship. Children born within the United States automatically become citizens, regardless of their parents' immigration status. And, as noted in the preceding chapter, the US Constitution prohibits most state laws that discriminate against noncitizen immigrants. Compared to many other wealthy countries, the United States is relatively welcoming to its newcomers.[4]

The United States is also known, less kindly, as the only developed nation that fails to recognize a right to health, or provide health insurance to all of its citizens. Even after the implementation of the Affordable Care Act (ACA), a law designed to expand access to care, over 30 million Americans remain without access to health insurance.[5]

These two distinctions—the United States's relative openness to immigrants, and its lack of universal health insurance—are not unrelated. Not only are many of the uninsured in the United States immigrants— both documented and undocumented—but concerns about the costs of providing health care to immigrants, as well as a widely shared belief that immigrants are not fully deserving members of the community, have helped to undermine efforts to provide universal coverage. This became dramatically apparent in 2009, during debates over the passage of the ACA. Although the act's opponents raised many objections, the erroneous claim that it would cover undocumented immigrants was among the most powerful,[6] as was evident when Congressman Joe Wilson falsely accused President Obama of lying about the act's coverage of undocumented immigrants. Wilson, like many other ACA critics, would rather have left many citizens uninsured than support insurance for undocumented immigrants.

The role of immigration in the debates over the ACA illustrate the many ways in which anti-immigration sentiment, and fears about immigrants' use of health care services, have influenced and undermined health policy in the United States. Laws relating to immigrants' access to care reflect varying and often inconsistent conceptions of the government's role in securing access to health care, as well as deservingness and belonging. Newcomers are especially vulnerable to these tensions. Indeed, as more citizens become insured as a result of the ACA, the continued exclusion of immigrants serves as powerful reminder of the limited and exclusionary nature of the American health insurance system. It also adds to the system's cost and complexity. But, as chapter 5 will show, the treatment of immigrants in the United States turns out to be surprisingly similar to the treatment newcomers receive in many nations that purport to have a universal health care system. When it comes to newcomers, few if any nations provide truly universal care.

Denying Newcomers Benefits

In the modern period, fears about immigrants' use of health care first reached prominence in the United States in 1994, in California, the state with the largest population of immigrants. As immigration from Mexico and Central America surged, nativist sentiment, much of it racially tinged, intensified. But rather than make explicitly racist attacks against immigrants, critics emphasized the supposed heavy tax burden created by undocumented immigrants' use of public services. To these critics, the notion that taxpayers should support those who broke the nation's immigration laws seemed outrageous.[7] Immigrants, especially those who were brown and undocumented, were not viewed as worthy members of the community. Rather, they were seen as lazy, freeloading outsiders who came to America to feast on taxpayers' largesse.

To reduce the supposed burden that undocumented immigrants placed on taxpayers and to deter immigrants from coming to America to obtain benefits, immigration opponents put forth a ballot initiative in California known as Proposition 187, or the Save Our State initiative. Endorsed by Republican governor Pete Wilson, the initiative denied undocumented immigrants access to most state-funded benefits, including all but emergency health care.[8] It also required police, school officials, and health care workers to report to state and federal authorities anyone who they suspected of being an undocumented immigrant.[9]

In their campaign for Proposition 187, supporters emphasized the high costs of providing undocumented immigrants with health care. With less than a week before the election, state health officials released a controversial and much-disputed report claiming that state Medicaid costs for undocumented immigrants had skyrocketed in 1993 to $340.8 million in Los Angeles County alone.[10] Although undocumented immigrants were only eligible for emergency care—services that hospitals were required to provide under federal law, and that would not be affected by Proposition 187—Sandra R. Smoley, the state's secretary of health and welfare stated: "[a]t a time when the state has been forced to reduce or freeze spending on programs for the most vulnerable Californians, it is wrong that we are spending hundreds of millions of dollars for illegal immigrants."[11] Although she did not say so explicitly, her underlying assumption was clear: undocumented immigrants did not deserve taxpayers' support.

Voters were persuaded; they approved Proposition 187 by a wide margin. Although the act was quickly halted by a federal court that found it violated federal law,[12] it left a lasting impact on US health policy. Denying immigrants public benefits quickly rose to the top of the national political agenda. In 1996 Congress, which unlike the states has broad power over immigration, enacted the Personal Responsibility and Work Opportunity Reconciliation Act (PRWORA).[13] Best known for reforming welfare, much of PRWORA's impact and cost savings came from restricting immigrants' access to public benefits. Echoing the policy embedded in the public charge provision of the immigration act, PRWORA declared: "Self-sufficiency has been a basic principle of United States immigration law since this country's earliest immigration statutes."[14] The act further stated that US immigration policy aimed at preventing public benefits from serving as an incentive for immigration. Congress thus codified nativists' views that immigrants are not worthy of public benefits. To the extent that social solidarity is embedded in laws providing support to those who need health care, PRWORA exclaimed, it doesn't extend to immigrants.

In chapter 9 we will argue in support of a version of solidarity for health that embraces newcomers. For now, it suffices to note that the views that animated Proposition 187 and were expressed in PRWORA— the belief that access to public health insurance encourages many high-cost, undocumented immigrants to the health care system—are unfounded. Although there is no way to know for sure how many unhealthy immigrants would come to the United States if newcomers had greater access to insurance, immigration did not slow down after PRWORA restricted immigrants' eligibility for public insurance programs.[15] This suggests that immigrants didn't come in large numbers for insurance when it was available, and they didn't stop coming in large numbers once it was no longer available. Indeed, although some immigrants undoubtedly come to the United States to gain access to health care, most come to find work, reunite with their family, or escape violence or persecution.[16] There is simply no credible evidence to support the widespread belief that large numbers of immigrants would come to the United States if they had greater access to public insurance programs.

Rather than freeload upon taxpayers, both legal and undocumented immigrants help to sustain the American health insurance system. For example, between 2002 and 2009, immigrants contributed more than $100 billion more into the trust fund that supports Medicare, the federal insurance program for people over 65, than they cost the program.[17] This is because the immigrant population is younger and healthier than the native-born population,[18] due in part to self-selection and healthier lifestyles, as well as the health requirements established by immigration law. Moreover, immigrants of all ages use fewer health care services and incur fewer health care costs than do native-born Americans. Even their citizen children, who are eligible for publicly funded health care, use less health care than citizens.[19] Although these lower user rates may be explained in part by difficulties immigrants face in obtaining health insurance, as well as fear of immigration authorities, they belie the belief that newcomers jeopardize the financial viability of public insurance programs.[20] Indeed, without young immigrant workers, the health insurance premiums of citizens would rise. Nevertheless, the misperceptions that immigrants burden the health insurance system and that publicly subsidized insurance would serve as a magnet for unhealthy immigrants have led politicians to enact a series of laws restricting immigrants' access to publicly funded health insurance. These laws harm the health of both immigrants and natives.

Uninsured Immigrants

Newcomers are not the only ones in the United States without health insurance. Even after the ACA was implemented, more than 16 percent of the nonelderly US population remains uninsured.[21] Although most of the uninsured are citizens, noncitizens are far more likely than citizens to be uninsured.[22] And because many noncitizens are denied the benefits of the ACA, newcomers are expected to form a larger share of the uninsured as more citizens obtain insurance.[23]

Given their heterogeneity, it is not surprising that rates of insurance coverage vary among different groups of newcomers. Immigrants from some regions, such as Latin America, who tend to have less education and work in low-wage jobs, are especially likely to lack insurance.[24] Lack of insurance is particularly widespread among undocumented immigrants who often work in low-wage jobs; more than 65 percent of undocumented immigrants lack insurance.[25] But even immigrants who are naturalized citizens are more likely to go without insurance than are native-born citizens. The US-citizen children of immigrant parents are also more likely to lack health insurance than are the children of native-born parents.[26]

The high rate of uninsurance among immigrants is due to several factors. Most important is the heavy reliance in the United States on employer-provided health insurance. This coverage is often unavailable to newcomers, who are disproportionately employed in low-wage jobs in the agricultural and services sectors in which employers are less likely than other employers to provide health insurance benefits.[27] Latino immigrants are especially likely to be employed in such industries, and therefore to be uninsured.[28]

Americans who are not insured through the workplace are forced to rely on a complex patchwork of private, or, more precisely, quasi-private, and public programs, each with their own eligibility criteria. Many of these programs are closed to some classes of noncitizens. On the other hand, there are many exceptions to these exclusions and there are many programs that cover only immigrants who are denied access to mainstream programs. The result is a messy and very confusing hodgepodge of exclusions, inclusions, and exceptions that reflect the nation's deep ambivalence about whether health care is a matter of social responsibility, and if immigrants deserve the health care they need.

Much of the complexity was created by PRWORA which, as noted earlier, sought to prevent public benefits from serving as an incentive for immigration. To do so, it established a complex and poorly drafted set of categories, restrictions, and exceptions that were layered on top of preexisting eligibility criteria for most federal benefits programs, including Medicaid, the largest federal-state program that covers low-income children and families; and the Children's Health Insurance Program (CHIP), a federal-state program that provides insurance for children in families whose income is above the eligibility limits for Medicaid. As a result, PRWORA made an already complicated health care system ever more byzantine. Although PRWORA discriminates on the basis of immigration and even national origin, preferring immigrants from some countries, such as Cuba, over those from other countries,[29] the Supreme Court has held that Congress can discriminate pretty much at will when it comes to immigration.[30]

PRWORA accomplishes its discrimination through the creation of multiple classes of favored and disfavored immigrants. In brief, under PRWORA all lawful permanent residents as well as immigrants with several other types of immigration status, such as refugees and asylum seekers, are considered "qualified aliens."[31] All other noncitizens are "unqualified." Undocumented immigrants fall within this category (though they become qualified, for example, if they successfully seek asylum), as do tourists and other nonresident aliens.

Not surprisingly, immigrants who are unqualified under PRWORA are ineligible for most federally funded benefits programs.[32] They remain eligible, however, for emergency medical assistance, and for public health programs, such as immunizations.[33] They are also eligible for state health benefits if the state enacted a law after 1996 affirmatively providing for their eligibility.[34]

The more startling effect of PRWORA arises from its treatment of qualified aliens. One might think that immigrants who are deemed by Congress to be qualified would in fact be eligible for federal benefits so long as they meet other criteria (like having a sufficiently low income). That isn't the case. Under PRWORA most qualified immigrants who arrived in the United States after the law's enactment (exceptions are made for certain favored aliens, such as refugees, asylees, and veterans) are ineligible for most federally funded benefits, not including emergency medical assistance and public health programs, for the first five years after they achieve qualified status. In other words, even lawfully permanent resident aliens cannot receive benefits under Medicaid or CHIP for the first five years after they receive their green card.[35] But even after the five-year ban passes, states may continue to deny coverage to most qualified legal immigrants.[36] Several states, including Texas and Virginia, do just that.[37]

As with unqualified aliens, PRWORA allows states to be more generous to qualified immigrants as long as they use their own funds. In the immediate aftermath of PRWORA's enactment, many states used their discretion and own money to provide health benefits for low-income legal immigrants who would have been eligible for Medicaid but for PRWORA. However, when state budgets were squeezed, first in the recession of 2001–2002, and then in the wake of the Great Recession of 2007–2009, several states cut health benefits they had previously funded for immigrants who were ineligible for Medicaid as a result of PRWORA.[38] More recently, some states have moved to restore or expand coverage for newcomers. For example, in 2015, California enacted the Health for All Kids Act which set aside $40 million to provide health care to undocumented children.[39] The original version of the law would have covered all undocumented residents in the state. It was tabled as too costly.

Advocates for immigrants have challenged many state laws cutting back on health coverage for immigrants as a violation of the principle of equal protection.[40] Some courts agreed and restored coverage; other courts, finding that PRWORA establishes a uniform federal policy to limit immigrants' access to public benefits, have upheld state laws eliminating coverage for immigrants.[41] As of 2014, only eleven states provided some state-only funded health program for immigrants.[42]

Reflecting both the oscillating views about whether newcomers deserve health benefits and the reality that it costs states more money to postpone care for newcomers, Congress has also granted states the option of covering prenatal care of immigrant women under the so-called unborn child option.[43] As of 2014, five states did so.[44] Likewise, the 2009 Children's Health Insurance Program Reauthorization Act, reauthorized in 2015, permits states to use federal funds to enroll lawfully residing children in CHIP up to age nineteen and lawfully residing children until twenty-one and pregnant women through sixty days postpartum in Medicaid.[45] According to the Kaiser Family Foundation, as of 2015, twenty-eight states covered children and twenty-three covered pregnant women.[46] Other states have been less generous, reflecting the view expressed by Governor Dave Heineman of Nebraska, who claimed that the provision of prenatal care to undocumented women would serve as a "magnet" for undocumented immigrants. Heineman added, "This is an issue of fairness. . . . Illegal aliens who don't pay taxes and don't obey the laws should not be receiving taxpayer-funded benefits."[47] What Heineman neglected to consider was that by denying prenatal care to undocumented mothers, the state was harming children who would be citizens as a result of their birth in the country. And as citizens, the children would be eligible for Medicaid. Hence taxpayers end up paying for health care for costs that could have been avoided by appropriate prenatal care.

Nevertheless, for noncitizens, PRWORA creates a large hole in the health care safety net. Exactly how large a hole is difficult to ascertain because of the complexity of PRWORA's categories and the variation among and the ever-changing nature of state eligibility rules.[48] Nevertheless, studies have found that PRWORA was associated with a 9.9 percent to 12.9 percent increase in uninsurance among some groups of immigrants, although other groups were found not to have been affected.[49] Not surprisingly, Medicaid participation rates fell significantly in states that did not use their own funds to insure immigrants who were barred from federal programs.[50]

PRWORA's exclusions, however, are not the only barriers that Congress has placed on immigrants receiving health insurance. The Illegal Immigration Reform and Immigrant Responsibility Act (IIRIRA) requires certain sponsors of immigrants (usually a family member) to sign a legally enforceable affidavit of support promising to assume financial responsibility for immigrants they sponsor.[51] Following IIRIRA's passage, some immigration authorities interpreted an immigrant's use of Medicaid benefits as a "public charge," in violation of the affidavit of support and potentially warranting deportation or denial of reentry.[52] According to a study conducted by Lisa Sun-Hee Park, Latina and Asian women were especially targeted. Park tells the story of one woman who was stopped at an airport and told that she could not reenter the United States until she paid back Medicaid's costs for prenatal care and the delivery of her child.[53] Eventually the Immigration and Naturalization Service (INS) clarified that Medicaid and other public health insurance programs were not to be considered public charges.[54] Nevertheless, a provision in the 2005 Deficit Reduction Act requiring states to document the citizenship status of Medicaid applicants led to further delays and inappropriate denials of Medicaid coverage,[55] even to US-citizen infants born to immigrant mothers.[56] This requirement was overridden in 2009.[57] Still, the complexity of the Medicaid application process, which can be daunting even for low-income, English-speaking applicants, and the fear that many immigrants have that their use of public health insurance benefits will affect their immigration status, deters many eligible immigrants from enrolling.[58]

Enacted in 2010, the ACA continued the preexisting pattern of both excluding and including immigrants in the health insurance system through a complex maze of criteria. Under the act's so-called individual mandate, most citizens and legal immigrants are required to maintain health insurance or pay a tax penalty.[59] To enable those who are required to have insurance but don't receive it through their workplace or a preexisting public program to obtain it, the act established insurance exchanges in which private insurance companies sell policies that meet regulated standards. Citizens whose incomes are between 100 and 400 percent of the Federal Poverty Level (FPL) are eligible for tax credits and subsidies to help them purchase the insurance sold on the exchanges.[60]

The ACA reflects the nation's conflicting attitudes about noncitizens' membership in the health care community and their right to health care. For example, non-citizens who are "lawfully present," a technical term that applies to all legal permanent residents, immigrants with legal residency visas, and some undocumented immigrants whose status is known to immigration officials, are allowed to purchase insurance on the exchanges and to receive income-based credits and subsidies to help them do so.[61] Indeed, although citizens must have incomes over 133 percent of FPL to receive such support, lawfully present immigrants can do so if their incomes are under 100 percent of FPL.[62] This apparent treatment in favor of immigrants was established because Congress had assumed that citizens with incomes under 133 percent FPL would be covered by an expanded Medicaid program, but that many immigrants, as a result of PRWORA, would lack that option. Thus lawfully present low-income immigrants were granted support, denied to citizens, to purchase insurance on the exchanges. However, in 2012 the Supreme Court struck down the provision in the ACA requiring states to cover adults with incomes less than 133 percent of FPL in their Medicaid program.[63] Many states then chose not to expand their programs. As a result, in states that have not expanded their Medicaid programs, lawfully present immigrants with incomes under 100 percent of FPL can receive public support to purchase insurance even though citizens with the same income lack any public options.[64] It remains to be seen, however, whether the exchange plans will be meaningful for immigrants with very low incomes, as the plans were not designed with this income group in mind. Moreover, the insurance provided on the exchanges is less comprehensive than that offered by Medicaid. In particular, unlike Medicaid, the plans on the exchanges don't cover long-term care.

Although the ACA has expanded coverage for some immigrants, it also makes it harder for those who are not lawfully present to have insurance. All of these immigrants are prohibited from purchasing insurance on the ACA exchanges.[65] This bar applies even to employer-provided insurance offered through the exchanges. Hence, many newcomers will lose their health insurance if their employer decides to rely on the exchanges, as millions of employers are expected to do. To enforce the bar against those who are not lawfully present, the ACA requires that exchange applicants provide their Social Security number, and in the case of noncitizens, immigration status, and that such information be verified by the Department of Homeland Security.[66] In 2014 federal officials warned hundreds of thousands of people who had purchased insurance on the exchanges that they might lose their insurance because of their immigration status.[67]

Thus, even after the ACA promised to provide insurance for all, millions of newcomers are left without access to either publicly funded safety net health insurance programs or the private plans available through the ACA exchanges. By leaving these immigrants uninsured, the United States maintains the illusion that health care is not a human right, available to all. Rather, it is a privilege, granted only to those deemed worthy of belonging to the community. In effect, the exclusion of some immigrants from the health insurance system underscores the supposed deservedness of those who are granted public benefits. Both immigrants and natives pay a high price for that illusion.

Lack of Coverage: The Impact on Immigrants

The many barriers that immigrants face in obtaining health insurance have a profound impact on their health. In 2008 the *New York Times* reported the story of Luis Alberto Jiménez, an undocumented immigrant from Guatemala who was working as a gardener in Stuart, Florida, when a drunk driver struck a car he was driving, leaving him with severe physical injuries and brain damage.[68] Uninsured, he was taken by ambulance to Martin Memorial Hospital, but after months of treatment, he remained in need of substantial care. Eventually he was placed in a rehabilitation facility that the *Times* speculated was willing to take him in anticipation of an insurance settlement.[69] Perhaps because no settlement materialized, the facility returned Jiménez to Martin Memorial.

Unable to find any skilled nursing facility willing to treat Jiménez, and uncompensated for all but $80,000 of the over $1.5 million it had spent on his care, Martin Memorial went to court asking for an order authorizing what is known as a medical repatriation or deportation, the involuntary return of a patient to his or her country of origin.[70] With the order in hand, the hospital leased an air ambulance for $30,000 and flew Jiménez to Guatemala,[71] where he lived in a one-room house with his elderly mother in a remote village. He received no medical care. Not surprisingly, his conditioned deteriorated.

After Jiménez's return to Guatemala, his guardian, his cousin Montejo Gaspar Montejo, asked an appellate court to overturn the lower court decision. In its ruling, the appeals court found that the hospital had not followed either federal law or its own discharge policy and that the lower court lacked jurisdiction to authorize the repatriation.[72] That court's decision, however, came too late for Jiménez, who was already out of the country and could not return without the approval of immigration authorities. Montejo, nevertheless, continued to challenge the discharge by suing the hospital for false imprisonment. In 2006, the appeals court rejected the hospital's claim for immunity and ruled that a jury should decide whether the hospital's actions were reasonable.[73] Three years later an all-white jury concluded that Martin Memorial did not act unreasonably, sparing the hospital from any legal liability.

The Jiménez case was unusual in two respects: first, it received a flurry of national media attention; second, it provoked an extensive court battle. In all other ways, the case was prototypical of what happens in the United States when uninsured immigrants require costly medical care. First, they receive emergency care. Then the trouble begins.

Despite the many policies designed to keep immigrants from using public health benefits, US law has long required hospital emergency departments to treat everyone needing emergency care. Since 1986, the Emergency Medical Treatment and Active Labor Act (EMTALA) has codified this principle by requiring all hospitals with emergency rooms that participate in the Medicare program, which means most hospitals, to provide an "appropriate medical screening" to anyone who presents in the emergency department.[74] Patients with a medical emergency must be provided with the treatment necessary to stabilize the condition. Although the hospital may bill the patient for the treatment provided, the care must be offered even if the patient is uninsured and has no means of payment.[75]

Despite PRWORA, the federal government has enacted several programs designed to help hospitals with some of the uncompensated costs created by EMTALA. For newcomers, the most pertinent measure is the so-called Emergency Medicaid program.[76] Despite its name, Emergency Medicaid is not a health insurance program. Rather, it offers federal financial support in participating states for hospitals that provide emergency care to undocumented immigrants who have an "emergency medical condition" and would have been eligible for Medicaid but for their immigration status.

The criteria for Emergency Medicaid are relatively stringent and closely adhere to the definitions set forth in EMTALA. Coverage is available only if the immigrant has an emergency medical condition, which is defined relatively narrowly to apply only to labor or "acute symptoms of sufficient severity" that serious harm will result in the absence of immediate treatment.[77] Coverage is never available for an organ transplant, no matter its necessity.[78]

A large percentage of the immigrants who receive care under the Emergency Medicaid program do so for childbirth and related complications.[79] Many immigrants with very severe health problems, however, do not qualify for the program. For example, in 2000 Hector Diaz, a native of Guatemala, was living in North Carolina when he began experiencing nausea, bleeding gums, a sore throat, and lethargy. Eventually he went to Moses Cone Memorial Hospital in Greensboro, where he was diagnosed with acute lymphocytic leukemia.[80] He was treated with chemotherapy until 2002, at which point he gave the hospital permission to seek compensation from the state's Emergency Medicaid program. The state refused, claiming that the treatment rendered was not emergency care. The North Carolina Supreme Court affirmed that refusal on the theory that Diaz's leukemia began to improve shortly after chemotherapy commenced. At that point, "his condition was stable, and therefore, he was no longer entitled to Medicaid coverage."[81] This was the case, the court concluded, even though if the chemotherapy ceased, Diaz would have "regressed into a state of an emergency medical condition."[82] In other words, Diaz could not receive coverage for his treatment until the hospital stopped treating him and his condition once again became urgent. Appropriate medical care, not to mention humane treatment, was not covered by Emergency Medicaid. This strict if nonsensical state of affairs was chosen by Congress, the court stated, to further the "compelling government interest to remove the incentive for illegal immigration provided by the availability of public benefits."[83]

Immigrants with serious chronic conditions have also been found to be ineligible for Emergency Medicaid. For example, W. T., an undocumented immigrant who was left incontinent with impaired mobility and difficulty swallowing after a stroke, was placed in Spring Creek, a long-term care facility.[84] Spring Creek sought and was denied financial support from the Pennsylvania Emergency Medicaid program. Once again the court upheld the state's denial, quoting an Arizona court in stating that the symptoms for which the patient was receiving care "must not only have arisen rapidly, but, more importantly, . . . they [must] be short-lived. In other words, a medical condition manifesting itself by chronic symptoms is not an emergency medical condition, even though the absence of medical care might lead to one of the three adverse consequences list [in] the statute."[85]

Although not all courts have read the criteria for Emergency Medicaid so narrowly,[86] many have,[87] which helps to explain why Luis Alberto Jiménez was repatriated to Guatemala. Once Martin Memorial Hospital had stabilized him, as required under EMTALA, it could no longer receive government reimbursement for his treatment. Moreover, any long-term care facility that agreed to take him would probably have suffered the same fate as Spring Creek. It would have been saddled with enormous unpaid expenses. It therefore isn't surprising that Martin Memorial could not find an appropriate rehabilitation facility to provide Jiménez with the care he needed. The hospital faced two bad choices: keeping Jiménez as an inpatient without receiving any payment, or flying him to Guatemala. Not surprisingly, the hospital picked the latter option, which might have been the very result that Congress wanted when it proclaimed that immigrants were supposed to be self-sufficient.

Many other hospitals have reached a similar conclusion. A report by Seton Hall Law School and New York Lawyers for the Public Interest reports that there were at least eight hundred medical repatriations between 2006 and 2012.[88] One hospital, the one that treated Sonia del Cid Iscoa, admitted to deporting ninety-six immigrants in just one year.[89] The practice is so common that one company, Mexcare, specializes in arranging care for the "unfunded Latin American national" back in their home country.[90]

Even immigrants who have health insurance have faced medical repatriations. In 2008, for example, Jacinto Rodríguez Cruz and Jose Rodríguez Saldana each suffered a traumatic brain injury in a car accident. After they were stabilized at Iowa Methodist Medical Center, the hospital was unable to convince a nearby rehabilitation hospital to treat the men, who had health insurance but were undocumented immigrants ineligible for Medicaid's long-term care coverage. Iowa Methodist then found a hospital in Veracruz, Mexico, that was willing to accept the men. After speaking with the patients' families in Mexico, the hospital had the semi-comatose men flown to Veracruz. About a month after they arrived, they were released to the care of their families.[91] Their families eventually sued the hospital for false imprisonment. An appeals court ruled for the hospital, finding that the families did not protest sufficiently against the transfer to establish their lack of consent.

Legal immigrants and even US citizens have also been caught up in the web of medical deportations. In 2008 the *New York Times* reported on the case of Antonio Torres, an uninsured legal immigrant who was sent to Mexico by St. Joseph's Hospital in Phoenix after a car accident put him in a coma.[92] According to Sister Margaret McBride, one of the hospital's vice presidents, St. Joseph's was just trying "to be good stewards of the resources we have."[93] Eventually, Torres's family found a hospital in California willing to treat him. They drove him to El Centro Regional Medical Center in California, which treated him until he was transferred to a California rehabilitation facility. With the care he received in California, Torres recovered from his coma and relearned to walk and talk.[94]

The case of Elliott Bustamante is perhaps the most surprising. He was born in 2007 with Down syndrome and a heart defect at University Medical Center in Tucson.[95] Although his parents were Mexican immigrants, he was a US citizen by virtue of his birth in Tucson. As such, PRWORA did not apply to him; he was entitled to Medicaid. That did not seem to matter to University Medical Center. Citing its policy to transfer patients to their "community of residence" for continuing care, the hospital arranged for Bustamante's transfer to Mexico. In the end, the transfer didn't occur because his parents contacted the Mexican consulate, which then arranged for a lawyer, who called the police as the child was being taken to the airport.[96]

Medical deportations have not been limited to immigrants who require inpatient care. Ambulatory patients with expensive conditions have also been flown to their native countries. The best-known example of this occurred in 2009 when Grady Memorial Hospital, Atlanta's primary safety-net facility, decided to close its outpatient dialysis unit in response to severe budgetary woes.[97] Because of a special provision in federal law, Medicare covers the cost of dialysis and transplantation for most citizens with end-stage renal disease (ESRD).[98] Many legal immigrants, and all undocumented immigrants, however, are ineligible for that coverage. Immigrants who are not privately insured often have to rely on state programs, Emergency Medicaid, or charity care. This can be especially challenging for ESRD patients because the Emergency Medicaid program does not cover organ transplants.[99] Only a few states—Arizona, California, Massachusetts, New York, and North Carolina—support maintenance dialysis for immigrants.[100] Unless charity care is available, uninsured patients in the states that do not cover maintenance dialysis must "wait for ESRD complications that are considered to be emergent (such as refractory hyperkalemia, volume overload, or acidosis or complications of uremia) to arise before receiving dialysis."[101] Not surprisingly, patients who are forced to wait for such complications have higher rates of hospitalization and death.[102] Overall costs of treating patients who are forced to rely on emergent dialysis are also far higher—up to 3.7 times higher in one study—than those of providing patients with maintenance care.[103]

Georgia is one of the states that does not support outpatient dialysis for immigrants.[104] When Grady Memorial Hospital decided to close its dialysis unit, its patients were left with some hard choices. One option Grady offered was to return them to their native country. As the *New York Times* reported, patients such as thirty-four-year-old Monica Chavarria found "no relief back home."[105] Chavarria lived in an Atlanta suburb with her husband of fifteen years and US-citizen child. After Grady closed its clinic, Chavarria took up Grady's offer of a flight and thirty free dialysis sessions in Guadalajara. But when she exhausted the treatments paid for by Grady, she found that she was ineligible for public insurance in Guadalajara and that the long waiting list for free dialysis went on for months. As a result she was forced to pay for her care and try to raise funds for a transplant. At least two Grady patients who returned to their native country died shortly thereafter, though the hospital claimed that their deaths were not due to the lack of treatment.[106] Morbidity rates for dialysis patients in Mexico, however, are far higher than in the United States.[107]

Most of the Grady patients who stayed in Atlanta eventually found relief. Although a lawsuit filed by patients protesting the closing was unsuccessful, the hospital ultimately contracted with an outpatient dialysis provider, Fresenius Medical Care, to dialyze its patients.[108] A dispute with Fresenius in 2011, however, interrupted care once again. During this episode, some patients were denied dialysis when hospital emergency room physicians determined that their condition was not yet severe enough to warrant emergency dialysis. At least one patient who was denied care flew back to Honduras.[109]

Of course, most immigrants are healthy and do not require expensive health care. Still, the laws that make it difficult for immigrants to obtain health insurance almost certainly affect their health. In 2002 the Institute of Medicine estimated that more than 18,000 people died each year in the United States because of lack of health insurance.[110] Harvard researchers later concluded that the lack of insurance was responsible for over 44,000 deaths among people eighteen to sixty-four years old in the United States each year.[111] Although researchers have not calculated how many immigrants die each year as a result of a lack of insurance, the high rates of uninsurance among immigrants suggest that many of them experience preventable deaths.

Many more immigrants suffer less-drastic health impacts. Although immigrants as a group are healthier than native-born Americans, and have lower health care costs than the native population, their health deteriorates the longer they stay in the United States.[112] One reason for this may be acculturation to unhealthy behaviors common in the US environment, such as eating fast food.[113] Another reason may be lack of access to medical care, including primary care.[114] Considerable evidence supports the suspicion that the health problems of immigrants are exacerbated by the difficulty they have in accessing primary and continuing care. Immigrants, including immigrant children, are less likely than native-born Americans to have a usual source of care.[115] In some subgroups the differential is especially large: immigrants from Mexico and Central America, for example, are twice as likely as citizens to lack a usual source of care.[116] Lacking a usual source of care, noncitizens are less likely to see a physician, dentist, or mental health professional than are citizens.[117] Immigrant children also have higher per capita emergency department costs than do native-born children, suggesting that minor problems are often left untreated until they become more serious and more expensive to treat.[118]

Immigrants also have less access than natives to preventive care. Although there is considerable heterogeneity based on ethnicity, age, and location, immigrants as a group are less likely than the native born to receive a wide range of preventive health services, including mammograms, cholesterol screenings, and flu shots.[119] At least one study suggests that cholesterol screenings for immigrants declined in the wake of PRWORA.[120] Foreign-born children are also 50 percent less likely than US-born children to be fully vaccinated.[121]

Inadequate access to these types of preventive and primary health care allows health problems to go untreated until they become emergencies. This may explain why costs for emergency department visits for immigrant children are three times higher than for native-born children, despite the fact that immigrant children's overall health care costs are 74 percent lower than native born children's cost, even adjusting for insurance and health status.[122] As the chief operating officer of a San Diego hospital that serves a large immigrant population told researchers: "Everybody arrives in a catastrophic condition because they do not receive proper medical care on a regular basis."[123] Not surprisingly, it is more expensive to treat conditions when they become catastrophic than when they are less severe.

Lack of insurance, although a critical factor, is not the only reason immigrants delay care. Immigrants are less likely than the native-born to receive medical care even if they are insured.[124] In some cases, this may be because they come from cultures that place less weight on Western medicine than does the dominant US culture.[125] Other immigrants who want medical care have settled in parts of the country that lack a well-developed support network that can help them find appropriate, culturally competent care.[126] Stigmatization and anti-immigrant hostility further deter immigrants from seeking needed care. Kathryn Pitkin Derose, José J. Escarce, and Nicole Lurie have noted that "[b]eing part of a stigmatized group can make immigrants reluctant to seek care because of concerns of poor treatment."[127]

Fear of immigration authorities also discourages immigrants from accessing health care.[128] Even though enforcement of Proposition 187 was almost immediately stopped by a federal court, its passage led to a sudden decline in immigrant visits to health clinics in southern California.[129] According to the *Los Angeles Times*, physicians at an East Los Angeles clinic "became concerned when Lilian Morales uncharacteristically missed an examination for precancerous lesions on her uterus. Reaching her by telephone at home, health workers soon ascertained what had happened: Morales, an illegal immigrant from Mexico, feared she would be reported to immigration authorities. So she stayed away."[130] Even more dramatic was the case of twelve-year-old Julio Cano, whose parents said they delayed treatment for his leukemia because of fear of deportation.[131] Although Julio may well have died even if he had been treated earlier, his parents' decision to delay care exemplifies the tragic human cost of imposing immigration measures on the health care system.

The Cost to Communities

Immigrants are not the only ones who pay a price when punitive immigration policies are inserted into the health care system. Because health has global public good qualities, both the communities that immigrants live in and those they come from also suffer. Medical deportations, whether forcible as in the case of Jiménez or "voluntary" as in the case of Chavarria, illustrate the impact on the communities from which immigrants come. The United States benefits from the labor of and taxes paid by immigrants, but when they experience serious accidents (even as in the case of Jiménez, as a result of wrongdoing by US citizens) or illnesses, they are sometimes sent back to their native countries, straining those nations' already burdened health care systems. As Nathan Cortez explains, foreign hospitals have become a "perverse form of safety net" for US hospitals.[132] However "perverse," this outcome should not be surprising. It is precisely the result the US Congress intended when it decided that immigrants should be able to stay in the United States only if they are self-sufficient and not in need of public support. In effect, US policy calls for sending the health care costs of immigration back to the communities from which immigrants came, even when the health care need results from conditions and incidents within the United States.

Not all of the costs can be shifted across the border. Many costs are shifted within the United States. Most obviously, US hospitals and other

health care providers bear the cost of the care they provide—sometimes
the care they are legally obligated to provide—to uninsured immigrants.
Claims about the cost of uncompensated health care, especially to immigrants, are notoriously difficult to verify, given the complexities of medical billing, the fact that hospitals do not routinely keep track of patients'
immigration status, and the frequent cost shifting in the health care system. That's why in 2004 the General Accounting Office concluded that
it could not ascertain hospital costs relating to uncompensated, undocumented immigrants.[133] Still, given the high rates of uninsurance among
immigrants and their limited access to primary and outpatient care, it
is almost certain that care for immigrants accounts for a disproportionate share of hospitals' uncompensated care costs. A 2007 Perspective in
the *New England Journal of Medicine* suggested that the uncompensated
costs for treating undocumented immigrants in California might be as
high as $740 million per year.[134] Per capita uncompensated care costs
for immigrants may be even higher in states such as Texas that fail to
provide Medicaid coverage even to many legal immigrants who could
be eligible under PRWORA. A study from Methodist Dallas Medical
Center provides a window into the extent of uncompensated care costs
for undocumented immigrants.[135] The authors reviewed the charges in
their own hospital associated with treating uninsured undocumented
patients as well as all of the reimbursement sources available from the
government. They concluded that if anticipated cutbacks in government
support for safety-net hospitals were considered, the hospital would
have faced a net loss for treating undocumented immigrants of $7.9 mil-
lion over the study period.[136] This figure did not include the costs of
treating uninsured legal immigrants.

The costs of uncompensated care are not felt simply by hospitals.
In an increasingly difficult economic environment, many hospitals,
especially safety-net providers that serve large numbers of uninsured
patients, face severe financial pressures.[137] The costs they bear for treating uninsured immigrants invariably impact other patients and payers
through cost shifting,[138] reduction in services, and even hospital clos-
ings. Grady's decision in Atlanta to close its dialysis unit is evidence of
this impact. Although two-thirds of the dialysis unit's patients were immigrants, citizens were also harmed when the uncompensated costs of
treating immigrants led the hospital to shutter its dialysis unit.

Physicians and other health care providers who treat uninsured immigrants in their hospitals and practices also pay a large price for policies that make it difficult for immigrants to be insured. A study by Mark V. Pauly and José A. Pagán found that physicians who practice in communities with high rates of uninsurance tend to be less satisfied about their careers and perceive themselves as providing lower-quality care than do physicians in communities with low rates of uninsurance.[139] The pressures to contain costs for uninsured patients, it seems, undermines physicians' sense that they are doing well by their patients.[140] Although this applies to all uninsured patients, immigrants form a disproportionate share of the uninsured population.

Medical deportations create special ethical strains for physicians. Responding to the practice in 2008, the California Medical Association passed a resolution condemning medical deportations and asked the American Medical Association (AMA) to do likewise.[141] The AMA responded by referring the matter to its Council on Ethical and Judicial Affairs, which issued a report affirming that a physician's "primary ethic requires that the physician first try to ensure that the discharge plan appropriately meets the individual patient's needs and is safe for the patient."[142] The report continued by noting that "[e]nsuring a safe discharge for patients can be extremely challenging for physicians when adequate post-discharge options are severely limited"[143] and that immigration status can limit those options. The council concluded that "physicians should not authorize a discharge unless they have confirmed that the intended destination has adequate human and material resources for the patient's needs,"[144] and that physicians should not approve of involuntary transfers.[145] Nevertheless, given the financial pressures that hospitals face due to the government's refusal to support long-term care for seriously injured immigrants, hospitals are likely to continue the practice. The costs to the doctor-patient relationship are high, and they reverberate beyond the particular patient. Professionalism, a source of trust, is eroded when physicians have to terminate care for non-medical reasons.

Nephrologists have been placed in an especially compromised ethical position by laws that prevent undocumented and many documented immigrants with end-stage renal disease from receiving insurance coverage for either transplants or maintenance dialysis.[146] A study of nephrologists found that although 64 percent reported having performed dialysis on undocumented patients in the past year, 24 percent reported advising their patients to relocate to another country because they were unable to receive necessary care. Another 13 percent reported suggesting to their patients that they relocate to another country or state.[147]

A 2011 Perspective in the *New England Journal of Medicine* by two Texas nephrologists, Rajeev Raghavan and Ricardo Nulia, described the ethical dilemmas created by laws denying immigrants access to dialysis.[148] Writing about their sick immigrant patients who must wait to be sick enough to receive emergency dialysis, Raghavan and Nulia asked if they had "an ethical duty to provide the same standard of care for all sick patients within our borders? Or would mandating the provision of health care (and of maintenance dialysis treatments) create an incentive for illegal immigration and worsen the current situation?"[149] Concluding that there was "no easy solution," they argued for the "standardization" of care for undocumented ESRD patients throughout the country.[150] What exactly that would mean they didn't say, but their story about their patient, Santiago, who by "any moral or medical standard" should have received dialysis, but could not because as a noncitizen he was only entitled to emergency care tells all. The interjection of immigration policy into health care has turned healers into gatekeepers who must watch the sick become sicker before they can offer relief. Although physicians play this role—often with discomfort—for other patients who are uninsured or underinsured, the lack of any true safety net for many immigrants magnifies the tensions.

The costs of denying immigrants health insurance are not confined to health care providers. Laws denying immigrants access to health benefits jeopardize the health of the native population. In 2007, Mark V. Pauly and José A. Pagán reported that even insured adults in communities with high rates of uninsurance were "less likely than their peers in low-uninsurance communities to have a place to go when they were sick or in need of advice about health, less likely to have visited a doctor, and less likely to have had a physical exam or checkup within the past year."[151] Insured patients in communities with high rates of uninsurance were also more likely than other insured patients to have unmet medical needs and less likely to have a mammogram.[152] In a later paper Pauly and Pagán further described their results and the economic mechanisms that explain how low rates of insurance lower quality of care for the insured.[153] Briefly, lack of insurance lowers demand, which reduces the number of providers available to perform services with high fixed costs. In addition, to the extent that health care providers offer charity care, their costs rise, leading to either increases in prices to the insured or a reduction in the quality of care for all.[154] Either way, even insured citizens suffer when their providers have to absorb significant uncompensated costs.

Denying immigrants health insurance can also affect the health of communities through mechanisms that operate outside the medical system. As Arijit Nandi, Sana Loue, and Sandro Galea have noted, barriers to accessing preventive health services may increase the proportion of a population susceptible to infectious diseases.[155] This in turn can weaken herd immunity. The low rates of immunization among the children of immigrants provides a perfect example of the problem. Low vaccination rates allow diseases such as measles and pertussis to break out in communities in which they were once rare. Likewise, as discussed in chapter 3, restrictions on access to health care, including primary care and a usual source of care, may delay treatment for communicable diseases, including sexually transmitted infections (STIs) and tuberculosis, that can spread from immigrant populations to native-born populations. After reviewing the problem, Nandi, Loue, and Galea conclude that "evidence suggests that factors that influence the level of access to basic health services among immigrants may directly impact the burden of infectious disease in the general population."[156] If so, a great paradox is at work: restrictive immigration policies that reflect, in part, fear of the health risks presented by immigrants operate to exacerbate those risks.

The interjection of immigration laws into health policy also undermines efforts to ensure an efficient health care system. The many laws that limit immigrants' access to publicly funded health insurance, and the many partial exceptions to those laws, add enormous complexity to an already complicated health insurance system. The US health care system is notable among those of wealthy countries for its high administrative costs.[157] Although hard to quantify, immigration policies add to the costs of the health care system by inserting untold restrictions and exceptions to those restrictions into the regulatory environment. Immigration policies also fragment public health insurance programs, such as Medicaid, into those available to citizens and those available to noncitizens, requiring health care providers to bill even more programs and payers than they otherwise would. And immigration policies prompt states and localities with large numbers of immigrants to develop their own programs and ways of caring for those denied insurance by PRWORA.

The most important effect of the intersection of immigration and health policies may, however, be political. Empirical research by Benjamin R. Knoll and Jordan Shewmaker suggests that anti-immigrant sentiments helped to drive opposition to the ACA.[158] They also found that Republican opponents of health reform "were generally successful" in framing the ACA as un-American. The very prospect of covering immigrants, and even of providing broad coverage, was deeply unsettling to many Americans. Thus, a nation of immigrants recoils from recognizing that health is a public good, yet only by providing health care to all who need it can it have an efficient and effective health care system.

However, as much as some may regret it, newcomers are a part of the American community. They live and work in the United States, helping to grow the economy and support the financial viability of the health care system. Although they are generally healthier than natives, like everyone else, they sometimes need health care. By excluding many of them from coverage, the United States has not made immigrants' need for health care, or the costs of their care, go away. It has only created a complex and incoherent system of exclusions and cost shifting, a morass that harms immigrants, strains health care providers, and undermines the efficiency of the system as a whole. In the next chapter, we apply our exploration of the accessibility of public health care systems to other countries.

5

Denying the Right to Health

In 2012, Aisha, a young woman living in Scarborough, Ontario, experienced symptoms related to sickle-cell disease.[1] Aisha was fifteen when her parents sponsored her immigration from Grenada to Canada. After her parents separated, her sponsorship lapsed, leaving her living in Canada without legal status. When she was eighteen and attending college, her disease flared up, sending her to a community health clinic in Scarborough, which referred her to the emergency room. Once there, she was told she would not receive care without paying CAD 350 for it upfront, unless her condition worsened. Unable to pay, she sat in the emergency department waiting for her condition to worsen to the point at which she became unconscious. Only then, was she admitted to the hospital. After a three-day stay, Aisha was billed more than CAD 5,000.[2]

International human rights law recognizes that health is a fundamental human right. Without access to health care, individuals such as Aisha can experience unnecessary pain, loss of function, and even premature death. Their ability to be productive members of the community and to participate in civic and political life, as well as fulfill their own capabilities, is diminished. Further, public health may be endangered, as communicable diseases such as influenza, tuberculosis, or even Ebola can spread when individuals lack access to timely treatment and preventive measures, such as vaccinations.

The recognition of a human right to health dates back to the Universal Declaration of Human Rights, which was adopted by the United Nations in the aftermath of World War II. The declaration asserts that everyone "has the right to a standard of living adequate for the health and well-being of himself and of his family, including food, clothing, housing and medical care."[3] This principle was reaffirmed by the international community years later in Article 12 of the International Covenant on Economic, Social and Cultural Rights (ICESCR), which requires states to respect "the right of everyone to the enjoyment of the highest attainable standard of physical and mental health."[4] Support for the right to health can also be found in numerous other sources, both hard and soft, of international law, including the International Convention on the Rights of the Child, the International Convention on the Elimination of All Forms of Racial Discrimination, the Declaration of Alma-Ata, and the Constitution of the World Health Organization.[5]

Under international law the right to health creates both a negative right of noninterference and a positive entitlement. The latter obligates states that have ratified the ICESCR to undertake disease-control measures and address a "wide range of socio-economic factors that promote conditions in which people can lead a healthy life, and extends to the underlying determinants of health, such as food and nutrition, housing, access to safe and potable water and adequate sanitation, safe and healthy working conditions, and a healthy environment."[6] It also demands the "creation of conditions which would assure to all medical service and medical attention in the event of sickness."[7] The right is widely understood to include an obligation to ensure that necessary health services are available regardless of ability to pay.[8] In other words, the right to health demands redistribution to support the costs of necessary care for those like Aisha who lack the means to pay for it.

Nations can and do fulfill their obligation to assure access to health services in varied ways. Across the globe, states organize their health care delivery and finance systems in many different manners. This is not incompatible with respect for the right to health. Fulfillment of the right does not demand any particular organizational or financial structure. In addition, the scope of redistribution and the particular benefits and treatments offered vary across the globe. Some nations offer a relatively comprehensive array of services; others a more limited set. This is permissible. Not every health service is essential; nor is every service affordable for every nation. International human rights law recognizes this, requiring that states act only "to the maximum of [their] available resources, with a view to achieving progressively the full realization of the rights recognized."[9] Thus low-income countries need not offer expensive, high-technology treatments and services that wealthier nations are obligated to provide. And even wealthy nations need not cover services that are elective, or beyond their means.

Regardless of these significant variations, all high-income nations, even the United States, which has refused to recognize a general right to health and has not ratified the ICESCR, although it did sign it, undertake significant steps to help their citizens access both public health protection and essential health care services. No nation leaves access to health care solely to either the vicissitudes of the market or the beneficence of charity. All countries heavily regulate their health care systems, and all provide significant public financing for health care for their citizens.

But what about noncitizen newcomers? Does the right to health apply to them? Must nations provide them with the same levels of care they offer their own citizens? The ICESCR appears to say yes, as it prohibits discrimination "of any kind" with respect to the "right" to health.[10] The WHO and United Nations High Commissioner for Human Rights concur, stating that "[n]on-discrimination is a key principle in human rights and is crucial to the enjoyment of the right to the highest attainable standard of health."[11] They add that states must "recognize and provide for the differences and specific needs of groups that generally face particular health challenges."[12] This suggests that the nondiscrimination principle requires more than formal equality; it requires states to address the particular health needs of marginalized populations.

The nondiscrimination principle would appear to apply to newcomers, and to obligate nations to ensure that noncitizens have equal access to medical services. The United Nations committee charged with interpreting the ICESCR has stated that nations must "*respect* the right to health by, *inter alia*, refraining from denying or limiting equal access for all persons, including prisoners or detainees, minorities, asylum seekers and illegal immigrants, to preventive, curative, and palliative health services"[13] and that "all persons, irrespective of their nationality, residency or immigration status, are entitled to primary and emergency medical care."[14] The 1985 United Nations Declaration on the Human Rights of Individuals Who Are Not Nationals of the Country in Which They Live agreed, albeit with a caveat, stating that noncitizens have the "right to health protection [and] medical care" in their country of residence "provided that they fulfil the requirements under the relevant regulations for participation and that undue strain is not placed on the resources of the State."[15]

Many international entities concur that the right to health extends with equal force to noncitizens. For example, in 2008 the World Health Assembly, the WHO's legislative body, called upon member states to promote "equitable access to health promotion, disease prevention and care for migrants, subject to national laws and practice, without discrimination on the basis of gender, age, religion, nationality or race."[16] Likewise, a 2013 report by the International Organization for Migration, WHO, and United Nations Human Rights Office of the High Commissioner asserted that international law requires that all persons have access to health care and that states make health care facilities available and accessible to migrants.[17]

Regional bodies have also affirmed that newcomers have an equal right to health. For example, the American Convention on Human Rights in the Area of Economic, Social and Cultural Rights states that the right to health care must be exercised "without discrimination of any kind for reasons related to race, color, sex, language, religion, political or other opinions, national or social origin, economic status, birth or any other social condition."[18] In 2007 European ministers of health issued the so-called Bratislava Declaration on Health, Human Rights and Migration, which called upon member states to eliminate the "practical obstacles and barriers to the enjoyment of any access to appropriate protection of health of all people on the move, including those in an irregular situation as far as emergency health care is concerned."[19] And in 2009 the European Parliament urged member states to ensure that undocumented immigrants were given access to health care.[20]

Despite these and similar assertions by influential international bodies, some uncertainty remains as to the full scope of states' legal obligations to non-citizen newcomers. Neither the ICESCR nor any other binding United Nations treaty explicitly recognizes an unqualified right to health for non-citizens. Moreover, some of the international treaties and declarations that refer to newcomers' right to health contain some notable qualifications. For example, Article 28 of the International Covenant on the Protection of All Migrant Workers and Their Families affirms that migrants have the right to receive "medical care that is urgently required for the preservation of their life or the avoidance of irreparable harm to their health on the basis of equality of treatment."[21] The covenant is silent, however, about migrants' right to nonurgent care, giving rise to the suggestion that migrants might not in fact be entitled to wholly equal care. Similarly, the Bratislava Declaration speaks only of the right of unauthorized immigrants to emergency care, leaving states' obligation to provide other needed forms of health care undefined. And the 1985 United Nations Declaration on the Human Rights of Individuals Who Are Not Nationals of the Country in Which They Live implies that immigrants' right to health is limited to the parameters established by the laws of the receiving nation. Likewise, when the Council of Europe addressed newcomers' right to health in 2011, it called upon European nations to provide migrants with "adequate entitlements to use health services,"[22] as opposed to equal entitlements to health services.

These caveats reflect common practice. Despite widespread recognition outside the United States of the right to health, most wealthy nations fail to treat noncitizen newcomers equally with respect to access to health care. Indeed, many states follow the Bratislava Declaration and guarantee some classes of newcomers, especially unauthorized newcomers, only emergency care. Other nations do not even offer that minimal level of care.

As we discussed in chapter 4, the frequent claim that the provision of publicly subsidized health care to immigrants acts as a magnet drawing undocumented immigrants is not supported by the evidence. Also unfounded is the common contention that the health care costs of immigrants tend to create unbearable strains on national health care systems. Although sharp spikes in migration, such as Europe experienced in 2015, can impose strains on local health care systems, more generally there is little reason to believe that migration burdens health care systems. The Organisation for Economic Co-operation and Development (OECD) has stated, "Regarding healthcare expenditure, although little direct information is available, there are a number of indications suggesting that immigrants are on average less costly for the public purse than the native-born."[23]

Before returning to these issues, in this chapter we review how nations that recognize the right to health treat their newcomers. As we show, countries that typically give lip service to the right to health discriminate against some classes of newcomers, denying them access to a wide range of necessary medical services. In effect, nations treat newcomers, especially those who are undocumented, as outsiders, excluded from the "universe" covered by their universal health care system.

Newcomers' Access to Care in Canada

Aisha lives in a nation that has ratified the ICESCR. Although the Canadian Constitution does not explicitly recognize a right to health, the 1984 Canada Health Act states as its goal, "to protect, promote and restore the physical and mental well-being of residents of Canada and to facilitate reasonable access to health services without financial or other barriers."[24] To fulfill that goal, the act set forth criteria that Canadian provinces must follow in providing health insurance, and helped pave the way for Canada's single-payer health care system. The system, which has long been the envy of many would-be health care reformers in the United States, provides relatively comprehensive care to all Canadian citizens, but not to all newcomers.

Canada is truly a nation of immigrants. Approximately 20 percent of its population is foreign born.[25] Immigrants to Canada tend to be older, be better educated, and have lower incomes than native-born Canadians. They are also more likely to be members of racial minorities.[26] As in other wealthy countries, immigrants tend to be healthier and use fewer health care resources than do natives.[27]

Compared to its peers, Canada is relatively generous to newcomers when it comes to health care access. Almost all immigrants who legally reside in Canada are entitled to coverage under the provincial health plans that implement the Canada Health Act. Researchers have suggested that this broader access to insurance may help explain why Canadian immigrants are more likely to have access to regular health care services than their counterparts in the United States, even when socioeconomic factors are taken into consideration.[28]

Despite the broad coverage for immigrants who legally reside within Canada, many newcomers face significant gaps in coverage. Some of the most populated provinces, including Ontario, Quebec, and British Columbia, impose a three-month waiting period before most newly arrived permanent residents can receive coverage from the provincial insurance plan.[29] Yet in a pattern evident in other nations, some favored groups of newcomers are given special treatment. For example, Quebec provides immediate coverage for pregnant women or victims of violence.[30]

Immigrants who lack permanent residence status fare worse. Refugees who are awaiting permanent residence status or are having their claim reviewed, and immigrants with a so-called temporary resident permit, receive their insurance through the Interim Federal Health Program (IFHP) which was established in 1957 to "provide urgent and essential health services to immigrants."[31] In April 2012, the minister of Citizenship and Immigration announced significant cuts to that program.[32] As a result, some newcomers were denied funding for any health care, while others lost access to basic services or lifesaving medications such as insulin. In response, several Canadian provinces established programs to fill some of the gaps, but not all did.[33] The 2012 cutbacks were challenged in court by physicians and lawyers who worked with refugees. In an earlier case brought by an undocumented immigrant who lacked access to health care, the Federal Court of Appeal had quoted with approval a statement by the lower court that expressed the widely held but unsupported claim that the provision of health care to unauthorized immigrants leads to increases in illegal immigration:

> I see nothing arbitrary in denying financial coverage for health care to persons who have chosen to enter and remain in Canada illegally. To grant such coverage to those persons would make Canada a health-care safe-haven for all who require health care and health care services. There is nothing fundamentally unjust in refusing to create such a situation.[34]

In adjudicating the constitutionality of the cutbacks to the IFHP program for refugees and others seeking the government's protection, the federal court in *Canadian Doctors for Refugee Care v. Canada* sounded a somewhat different chord. Although the court conceded that the Canadian Charter of Rights does not guarantee "the positive right to state funding for health care,"[35] and that international law was not binding on domestic courts, it ruled that the rights recognized in international conventions, including specifically the Convention on the Rights of the Child and the Convention Relating to the Status of Refugees, can serve "as interpretive guides" to an analysis of the rights established under the Canadian Charter of Rights and Freedoms.[36] With that backdrop, the court went on to conclude that the cutbacks were unconstitutionally cruel and unusual treatment, especially in their application to children, and that they "potentially jeopardize the health, and indeed the very lives, of these innocent and vulnerable children in a manner that shocks the conscience and outrages our standards of decency."[37] In reaching this conclusion, the court noted that a refugee child with asthma "may be able to access emergency room treatment for an acute asthma attack, but could later be left gasping for breath if his impoverished refugee claimant parents could not afford the cost of the child's asthma medication," and that an HIV-positive child who was entitled to an even lower level of benefits might be left without any treatment, "effectively condemning the child to an early death."[38] The court further found that by relying on country of origin to determine the tier of care to which an applicant was eligible, the government had unconstitutionally discriminated on the basis of national origin.

In response to the court's order, the government issued an interim policy eliminating the reliance on country of origin and restoring some but not all benefits.[39] Notably, individuals whose refugee claim was suspended or rejected remain eligible only for coverage "to prevent, diagnose or treat a disease posing a risk to public health or to diagnose or treat a condition of public safety concern."[40] The government appealed the court's decision.

While the appeal was pending in 2016, the new Liberal government led by Prime Minister Justin Trudeau reversed course, restoring the benefits that were cut and expanding the program to cover certain services for refugees prior to immigration.[41] But some who have had their refugee claims denied, or those like Aisha who lack any legal status, may continue to fall through the cracks and will be forced to rely on community health centers, where they are available and appropriate, or emergency departments. As the court found in *Canadian Doctors for Refugees*, this can harm the health of newcomers and lead to more expensive and uncompensated care, putting a significant financial burden on hospitals and community health care centers. It can also create painful ethical dilemmas for health care workers who have patients who need but cannot afford health care. As one physician told the court in *Canadian Doctors for Refugees*, "Once you assume care for an individual I think ethically it's highly problematic to say two visits, three visits, sorry, you don't have TB. We don't care what you have, please move on."[42]

Cracks in the European Welfare State

Canada is not the only nation that fails to respect the right of all newcomers to health, despite nominal recognition of a right to health. Europe is the birthplace of the welfare state. Otto von Bismarck established the first national health insurance program in Germany in 1883. In the ensuing decades, other Western European countries adopted their own national health care laws. Some moved toward so-called universal health care incrementally; others, like the United Kingdom, did so through the passage of a single sweeping piece of legislation. Today, all Western European nations purport to recognize the right to health; indeed, the constitutions of several European countries explicitly proclaim the right. Moreover, access to high-quality health care has become a hallmark of European citizenship and identity. Nevertheless, the robustness of European health care systems and the health security they once promised have been called into question in recent years, as so-called austerity programs have been implemented across Europe and rapid migration has challenged Europeans' willingness to support newcomers.

European nations fulfill the right to health in a variety of ways. Building on the work of Gøsta Esping-Andersen, Gudrun Biffl identifies five different approaches for organizing and paying for health care utilized across the continent.[43] The Scandinavian model emphasizes the universality of welfare rights, including the right to health, and does not rely on means testing. Under the Anglo-Saxon model, employed in the United Kingdom and Ireland, health care services are delivered by the public sector and are at the point of entry. The Continental European, or Bismarck, model utilizes a social insurance system that is funded by contributions from employers and employees, with transfer payments used to support those in need who would otherwise be left out of the employment-based system. In the Southern European model, health services are universally accessible, while income protections are provided via the Continental model. Finally, the Central and Eastern European model builds upon the socialist histories of those countries, and relies to a significant degree on the public sector.

At least in theory, European countries accept that the right to health extends to newcomers. As noted earlier, in 2007 EU ministers endorsed the Bratislava Declaration and called upon their nations to address the health care needs of migrants (the English term most frequently used in Europe to refer to noncitizens). All EU countries have also signed the Convention Relating to the Status of Refugees, which requires states to treat refugees the same as nationals "with respect to public relief."[44] According to the European Committee of Social Rights, which oversees the implementation of the European Social Charter, the denial of medical assistance to foreign nationals violates the charter.[45]

Despite these assertions, European nations have been reluctant to grant noncitizen migrants, especially undocumented immigrants, the right to health. Although migrants from within the European Union and guest workers are for the most part eligible to participate in national health programs, significant gaps remain for other immigrants from outside the European Economic Area. For example, although many of the migrants from the Middle and Near East in 2015 received limited health care, often from NGOs in refugee camps when they first reached Europe, access to care was thereafter limited.[46] In Germany, the nation that accepted the most migrants in 2015, asylees are entitled to free care, but only after they obtain documentation, which can be challenging.[47] In many other countries, asylum seekers are only entitled to care for acute illnesses.[48]

Throughout the continent, undocumented immigrants face especially high barriers in accessing needed health services. In a study of the policies in European nations published in 2012 as part of the "Health Care in NowHereland" Project, Carin Björngren Cuadra concluded that twenty-two out of twenty-seven European states studied failed to fulfill undocumented immigrants' right to health as required by international law.[49] Interestingly, Björngren-Cuadra found no relationship between the type of health system the nation employed and its treatment of immigrants.[50] Wealthy nations with robust welfare states were no more likely than less wealthy nations to respect immigrants' right to health.

Björngren-Cuadra's report identified ten European states that provided undocumented migrants "less than minimum rights" to access health care. In these countries—Finland, Ireland, Malta, Sweden, Austria, Bulgaria, the Czech Republic, Latvia, Luxembourg, and Romania—undocumented migrants face significant affordability barriers, even for emergency care. For example, in both Sweden and Austria, undocumented immigrants may have to pay the full cost of emergency care.[51]

In twelve other countries—Cyprus, Denmark, the United Kingdom, Belgium, Estonia, Germany, Greece, Hungary, Lithuania, Poland, Slovakia, and Slovenia—undocumented migrants receive "minimum rights of access to health care."[52] In these nations, undocumented migrants can generally receive emergency care, and sometimes other health services, regardless of ability to pay.[53] But significant restrictions remain on some forms of needed care.

The United Kingdom and Germany provide some but not all necessary care to undocumented newcomers. The policies in both nations are confusing and contradictory, and like the policies within the United States, send inconsistent messages about whether newcomers are members of the community covered by each nation's health care system. In the United Kingdom, for example, all legal residents and EU citizens are entitled to treatment free of cost from the National Health Service.[54] Undocumented immigrants are entitled to free care from hospital emergency departments, as well as treatment for certain communicable diseases.[55] However, free care is not available to undocumented immigrants for HIV treatment unless and until the individual requires emergency care.[56] Moreover, the National Health Service does not provide financial support for other forms of care required by undocumented patients in hospitals. Indeed, hospitals are obligated to determine whether undocumented patients are able to pay for their own care. If they are not, and the hospital nevertheless provides the care because it is medically necessary, the hospital is forced to bear the cost.[57] As a result, nonurgent secondary care can be quite difficult for undocumented immigrants to access. And those who receive such care can face very high charges. In addition, although general practitioners may register undocumented immigrants as patients, they are also permitted to refuse to treat undocumented residents or to demand payment from them. Although most general practitioners will accept undocumented immigrants as patients, immigrants often face problems finding a general practitioner willing to accept them as a patient.[58]

German policies likewise reflect inconsistent attitudes toward immigrants' participation in the nation's health care system. Under the Asylum Seekers' Benefits Law, undocumented migrants can receive emergency care from a hospital or practitioner regardless of their ability to pay.[59] As previously mentioned, additional benefits are available under a program available to asylum seekers, but documentation is required for all but emergency care,[60] and health care providers can face legal action for failing to report on undocumented migrants.[61]

According to Björngren-Cuadra, in 2012 only five European nations, Italy, Portugal, France, the Netherlands, and Spain, provided more than minimal rights to health to undocumented immigrants.[62] As in the United States, however, European countries in recent years have frequently changed policies regarding coverage of migrants, sometimes restricting care, other times expanding it. As of 2015 only Belgium, France, the Netherlands, Portugal, and Switzerland provided close to full coverage for undocumented migrants.[63] Even in the countries that purport to provide full coverage, undocumented migrants face barriers that do not exist for legal residents. For example, in France migrants are entitled to access publicly subsidized health care subject to certain conditions if they have been residents for three months or more, or meet income criteria; they may also access general practitioners free of charge after a three-year length of stay.[64] Emergency care is available regardless of length of stay.[65] In the Netherlands, access is even broader, although the so-called Linkage Law, makes clear that entitlements to public benefits are dependent upon lawful residence.[66] As a result, the care of undocumented immigrants is financed through a mechanism distinct from that available to pay for the care of legal residents. Notably, providers are obligated to bill undocumented patients, and representatives from the Ministry of Health have told researchers that so as not to incentivize "health tourists," providers should not offer undocumented immigrants immediate access to nonurgent care.[67] Ultimately, however, providers in the Netherlands are partially reimbursed for care that the patients cannot afford through mechanisms that run "parallel to the normal payment systems."[68]

As the backlash against immigration has grown in the wake of rapid increases in immigration from non-Western regions and slow economic growth, many European nations have cut back on the coverage they once provided for immigrants. For example, in 2013, the National Health Service in England increased charges for individuals who are neither UK nor EU citizens, nor "ordinarily resident" in the country.[69] And as noted previously, in 2012 Spain, which previously had one of the most generous programs for immigrants, dramatically reduced access.[70] Likewise, in 2011 the Netherlands cut back on subsidies for interpretation and translation services for health care.[71] These cutbacks reflect newcomers' tenuous status in their European homelands.

Although migrants with permanent residence status theoretically have a right to full participation in European health care systems, in many nations migrants face great barriers in attaining such status. Indeed, in some countries, immigrants need to wait up to eight years, and pass language and cultural tests, before becoming long-term residents.[72] Citizenship can also be extremely difficult to achieve in many European nations. Some European countries, most notably Germany, Austria, and Switzerland, restrict citizenship for the most part by ancestry.[73] Other nations require noncitizens to wait up to ten years to achieve citizenship.[74] In several European countries, even the native-born children of immigrants may be denied citizenship.[75]

As in other countries, the restrictions on noncitizens' participation in health programs are widely defended as necessary to prevent immigrants, especially those without legal status, from migrating to Europe for health benefits.[76] Critics of coverage also argue that immigrants' health care costs can pose unbearable burdens on state health care systems.[77] However, as discussed in chapter 1, people do not generally immigrate for health care. Moreover, the health care costs of newcomers are generally lower than those of citizens. Indeed, in 2000 Spain increased access to care for undocumented migrants, a policy later reversed, after an official study concluded that the costs of doing so would be negligible.[78] Moreover, in some countries, social insurance systems might benefit if undocumented immigrants were allowed to participate equally with legal residents and were therefore expected to pay some of their own insurance costs.

Nevertheless, the claim that the provision of health for undocumented immigrants places extraordinary burdens on national health care programs and draws more, unhealthy undocumented immigrants, is widespread. These views have even appeared in judicial decisions. For example, in 2008, the European Court of Human Rights stated that Article 3 of the European Convention on Human Rights, which prohibits torture and degrading and inhumane treatment, "does not place an obligation on the Contracting State to alleviate such disparities [in care available in Europe and the country of origin] through the provision of free and unlimited health care to all aliens without a right to stay within its jurisdiction."[79] The court added that finding to the contrary would place "too great a burden" on states.[80] More recent decisions by immigration tribunals in the United Kingdom have offered a different perspective, suggesting that in some circumstances, the deportation of a noncitizen with significant health care needs that cannot be met in the country of origin might violate Article 8, which affirms a right to respect for private and family life.[81] In one recent case concerning the deportation of a legal immigrant who had received a kidney transplant in the United Kingdom, the Immigration and Asylum Chambers concluded that deporting the woman to Nigeria would violate Article 8, because she would die for lack of medical care shortly upon her return.[82] Still, the tribunal emphasized that such cases would be rare and that the individual's right had to be weighed against the public interest in safeguarding limited resources.[83] Likewise, in a decision concerning the deportation of a sick child, the tribunal noted that the United Kingdom was under no international obligation to be "the hospital of the world," but that the issue remained whether removal was disproportionate given the medical evidence.[84] In short, even the courts charged with protecting the right to health fail to do so for newcomers.

The Impact of the Denial of Care

The impact of the denial of newcomers' right to health in Europe is hard to gauge, primarily because data is sparse. Many European countries do not track health by immigration status, but look instead at ethnicity or national origin. As a result, the health of newcomers is often conflated with or masked by the health of native-born members of minority populations.

The data that exist suggest that in Europe, as elsewhere, immigrants as a group are healthier than citizens, but there is great variation. In some countries, migrants tend to have poorer health than the native population. Moreover, some groups of noncitizens face higher rates of particular illnesses and injuries than natives. For example, newcomers as a group appear to be more vulnerable than citizens to occupational injuries,[85] probably because of their disproportionate employment in low-wage, dangerous jobs. Newcomers also have higher rates of some communicable diseases, including tuberculosis, hepatitis B, and HIV, often as a result of premigration exposures.[86] In addition, in many European countries, infant mortality rates are higher for migrant mothers, especially those from non-Western countries.[87] Refugees, undocumented immigrants, and asylum seekers are also at greater risk than natives for mental health problems, probably as a result of the violence and traumas they have experienced in their native countries or during the migration process.[88]

Critically, migrants in Europe, especially those who are undocumented, are less likely than natives to use many important health services. For example, newcomers are less apt to receive important preventive services, including mammography and cervical cancer screenings.[89] They also have fewer prenatal health care visits, and some studies show that they access prenatal care later in pregnancy.[90] Newcomers also have more emergency room visits than natives. This may be because of the barriers they face in accessing other sources of care. Some HIV patients in the United Kingdom, for example, have been "left untreated until they've been admitted as emergencies to intensive care treatment units."[91]

Although the factors influencing newcomers' lower utilization rates are not fully understood, legal barriers to participation in state health programs undoubtedly play a role in reducing the health services used by undocumented newcomers. This was illustrated when Spain starting in 2002 allowed undocumented migrants to receive medical cards and access health care on the same terms as legal migrants. A study by Alberto Torres-Cantero and colleagues found that once Spain removed the legal barriers to coverage, undocumented immigrants used health care services at rates equivalent to those seen for legal migrants.[92]

Although legal barriers to immigrants' participation in health care systems likely affects their use of care, other factors are also at work, as even legal immigrants who are provided with health care coverage have lower utilization rates than natives.[93] Some studies, for example, suggest that some immigrants distrust Western medicine or experience significant cultural misunderstandings in their encounters with Western health care providers.[94] For this reason, health researchers and human rights advocates have stressed the need for culturally competent care.

The health impact of nations' failure to respect newcomers' right to health is not fully known. Again the dearth of data is notable and makes it difficult to reach firm conclusions about the health or economic impact of barriers to immigrants' access to health care. Nevertheless, studies suggest that migrants who have cancer present at later stages than natives.[95] A study from the Netherlands found that immigrants had elevated levels of avoidable mortality compared to nonmigrants.[96] Although some of the differential was explained by socioeconomic status, not all of it was.[97] It also seems plausible that higher infant mortality rates may be associated with reduced access to prenatal care (although other factors are certainly also at work). Other studies have suggested that lack of access to affordable care has forced immigrants who are HIV positive to rely on what are known as "African treatments" for their disease.[98] Lack of access to treatments may also undermine immigrants' willingness to be tested for the disease.[99] After all, what's the point of being tested if you cannot be treated if found to be infected?[100] Delays in testing, however, can have significant impacts on public health, as testing is associated with changes in behavior that reduce transmission.[101]

Lack of access to health care for immigrants, who tend to have higher rates of some communicable diseases than natives, poses a potential public health risk to the broader community, a risk that is often overstated. Indeed, the great irony is that while newcomers are often targeted and disparaged for the health threats they supposedly pose to natives, they are often denied access to the health care that would diminish those threats.

Likewise, although immigrants are frequently denied care on the theory that their health care costs burden receiving countries, the barriers imposed on the care they receive can actually add to overall costs. This is especially obvious with communicable diseases, which can spread to others if not quickly treated, adding to overall costs. Similarly, by denying immigrants routine access to care outside emergency rooms, nations effectively push them to emergency departments, the most costly site for care. As Tony Delamothe explains, "A public health doctor—or anyone, really—will tell you that emergency care is the most expensive way of providing healthcare and that it's preferable to treat illness as early as you can."[102]

Noting these concerns, international health and human rights organizations have decried the myriad restrictions placed upon newcomers' access to health. As a 2013 report by the International Organization for

Migration, WHO, and United Nations Human Rights Office of the High Commissioner explained, states' failure to respect immigrants' right to health can increase health care risks for both migrants and natives, while also leading to higher overall costs.[103] The report further noted that there is no evidence to support the contention that legal barriers to entitlements deter migration.[104]

In later chapters we explain that health is a global public good. As a result, norms of reciprocity and fairness obligate nations to recognize immigrants' right to health. We also explain why the absence of citizenship does not justify denying newcomers, even those who are undocumented, equal access to health care. Nor, we show, does the need for solidarity, which can support obligations to "carry costs" or support redistribution for others. Rather, because citizens and immigrants interact in close proximity in their roles as patients, health care professionals, caregivers, and neighbors, citizens have duties of solidarity to immigrants with respect to health.

For now, it suffices to observe that the common practice of discriminating against noncitizen immigrants regarding the right to health makes for "blatantly poor public health practice."[105] Denying newcomers equal access to health care does not deter migration, but it can lead to a less healthy workforce and population. It can also lead to the unnecessary spread of communicable diseases and the delivery and rearing of children with unmet health care needs. In effect, the right of citizens to live in a healthy community is undermined by the denial of newcomers' right to health.

Moreover, the health care needs of newcomers cannot be ignored for long. Serious health conditions that are left untreated eventually demand treatment, often in emergency departments and hospitals, where costs are higher than they are in other health care settings. Thus, for example, providing antiretroviral therapy to HIV-positive undocumented immigrants is more cost-effective than treating HIV patients only when they develop acute symptoms of their disease.[106] For these reasons, the United Nations Special Rapporteur on Migration has concluded that the denial of immigrants' right to health leads to higher health care costs.[107]

Like health-based immigration restrictions, restrictions on immigrants' participation in health care programs offer wealthy nations the mirage that newcomers' health care problems can be "kept out" and that their health care systems can be spared the costs, both physical and fiscal, of outsiders. The denial of immigrants' right to health also helps to sustain the illusion that health care benefits are available only to those who are "deserving" of them. Thus, restrictions on immigrants' health care access helps to perpetuate the myth that health care systems can be bounded and that only those within the boundaries merit care.

But these are only illusions. Unless global economic conditions change dramatically, newcomers will continue to migrate, live, and work in developed countries. Like everyone else, they will face health problems, often as a result of conditions they experience once they arrive in their new homelands. This reality has forced most nations to provide at least some access to emergency care, and many nations to establish policies providing newcomers with limited access to other health services. In short, despite strong anti-immigrant sentiment, receiving countries know that they cannot keep their newcomers fully outside their health care systems. Health care systems are not and cannot be closed to a discrete set of "deserving" members. Moreover, futile attempts to close health care systems simply increase the systems' costs and complexity, comprising not only newcomers' right to health, but that of citizens also.

6

Health as a Global Public Good

Smallpox

Smallpox, the variola virus, is among the most contagious diseases known to humankind. It first surfaced three thousand years ago in India or Egypt and has devastated entire communities. The virus was airborne and spread through face-to-face contact, and often through contaminated clothing and sheets. When people were infected with smallpox they first experienced a twelve- to fourteen-day incubation period during which there was no evidence of the virus. They didn't know that they were sick and could easily infect others. Following the incubation, flulike symptoms were experienced, including fever, headaches and malaise. When these subsided, lesions and pustules appeared, along with their scars. About 30 percent of people who were infected with smallpox died within a couple of weeks, and the majority of survivors were left with disfigured pox marks. The settlement of Plymouth, Massachusetts, in 1633, brought with it an outbreak of smallpox that devastated the Native American community. In the eighteenth century smallpox killed one in ten children born in Sweden and France, and every seventh child in Russia. This deadly virus spread across the globe. It moved from West Africa to South America in the nineteenth century. In industrialized countries it could spread through a ventilator, causing people throughout an entire building to become infected.[1]

In 1967 when smallpox threatened 60 percent of the world population, the WHO established a global plan to eradicate it. By 1977 that plan had succeeded. Not only were lives saved, but countries that donated money to eradicate the virus globally benefited as well. Preventing diseases in other countries can save money for the country contributing the money. Lincoln Chen, Tim Evans, and Richard Cash point out that the United States invested $32 million in the global campaign to eradicate smallpox. Taxpayers save this amount of money every twenty-six days in savings from not having to vaccinate and screen people for smallpox.[2] But the economic benefits pale in comparison to the lives that were saved because of the eradication of the disease. A world free from smallpox is a better world; individuals, populations, and the global community are healthier, wealthier, and happier. Health, free from smallpox, is a good: the benefits transcend individuals to include populations, the global community, and the global financial structure.

Public Goods

In this chapter we explain why health is a global public good. Public goods benefit the public, and their absence—which some people have referred to as public "bads"—harms the public. Health confers countless benefits on the public. This is not to say that individuals do not also benefit from their own health. But good health is not only or even primarily a benefit for the individual. Health fosters a strong and innovative workforce, contributes to national security, and creates happier communities.

The term "public good" is a term of art used in economics. Understanding health as a public good can inform the kind of health policies that are appropriate for newcomers. We argue that highlighting the public-good dimension of health can help us to devise effective and fair health policies. Public goods have two main characteristics: the benefits of public goods are nonrivalrous in consumption and nonexcludable. When something is nonrivalrous it can be consumed by one person without diminishing it or restricting what is available for others. Consider clean air. The air that one person breathes does not deprive others of clean air. In contrast, private goods, such as cars and computers, lose value when they are used. Public goods are different. Their value is not diminished through use. When something is nonexcludable it is difficult to keep other people from enjoying it. This is true for clean air. It is close to impossible to exclude people from breathing air. In contrast, it is easy to exclude them from cars and computers. Incidentally, some mechanisms that ensure health, such as antiretroviral drugs, are excludable, just like a car, though the consequences of excluding others from them are, of course, far more devastating. Public goods such as green grass in a park and clean air are different. Everyone enjoys the beautiful green lawn in the park, and it is difficult to restrict the pleasure it brings to those who pay taxes, or dutifully refrain from walking on it. Although public goods have enormous benefits for people, the very qualities that make them efficient for a community, nonrivalry and nonexcludability, make them unwieldy in the marketplace. It is difficult to price something to sell to people when it is possible for them to have it without paying for it.

Ensuring adequate public goods can be challenging because they are not easily accommodated by the free market. The nonexcludability of public goods means that they cannot be restricted to those who will pay for them. This, in turn, makes it impossible to enforce a price, leaving little incentive for anyone to sell public goods. People can have public goods even when they don't pay for them. Because of this public goods are vulnerable to being undersupplied, or, when available, some people may be unjustly enriched by the benefit of the good without contributing to its creation. People who enjoy a public good without contributing to it are unjustly enriched. Consider an example: Most people in a community refrain from walking on a lawn, to ensure that it is lush and green, while other people walk over it on a regular basis. Those who walk on the grass enjoy a benefit that others cannot enjoy and that is only possible because others have kept off the grass. This is the "free-rider problem," and it gives rise to concerns about fairness. Because the market doesn't work effectively with public goods, collective action is often required both to ensure adequate supplies of the good and to address free-rider problems.

Although it is relatively easy to specify the critical features of a public good, applying those features to particular goods is not straightforward. Public goods, such as clean air and peace, are frequently intangible, and excludability and rivalry are relative concepts.[3] In addition, public goods are rarely pure.[4] With these caveats in place we will show that health satisfies the crucial features of a public good.

Public goods change our moral obligations. From a utilitarian perspective, they can be valuable because they have the potential to affect large numbers of people; whatever we do to enhance them can benefit many people. For this reason, public goods can help maximize happiness. If public parks make people happy, their public dimension has the potential to make lots of people happy. Consider the eradication of smallpox. The creation of vaccination saved the lives of millions for generations forward. Moreover, the protection that is conferred on nonvaccinated members of a community when herd immunity is achieved means that the good didn't benefit only those who were vaccinated. Public goods are also morally significant for fairness reasons. Because public goods are both nonrivalrous and nonexcludable, people other than those who pay for them or contribute in other ways to their creation can enjoy them. People who are enriched by public goods but do not contribute their fair share to the goods' creation, give rise to concerns about fairness. If justice is conceived in terms of reciprocity, free riders may be in debt to the community.

If our sense of justice and fairness is not informed by reciprocity but is more inclusive, then we might view the beneficiaries who do not contribute to a public good not as free riders but as fair followers. This point was nicely made by Kevin Outterson, a law professor at Boston University. He argued that people in developing countries who enjoy the benefits of research and development done in rich countries in the way of free medicine are really fair followers.[5] If access to an essential medicine truly doesn't reduce innovation, and it is nonrivalrous, fairness considerations may dictate giving the medicine away. Denying people lifesaving medicines when they cannot afford to pay for them instead seems unfair and inhumane. At the heart of the concern about free riding, is a concern that if we simply give something away, others will be less inclined to pay for it, and given nonexcludability, it will be impossible to enforce payment. But if there is no harm done, and innovation will continue, it is difficult to see why anyone would object.[6] Although fairness concerns can arise with public goods, given a more inclusive perspective public goods may be celebrated for the benefits they can easily confer on others.[7] In either case, public goods have normative implications. They have the potential to bring people together by conferring benefits on fair followers, or drive them apart as they reflect on the unearned windfall of others—perhaps at their own cost.

Because public goods are not easily provided by the market, if they are going to be adequately supplied, non-market mechanisms may be required. Norms and law can be useful in ensuring an adequate supply of public goods. Consider the case of clean air again. Market mechanisms need to be supplemented with laws that regulate greenhouse gas emissions. Moral and nonmoral norms are also required so that individuals monitor adequately their personal use of cars, electrical appliances, and other items. In other words, if the market cannot supply public goods, additional effective mechanisms need to be created.

Global Public Goods

The concept of a public good is complex, and that complexity is exacerbated with global public goods. To qualify as a *global* public good, the good must have benefits that are quasi-universal in other countries, people, and generations.[8] Typically, when thinking of the public we think of nation-states, or smaller units, such as regions and cities. However, Inge Kaul, Isabelle Grunberg, and Marc Stern suggest that in thinking about *global* public goods, the focus should be on those who benefit from the good.[9] Global public goods should benefit more than one group of countries, or region of the world such as Europe or the Americas. It should extend over an array of the global population, including socioeconomic groups. Similarly, a global public good should meet "the needs of present generations without jeopardizing those of future generations."[10] In the end, they arrive at the following definition:

> A pure global public good is marked by universality—that is, it benefits all countries, people, and generations. An impure global public good would tend towards universality in that it would benefit more than one group of countries, and would not discriminate against any population segment or set of generations.[11]

According to this United Nations Development Program report, a "global public good" is a public good with benefits that are:

> quasi universal in terms of countries (covering more than one group of countries), people (accruing to several, preferably all, population groups), and generations (extending to both current and future generations, or at least meeting the needs of current generations without foreclosing development options for future generations).[12]

These definitions share an emphasis on *universality*: global public goods have a universal reach. They generate benefits for multiple nations, and socioeconomic groups, as well as future generations. Now that we have a definition of public good and global public good, let's see if health qualifies.

Health as a Public Good

In some quarters, health is viewed as a private good on the grounds that the primary beneficiary of health is the healthy individual. David Woodward and Richard Smith claim that "health per se is not a public good, either individually or nationally. One person's (or one country's) health status is a private good in the sense that he/she is the primary beneficiary of it. An individual's health remains primarily of benefit to that individual, although there may be some (positive or negative) externalities resulting from it, such as the exposure to others from a communicable disease."[13] In addition, they claim that health should be viewed as a private good because it is achieved through excludable mechanisms such as vaccinations and condoms. Thus health is nonrivalrous, but excludable, and more closely akin to a club good (which is a public good that is nonrivalrous but excludable, such as cable television).[14]

We call this the standard view. Arguments in support of the standard view are vulnerable. The economic perspective of man as isolated, opportunistic, and self-interested may underlie the standard view of health as a private good. However, if that world view is wrong, and people are by nature cooperative rather than competitive, flourishing when embedded in interdependent communities, the view that health is a private good is problematic.

Even the standard view acknowledges that health should sometimes be understood as a public good. When a communicable disease is prevented in one person, there are benefits for other people because their risk of infection is thereby reduced. Thus communicable diseases are nonrivalrous.[15] Because communicable diseases count for about 26 percent of deaths and 30 percent of the global burden of disease, recognizing the public-good quality of health in this context is significant.[16] For Woodward and Smith, eradication of a communicable disease is a pure public good: the benefits of eradication are neither excludable nor rivalrous. Even the standard view, which is predisposed to viewing health as a private good, accepts that health related to communicable diseases is a pure public good. We saw this in the case of smallpox. Its eradication was a significant global public good. Although we can only speculate, had the United States not viewed the eradication of smallpox as a global public good, it might not have contributed $32 million to the global effort to eradicate it. Here countries acted in solidarity with much success for global health.

Health is clearly good for people who have the good fortune to be healthy. The question is whether health can also be understood as a public good. Our view is yes. Health is not only good for individuals, it is also good for society. Health is nonrivalrous in consumption since one person's good health doesn't diminish the health of another. Very often one person's health can contribute to the health of others. Health can also be nonexcludable. It can be difficult to exclude people from good and bad health. For example, widespread vaccinations carry with them the phenomenon of herd immunity. People who have not been vaccinated are protected by the vaccination of others. This is not to say that health does not also have private good dimensions. Some of the access goods for health are private: medicines and medical devices, for example. But the fact that some of the access goods for health are private (and excludable) does not show in and of itself that health is a private good. Grass seed, mulch, and soil are excludable, yet the green grass in a park is public.

The question of whether or not health is a public good is different from the question of whether the access goods for health are public or private. In this respect, our concern is different from the one raised by philosopher Onora O'Neill, who explores the question of whether there are "true public goods that bear on health" and is skeptical both of such goods and of their importance for public health.[17] Unlike O'Neill, we argue that health itself is a global public good, and that this fact has important implications for health policy and for the health and wellbeing of newcomers.

The standard view has shortcomings. Although some access goods for health are excludable, others are not, or can only be excluded with considerable effort. For example, it has been shown that our place in a social network can impact our health and the health of others within the network. Obesity is a good example. In one study of 5,124 people, Nicholas Christakis and James Fowler observed clustering of obese people on a graph. The study found that the average obese person was more likely to have obese friends, friends of friends, and friends of friends of friends. A similar effect was found for nonobese people.[18] The researchers found that the obesity epidemic was multicentric—spreading from multiple locations. This suggests a couple of ways that obesity might spread, including imitation, encouraged by mirror neurons, and the spreading of norms, such as a norm about tolerable weight gain.[19] There have been similar findings with respect to clustering and depression—a significant factor in global morbidity and mortality.[20]

Mirror neurons give people the capacity to mirror the actions of others; they are one of the primary mechanisms human beings have to empathize with others and establish social ties with them. Neuroscientist Marco Iacoboni states, "It seems as if our brain is built for mirroring, and that only through mirroring—through the simulation in our brain of the felt experiences of other minds—do we deeply understand what other people are feeling."[21] In the case of obesity, people may mimic their obese social ties through mirror neurons.

The standard view focuses on the individual; it treats health as if it were a matter for only individuals. But this ignores public health and the health of populations. High rates of disease can devastate populations. The impact of HIV/AIDS in sub-Saharan Africa is a good example. The United Nations Programme on HIV/AIDS and the World Health Organization estimated in 2009 that there were 33 million people living worldwide with HIV/AIDS and that two-thirds of them lived in Africa, with an increasing number in rural communities.[22] In addition, around 70 percent of new infections occurred in sub-Saharan Africa and about 70 percent of deaths from HIV/AIDS took place in sub-Saharan Africa.[23] HIV/AIDS has reduced the workforce and agricultural outputs and has increased poverty. One of the adverse effects of HIV/AIDS at the population level has been with respect to the natural environment. For example, forests have been depleted as families turned to them for firewood to care for the sick and to make coffins.[24] One study found that the loss of human capital because of HIV/AIDS has impaired preservation efforts of endangered species such as elephants.[25] Absenteeism and reduction of available workers because of the impact of the disease on working-age people took its toll on the environment.

There are many other ways in which the HIV/AIDS epidemic in sub-Saharan Africa has impacted the well-being of the community, future generations, and the environment. We can only begin to see this when we shift from seeing health as a private good, good only for individuals, and begin to recognize its public good dimensions.[26] When the latter perspective is adopted, we can begin to appreciate how health is a public good with wide-ranging benefits for the community, the globe, and future generations. Although we would not deny that health can be viewed as a private good, there is no reason to think that it is only or primarily a private good.

As the examples of depression and obesity show, the role of social ties in health is not restricted to communicable diseases. Networks affect health even with noncommunicable diseases (NCDs). NCDs such as diabetes, cervical cancer, and stroke also afflict large numbers of people in developing countries, especially those living in urban slums. According to Thomas Bollyky: "The frequent onset of these diseases among younger populations consumes scarce health-care resources, saps labor from the work force and hinders economic development, and makes it harder for governments to address other threats, such as infectious diseases."[27]

In some quarters, NCDs are thought to underscore the private nature of health insofar as they are related to lifestyle choices: diet, exercise, and alcohol and tobacco consumption. "But for" the choices of individuals, some argue, people would not have these illnesses. Setting aside the obvious role of genes and luck, individual lifestyle choices do not take place in a contextual vacuum but are influenced and shaped by context, what's on offer, so to speak. Richard Thaler and Cass Sunstein refer to this in terms of choice architecture.[28] The framing of individual choice is shaped by a variety of factors outside individuals, pushing them in various directions. In different words, Linda Fried concurs: "As these behavioral and environmental risks have been imported from developed to developing countries, and as we learn that community norms and social networks reinforce the uptake of adverse health behaviors, this puts into question whether, in fact, we should consider these risk factors and the resulting diseases 'non-communicable.'"[29] Put differently, diseases that are quintessentially associated with individual behavior, such as stroke and heart disease, are similar to communicable diseases because norms and networks that foster them are nonexcludable. Our health is affected by the health of other people in a multiplicity of ways, and the health of one can affect the health of others. Thus, although the standard view depicts health as a private good because individuals are the primary beneficiaries,[30] there are a number of reasons for thinking this is not the case. Health is certainly good for the person who has it, but whether the healthy individual is the *primary* beneficiary is a very complicated matter.

If people are connected to others, as most are, their health is very much a public matter. When we think about people embedded in communities, it is difficult to identify health benefits as primarily individual. Looked at from the perspective of people within a social context, health is often for the sake of others. Healthy parents are better able to support their families; healthy spouses are better partners; healthy neighbors share in creating a vibrant and safe community. When we think about people embedded in their communities, it is difficult to see why individuals would be the primary beneficiaries of health. Someone who is embedded in a network benefits a range of people in that network, and calculating the primary beneficiary is complex. For example, who the primary beneficiary of a good is may depend on how many people are affected, and who is in greatest need, among those who are affected. One very reasonable way to understand "primary beneficiary" is as the person who benefits the most from something. A loaf of bread means something very different to someone who is hungry than to someone who has just finished dinner in a five-star restaurant. When it comes to being a beneficiary, all individuals are not equal. Assuming that individuals are the primary beneficiaries of health reflects a particular philosophical worldview. Individuals can be most easily viewed as the primary beneficiaries of their health only when we are predisposed to view the world through the lens of individualism. Looked at through another lens, whereby individuals are not primarily economic, self-interested agents, but rather other-oriented, it is just as easy to view other people as the primary beneficiaries of health. Thus it is a mistake to agree with Woodward and Smith that health is a private good because the primary beneficiary is the healthy individual.

Social Determinants

Some of the most significant factors affecting health are what have come to be known as the social determinants of health. According to the WHO, "The social determinants of health are the conditions in which people are born, grow, live, work and age, including the health system. These circumstances are shaped by the distribution of money, power and resources at global, national and local levels."[31] The social determinants of health include a wide array of social and economic factors as well as the physical environment. Income and social status are also associated with better and worse health. Inequality and social gradients are also associated with health; thus, income is not the only factor.[32] The health of each social gradient is associated with inequality and social status. Although the health of those on lower gradients is worse than of those at higher gradients, everyone's health is affected by social gradients.[33] Education levels are also associated with health; not surprisingly those with less education fare worse healthwise than those with more education. Early childhood education is a particularly important determinant of health. Other social factors, such as social capital and the support of families, friends, and communities are also important: isolation can be deadly.

Clean water, clean air, and safe communities can also affect health and can be viewed as social determinants. Employment and the conditions in which people work also affect their health. Some studies show that the more control people have over their work, the healthier they are.[34] Research has also shown that unemployment per se harms health.[35] Commenting on the social determinants of health, the WHO has the following to say: "The context of people's lives determine their health, and so blaming individuals for having poor health or crediting them for good health is inappropriate. Individuals are unlikely to be able to directly control many of the determinants of health."[36]

The social determinants of health are largely responsible for health inequities both nationally and globally.[37] The WHO considers the differences in health status within and between countries "unfair and avoidable."[38] For example, gender bias, as reflected in norms, values, and power relations, affects the health of girls and women. Poverty and its attending circumstances, such as the absence of clean potable water, food, and shelter, have an impact on health. Racism and discrimination have also been shown to have an adverse impact on health. Although it is clear how poverty hurts health, what is less clear is that simply providing clean water and nutritious food solves the problem. Sir Michael Marmot makes the point that how these "goods" are distributed is socially determined.[39]

Consider the relevance of this insight to the question of whether health is a public good. Given that so much of health is determined by social factors such as poverty, education, social status, social cohesion, and air quality, some of which are beyond the control of individuals, the social determinants of health show that some aspects of health are determined by public factors. Indeed, the observation that social status has an adverse impact not only on the poor, but also on the rich—those higher up the social ladder—evidences the nonexcludability of health. Only when we think of people through the lens of rugged individualism, as atomistic, isolated, and unembedded, is it plausible to view individuals as the primary beneficiaries of health. But surely it is wrong to think about people separate from from their activities, families, communities, and humanity. If the standard view holds that health is a private good because the access goods for health are private, then by parity of reasoning, since we have argued that in substantial ways the access goods are public and nonexcludable, it would follow that health is a public good.

Health is nonrivalrous in the sense that one person's health does not deprive others of health. Everyone can enjoy good health. Health is nonexcludable in the sense that it is difficult to exclude people who are embedded in communities from many of the access goods for health. Of course, there are circumstances in which an access good to health is genuinely scarce, such as a scarce organ or expensive patented medication. But many other significant access goods for health are nonexcludable. If anything, not only is health not rivalrous in consumption, healthy people can often improve the health of others. This is directly the case with herd immunity, and indirectly in relation to, for example, obesity. It is also reasonable to view health as a public good because of the massive role that the social determinants play in health. Since people cannot practically, legally, or ethically be sequestered from many of the social determinants of health, these access goods for health are nonexcludable. The benefits of health and the harms associated with its absence cannot be restricted when we view people as social beings embedded in communities. Nor is it only the health of the poor that is affected by the social determinants. In the case of inequality, the health of people at each social gradient is impacted.[40]

People Are Social Creatures

The standard view fails to take into account the extent to which people are social. Philosopher John Stuart Mill recognized the social nature of human beings: "there *is* this basis of powerful natural sentiment; . . . when once the general happiness is recognized as the ethical standard, will constitute the strength of the utilitarian morality. This firm foundation is that of the social feelings of mankind—the desire to be in unity with our fellow creatures."[41] People are social. Indeed, as discussed elsewhere in this chapter, recent studies on mirror neurons show that people are wired to be social insofar as they are neurologically predisposed to be empathic.[42]

People are socially embedded, and interdependent. What counts as a beneficiary of a person's health depends on the context. Infants are typically embedded in nuclear families, sometimes extended families, and in cohesive communities, neighborhoods. The health of an infant brings joy and well-being to many people. The elderly very often live "smaller" lives, but their value within their networks can be significant. There can be many beneficiaries of a person's health. People are deeply and widely embedded; they go to schools, have jobs, shop, buy homes, engage in volunteer work, raise families, care for friends and extended family, interact with friends, and travel the globe. For these people, the beneficiaries of their health are wide-ranging and abundant.

Beneficiaries of health can be determined not only by how many people are "touched" by a life, but also by the role that people play in the lives of others. If a person is the main breadwinner in a family or the primary caretaker of children and aging parents, all his or her dependents are beneficiaries. But so are employers, colleagues, and clients. The standard view holds that health should be viewed as a private good because the healthy individual is the primary beneficiary of health. Our analysis shows that it is a mistake to treat the individual as the primary beneficiary of health.

Under the standard view, health should be viewed as a private good because the individual is the primary beneficiary. We have argued that this is only true because of the underlying and unjustified assumption of individualism. Before leaving the standard view, it will be helpful to consider another example given by Woodward and Smith. They compare the private benefit of health to that of a garden, claiming that a garden is primarily a benefit to the homeowner because he sees more of it and spends more time in it.[43] This may be true of the proverbial secret garden, but not for most gardens. There is another way to look at this, according to which passersby are the primary beneficiaries of a garden. When a garden is visible to the public, as many are, neighbors and passersby may easily enjoy it. Indeed, they may well enjoy it more than homeowners, who may be fewer in number than passersby, and may only see it when they are outside their homes. When a garden is considered in the context of the community in which it's embedded, it is difficult to view the garden as primarily a benefit to the owner. In fact, many homeowners treat their garden as the gateway to the private domain, but not itself private. Gardens often provide a house with what real estate agents call curb appeal. Just as health benefits individuals, so too do gardens. Health has a private dimension. But the standard view seems to assume that because health benefits the healthy individual, it only benefits that individual. Philosophers call this the fallacy of composition. It takes place when one assumes that something which is true of a part is also true of the whole. But as Mill argued, people are social and live in communities. They benefit from the health of one another in countless ways: children are healthy, communities are robust, and economies flourish. Viewed in a social context, the benefits to the individual from good health seem relatively unimportant compared to the benefit to others from their health.

Health as a Global Public Good

So far we have argued that health is a public good. It is perhaps easiest to see that health is good for particular communities, regions, or nations. Arguably if health is a public good and we now live in a global context, health is also a global public good. It is often treated as such. Thus when the Ebola virus killed more than eleven thousand people in West

Africa in 2014 and 2015, Margaret Chan, director of the World Health Organization, declared the outbreak "a public health emergency of international concern," with the WHO emphasizing the need for countries worldwide to help because a "coordinated international response" was required to stop the spread of the deadly virus. Multiple nations donated expertise and money to combat the virus.[44] How is it that the elimination of an epidemic in West Africa, for example, is a good for people in Canada? The obvious answer is that today with frequent travel, illnesses in one country threaten people in other countries. Yet there are a number of ways that the health of people in our country affects those in other countries.

Today, many people travel for business, pleasure, or to begin new lives in new countries. Work is often outsourced to distant nations. In addition, many people work in the global public domain, for organizations such as the UN, World Bank, and Médecins Sans Frontières. In the case of Ebola, the first Americans to return to the United States with the Ebola virus were aid workers who had gone to West Africa to provide medical aid. Social and moral norms, laws, and the activities of multinational firms can also affect health transnationally. Norms flowing from rich countries to poor countries about diet, exercise, and other lifestyle matters affect the health of people worldwide. Sometimes norms are global, including norms about tobacco and sweet sodas. Eighty-four percent of the world's 1.1 billion smokers live in developing countries and account for 5 million tobacco-related deaths a year.[45] Smoking is increasing largely because of global marketing campaigns.[46]

Regulation of tobacco, alcohol, and processed foods is close to nonexistent in many developing countries. Poor countries are often reluctant to tax unhealthy products for fear that doing so will damage their fragile economies. Multinational companies have expanded their marketing efforts to poor countries. Coca-Cola is everywhere. Until recently, with the adoption of the World Health Organization Framework Convention on Tobacco Control,[47] tobacco companies advertised aggressively in poor countries, often targeting women and children with billboards, cartoon characters, and music sponsorship. Many of these marketing strategies are now prohibited in the United States and other rich countries. Tobacco sales have increased in Asia, Eastern Europe, and Latin America.[48] There are then a number of ways that the social determinants of health can be exported from rich to poor countries. If the social determinants of health can be exported from one nation to another largely by way of multinational corporations, travel, and communication flows, these determinants of health are nonexcludable on a global scale. This supports our understanding that health is both a public good and a global public good or "bad" as the case may be with both Ebola and tobacco, for example.

The activities of rich countries, multinational organizations, and individuals affect the choices available to people in poor countries and influence the health and public health of people worldwide. Some of the NCDs that are prevalent now are the result of social networks. Tobacco use, and its converse, smoking cessation, for example, have been shown to increase or decrease according to how widely tobacco is used within networks.[49] Today many networks are transnational. Lifestyles of one country can span the globe. So too do diseases, such as heart disease and stroke, which are fostered by international business practices. Therefore, although NCDs are often fostered by individual decisions, the choice architecture is public and the design global. Given globalization, it can be difficult to exclude people from health-impacting networks in a globalized context.

If health is a global public good, there are some important implications. First, we are all in this together. One person's health can adversely affect another's health, even when the other person is across the globe. Similarly, good health can benefit many. It is difficult to exclude people from enjoying the benefits associated with good health. Herd immunity testifies to that. When a sufficient number of people in a community are vaccinated against a contagious disease, they create a firewall of sorts that shields those who are not vaccinated. Thus the good health of some is conferred upon others, making health both nonexcludable and nonrivalrous. Likewise poor health is a global public bad; it often is difficult to exclude people from the harm.

We benefit from the good health of people globally, and suffer from their poor health. Health enhances people's human capital and fosters their talents and capacities to function within the global workforce. Health makes people better workers, and presumably more productive within the workforce. It also makes them healthier sexual partners for reproductive purposes.

Given the extent of migration flows for work, the benefits of good health can have positive effects for multiple countries and diverse people. Indeed, in the case of the medical brain drain, wealthy countries often recruit healthy and skilled medical workers to care for their sick and elderly, leaving poor countries without. In addition to migration flows, outsourcing work is a widespread practice. As we recently saw, when Apple outsourced the manufacturing of its computers to Foxconn in China, transnational business practices can be deadly for local workers. Foxconn, one of Apple's suppliers, subjected its employees to such grueling workplace practices that many jumped to their death.[50] The insatiable desire of Americans to consume iProducts, and Apple's failure to adequately monitor their suppliers, is, in part, responsible for the suicides and other harms to Chinese workers at Foxconn. Given the need to work, it is difficult to see how Chinese workers could avoid these working conditions. And the deaths of Foxconn workers are an externality of international consumer preferences and Apple's business practices. Given a global economy and financial system, it is difficult if not impossible to exclude people from the health of the global community. Thus many people in affluent countries benefit from the workforce of poor countries. (When we refer to affluent countries we do so broadly, to include nations, governmental organizations, nongovernmental organizations, companies, and individuals.) If rich nations do not acknowledge the global public-good dimension of health and contribute to ensuring health globally, they risk being free riders. Free riding of this kind harms the most vulnerable people in the world.

Once we acknowledge that health is a public good, and indeed a global public good, our understanding of what we owe newcomers must also be reconsidered. If health is impacted by social determinants, social capital, and norms, and we live side by side with newcomers, we cannot easily remain unaffected by their health. If the children of newcomers attend the same schools as those of natives, or later, the same universities, or work at the same jobs, and they smoke or consume sodas, natives will suffer. Alternatively, if natives smoke or have sedentary lives, and/ or live in communities with high pollution, they will adversely affect the health of newcomers. In other words, health is bilateral.

In a world governed by ethics and justice, harming others can trigger duties to them. We look at this closely in chapter 8. Justice requires us to compensate people for the harms caused to them, and not to unjustly benefit from others. Failure to recognize the public good dimensions of health can lead to free riding. Counterintuitively, there is some evidence that people in rich countries free ride on the health of newcomers. Against the background of health as a global public good, newcomers should not be sent "home" when they become ill, or denied access to medical care, but cared for as we would care for family.

7

Creating Global Health

In the preceding chapter we saw that health has public good dimensions—its benefits are both nonexcludable and nonrivalrous. Acknowledging this is important. First, it explains how the health of each person stands to impact the health of others and how the health of newcomers can affect the health of natives and vice versa. Because health is a global public good, it is in the interest of natives to craft health policy that will meet the health needs of newcomers. Second, the public-good dimension of health explains how health can be vulnerable to free riding. Natives may, for example, free ride on the healthy network effects of newcomers, without reciprocating appropriately. Despite the public-good dimension of health, many nations operate in ways that put health at risk, apparently blind to the shared interest all have in the health of all.

Although the public-good argument supports a more equitable approach to the health of immigrants, it is not the only argument that does so. In this chapter, we consider a second argument in support of meeting the health needs of newcomers. Before turning to it, we discuss the view that our obligation to health needs is a charitable one. In this view, if natives have a moral responsibility to support the health of newcomers it is a charitable or supererogatory responsibility based on the duty to aid others in need. According to David Heyd, supererogatory acts are "optional" and should be "distinguished from those acts which fall under the heading of duty. . . . [T]hey are *beyond* duty, fulfil *more* than is required, *over and above* what the agent is supposed or expected to do."[1] Consider an example. When the Gates Foundation donated $50 million to Ebola in West Africa, its largest gift to date,[2] most people would consider the gift a charitable or supererogatory one. Essentially, gifts are optional, and when people give them they are going above and beyond duty.[3] More specifically, it could be argued that caring for newcomers is a charitable act, but not an obligation. Crowd-funding websites, such as GoFundMe, provide opportunities for people to fund the health needs of newcomers and natives, among other things. For example, Funke, an African, had a campaign on GoFundMe, for surgery for cancer at a hospital in the United Kingdom.[4] If crowd-funding campaigns were the primary mechanism receiving countries used to meet the health needs of newcomers, they would be treating their responsibilities to newcomers as optional, supererogatory acts, and not as strict moral responsibilities that it would be wrong not to meet and on which newcomers could rely.

Understanding responsibilities for the health of newcomers as solely supererogatory has three shortcomings: (1) it is probably not an accurate account of the nature of the duty, (2) it would likely leave many newcomers without needed health care, and (3) it would fail to reflect health's global public-good dimension. When providing for the health needs of newcomers is optional, their needs are likely not to be met and the community as a whole is exposed to unnecessary health risks.

People also have negative duties not to harm others and are strictly responsible for remedying the harms they have caused. Negative duties, unlike supererogatory ones, generate mandatory obligations. The duty not to harm others is morally demanding in a way that the duty to help them is not. When people violate a negative duty, they are responsible for remedying the harm caused. Thomas Pogge has argued persuasively that global poverty is a violation of negative duties.[5]

In this chapter, we discuss examples that show that affluent countries have jeopardized the health of the global poor through international conduct and policies, and, in turn, fostered migration. If our argument is persuasive, it would justify imposing morally demanding responsibilities on newcomers as opposed to supererogatory ones. To this end, we consider the connection between poverty and health, and the role of affluent countries with respect to both; the role of international tax policy on global poverty and health; and the role of affluent countries in environmental harms, and the impact of those harms on health and migration. These are merely illustrative of the ways that affluent countries have compromised the health of people globally. Since newcomers may well be among those harmed and may migrate to seek refuge from that harm, or try to mitigate harm to their families by deploying remittances, it can be argued that receiving countries have a morally demanding duty to address the health harms of newcomers. Put differently, affluent countries have moral obligations for the health of newcomers because they have played a role in creating the global conditions that compromise health. Because newcomers are seeking a better life, often trying to escape poverty and environmental damage, they may well be among those harmed by such global policies. In chapter 9 we develop this argument further by showing that the moral and social preconditions for solidarity with newcomers are satisfied.

The social determinants of health are global. They include but are not limited to international law, the conduct of corporations, and governments. As we discussed in the preceding chapter, the social determinants play an important role in health, both domestically and internationally. A recent WHO Commission report explains:

> The Commission takes a holistic view of social determinants of health. The poor health of the poor, the social gradient in health within countries, and the marked health inequities between countries are caused by the unequal distribution of power, income, goods, and services, globally and nationally. . . . Together, the structural determinants and conditions of daily life constitute the social determinants of health and are responsible for a major part of health inequities between and within countries.[6]

The commission's point is well taken. The impact of the social determinants of health, including inequality within and among countries, adversely affects the health of the poor. The social determinants of health, including inequality, are largely the result of the policies nations adopt. If the WHO is right, those who perpetuate health-damaging determinants have a moral responsibility to address them. Poverty is among the most significant determinants of health.

In anticipation of an objection, it is important to be explicit about what we are not saying. We are not maintaining that affluent nations have only harmed poor nations, or even that affluent nations have primarily harmed poor nations. Our assessment of the obligations of affluent nations is consistent with the view that they have also helped the global poor. In general, people have a responsibility not to harm others. If people confer a good or benefit, in addition to conferring a harm, they are not thereby absolved of responsibility for the harm they have caused—at least in the absence of an agreement to that effect. The same is true for states and the harms that they cause. For example, if a nation, or affiliated organization, were to develop an oil field in a poor country, providing jobs and stimulating the economy but also damaging the environment and the health of indigenous people, the company is not exonerated from responsibility for the harms caused simply because it has also done some good. We might praise it for its good acts but require it to remedy the harms to the environment and local people. The same reasoning applies to affluent nations and their affiliated organizations.

The Connection between Poverty and Disease

According to the WHO, 45 percent of the diseases in poor countries are associated with poverty.[7] Conditions such as poor nutrition, indoor air pollution, and access to sanitation are among those that affect health. The diseases associated with poverty, such as TB and malaria, are often easily treatable and can be prevented altogether. Nets to prevent malaria, for example, are both inexpensive and effective.[8]

Studies have shown for some time that extreme poverty adversely impacts health.[9] Filth, parasites, unsanitary conditions, sewage, dirty water, toxic cooking fumes, malnutrition caused by a lack of resources, exposure to the elements, lack of education, and increased conflict and violence all take a toll on the health of the global poor.[10] In 2000, the importance of development for health and well-being was recognized when the leaders of more than forty nations came together and identified eight development goals, known as the Millennium Development Goals, for the global community, and dates by which those goals should be met. The Millennium Development Goals are:

1. Eradicate extreme poverty and hunger.
2. Achieve universal primary education.
3. Promote gender equality and empower women.
4. Reduce child mortality.
5. Improve maternal health.
6. Combat HIV/AIDS, malaria and other diseases.
7. Ensure environmental sustainability.
8. Develop a global partnership for development.

Some of these goals, such as 4, 5 and 6, directly target health. Others, such as 1, 2, and 3, indirectly target it. In a recent WHO document, the connection between health and sustainable development is nicely stated.[11]

> Healthy people contribute to sustainable development. At the same time, policies that promote sustainability benefit human health. The health of populations, and how equitably health is distributed, provide a yardstick to judge progress across all aspects of economic, social and environmental policy. Increasing evidence points to a causal link between per capita income and overall life expectancy. Better health is thus also an outcome of, and prerequisite to, reducing poverty.[12]

This acknowledges the connection among sustainable development, the reduction of poverty, and improved health, as well as the virtuous cycle of good health and development. That is, healthy people are better contributors to the economy. Likewise, healthy economies foster healthier people. In many cases, factors that adversely affect the economy will also adversely impact health and, in turn, the economy. We saw this in the case of HIV/AIDS in sub-Saharan Africa.

Global Policy and Global Poverty

When poverty is considered on a global scale, the scope of the problem appears mammoth, beyond the capacity of international efforts. Yet considerable progress has been made toward reducing global poverty. Although far too many people in the global community continue to live in extreme poverty, far fewer do so today than in the past. The Millennium Development's pledge to halve extreme poverty by 2015 has been accomplished. In 1990, 43 percent of people living in developing countries lived on $1 a day, or less (1.9 billion people).[13] As of 2010, 21 percent of people (1.2 billion) living in developing countries lived on less than $1.25 a day. In a period of twenty years, the global poverty rate was reduced by half.[14] Given the connection between poverty and poor health, this may bode well for health. The success of these recent international efforts shows that there is reason to be optimistic about what global efforts can achieve.

This success may indicate something about the cause of global poverty. Philosopher Thomas Pogge has argued in favor of the view that global poverty is the result of global institutions, and that these institutions could be rearranged so that they would not create poverty.[15] If Pogge is correct in viewing poverty as largely the result of institutional structures and institutions are human constructs, they are amenable to change by humans. This is also implicit in the Millennium Development Goals. Arguably, the harms associated with poverty, including the diseases of poverty, are the result of institutional structures in violation of a negative duty not to harm others.[16] Pogge also states that poverty violates the human rights of the world's poor. According to him, global poverty is the result of a specific institutional order: "the increase of intra-national economic inequality in nearly all countries is no longer under easy domestic control but rather driven by the increasingly important role that supranational rules play in constraining and shaping national legislation and in governing domestic markets for goods, services, labor, and investments."[17] Although, Pogge doesn't refer to these supranational rules as global social determinants of health, in some cases they qualify as such.

Pogge describes some of the ways in which wealthy societies contribute to global poverty. First, they often purchase, even if indirectly, huge amounts of natural resources from developing countries without regard to whom they pay for these resources. Sometimes they knowingly purchase them from corrupt leaders who retain the money for themselves instead of distributing it to the country's citizens. This happened in Sierra Leone with diamonds, and the issue was later made famous in the movie *Blood Diamond*. Charles Taylor, a warlord and former president of Liberia, was sentenced to fifty years for war crimes by an international tribunal for the role he played in the atrocities in Sierra Leone. Many of these crimes were financed by conflict diamonds—diamonds mined and sold to finance war.[18] Second, institutions, such as banks, from developed countries lend money to corrupt leaders and dictators who then spend it and impose the debt burden on the nation.[19] Poor countries are left to pay off loans, negotiated by corrupt leaders, never having benefitted from the money lent. Arguably, wealthy societies are responsible for exercising greater due diligence with respect to whom they lend money. Third, affluent societies tolerate embezzlement by allowing their banks to encourage illicit deposits. Bank transfers from local to foreign banks, sometimes from kleptocrats, and the absence of transparency and oversight, can encourage illicit financial flows. Secrecy jurisdictions (tax havens) make it difficult to regulate and oversee bank actions.[20] Fourth, developing countries lose billions of dollars because of the evasive tax practices of multinational firms.[21] We discuss this later in this chapter. Fifth, wealthy economies have harmed the global community by emitting greenhouse gas that affects all countries. Climate change, spurred by the manufacturing needs and consumer demand of developed countries, has already had an impact on the health of people in developing countries and will likely have a greater impact in the years to come.

Law, Poverty, and Health

International law is itself a social determinant of global health. A good example of how law can impact international health can be found with Trade-Related Aspects of Intellectual Property Rights (TRIPS), which governs property rights, including patent rights, to medicines that people need worldwide.[22] In 1994, every member of the World Trade Organization, including many developing countries, were made subject to the TRIPS agreement. In essence the agreement applies patent protection to all intellectual property, including patents on medicine. Prior to the agreement, countries had the ability to exclude medicines from patent protection and purchase their medicines through generics and other non-protected mechanisms. TRIPS was thought to be essential in order to incentivize innovation in research and development in pharmaceuticals. In effect, the Agreement puts many life-saving medicines beyond the reach of developing countries. Patents on pharmaceuticals make it impossible for financially strapped countries to have those medicines. Whether patent protection in developing countries is necessary to foster innovation is debatable, but clearly TRIPS and patent protection in the poorest countries adversely affects the health of many people. This illustrates how global social determinants, in this case the law, can hurt the health of the global poor.

Even if one were to argue that patents foster innovation, and that in the end innovation helps global health, it would nonetheless be possible to create a system in which patents didn't apply to people in developing countries. Indeed, such a system existed pre-TRIPS. Since poor countries do not pay for these medications in any case, there would seem to be little threat to innovation.[23] The pharmaceutical industry is a lucrative one and unlikely to be hobbled by the additional costs incurred by developing countries. Given the connection between health and the economy, not only has the global poor's health suffered because of patent protection, but the resulting unhealthy populations will, in turn, compromise the economies of developing countries. The impact of the HIV/AIDS pandemic on sub-Saharan Africa's environment and economy is a good example. Given the fragility of these economies and the health of their populations, it should not be surprising that migrants seek a better life in another country. There are other ways that international law fosters poverty and thereby adversely impacts health. We cannot review all of them, but before turning to a discussion of environmental harms, it is worth considering another example of the role of the law in global poverty, and, in turn, the role international actors play in the health of poor countries.

Tax Injustice

The responsibilities of states to their citizens, such as building infrastructure, providing social services, and protecting populations through a justice system and police force, are financed by governments through tax revenue. Fair and just taxation across the globe is therefore essential to eradicate poverty, and the diseases that follow in its wake. Today, two-thirds of the global poor live in middle-income countries such as India and China, where there is some economic growth and a potential to raise taxes to meet needs.[24] Tax revenue is an important part of the creation of economic self sufficiency for developing countries. Low-income countries collect on average only 13 percent of their GDP in tax revenue compared to 35 percent collected in OECD countries.[25] According to the United Nations, "if least developed countries raised at least 20 percent of their GDP, they would achieve all of the MDG."[26] In other words, revenue from taxation has the potential to lift the poor out of poverty and thereby also improve their health. Although nations are responsible for their own tax policy, many poor and middle-income countries extend incentives to wealthy individuals and foreign companies in order to attract investment.[27] Unfortunately, because of these practices, many of the poorest nations lose more money from lost taxes than they gain from foreign investment.[28] Since foreign direct investment increased by 2,000 percent between 1982 and 2011, to $1.5 trillion, the potential loss in tax revenue to developing countries is great.[29] To attract some of this cash flow, countries engage in practices in order to draw investments to their nations, and away from others. Tax-related incentives can figure prominently in the investment decisions of wealthy individuals and multinational corporations.[30]

Some countries reduce their corporate income tax rate; others grant generous tax incentives to foreign corporations, engage in lax enforcement of the prevailing tax laws, and tolerate secrecy around banking practices.[31] Corporations also engage in evasive tax practices, such as transfer mispricing and false invoicing. In the former, multinational companies with multiple subsidiaries in different countries can manipulate pricing in order maximize tax benefits to the corporation. False invoicing follows a similar pattern but among different companies.[32] According to Deloitte, 60 percent of world trade takes place among companies that are part of the same multinational corporation.[33] By manipulating transfer pricing, multinational companies are able to avoid paying for taxes, poor nations lose much needed revenue, and in the end companies can misrepresent their gains and losses. A company with subsidiaries in several countries could, for example, produce something in a poor country with a high tax rate but sell it for a subsidiary in a tax haven. According to one estimate, "30 percent of sub-Saharan Africa's annual GDP has been moved to secretive tax havens."[34] Banking assets are frequently held offshore in tax havens, and a substantial amount of foreign investment flows through them. Combined, these various strategies reduce revenues that could be used to promote development for some of the poorest countries in the world.[35] Interestingly, there is also evidence showing that African countries that collect more taxes have lower levels of undernourishment.[36] Not surprisingly, tax revenue can be used to end hunger and poverty.

Consider the case of India. Between 1990 and 2010 per capita income grew at about 5 percent a year. In India, the tax-to-GDP ratio is very low, just 16.8 percent. In Brazil, it is 34.2 percent and in South Africa 31.2 percent. Research also shows that there is a significant difference between the corporate income tax rate of 33 percent in India, and what is actually paid—only 24 percent. India has also experienced a loss of revenue because of widespread offshore banking by both individuals and corporations. Between 2011 and 2012, it was estimated that India lost $99 billion in revenue.[37] India is a poor country. In 2011, the World Bank estimated that 23.6 percent of the Indian people lived in poverty, that is, roughly 288 million people living below $1.25 a day.[38]

Multinational organizations have a strong presence in India. The top ten multinationals in India are Microsoft (USA), IBM (USA), Nokia (Finland), PepsiCo (USA), Ranbaxy Lab (India), Nestle (Switzerland), Coca-Cola (USA), Proctor and Gamble (USA), Sony (USA), and Citigroup (USA).[39] A thorough analysis of the tax practices of specific multinational companies is beyond the scope of this book. We do, however, want to underscore that the companies located in India are among the largest in the world, and most have their corporate headquarters in the United States. Whether these particular companies engage in "tax gaming" is unclear. But if there is "tax gaming" in India, much of it would be to the benefit of shareholders from affluent nations. Not surprisingly, major multinationals make an effort to protect their tax advantages. A 2014 article in the *Economic Times* reported that multinationals were eager to sign agreements (known as advancement pricing agreements) that would protect the tax pricing between subsidiaries and their foreign parent.[40]

The loss in revenue to poor and middle-income countries is staggering, and the revenue that they would have but for tax gaming could go toward reducing poverty, feeding the global hungry, and improving health. Some of the countries in which these practices are common are those from which there are large migration flows—for example, China and India. Put differently, the tax practices of many multinational companies sustain poverty, foster the poor health that follows in its wake, and undermine global justice. This has two important normative implications. First, far from developing the economic wherewithal of poor countries, and lifting people out of poverty, the tax practices of many multinationals maintain poverty. In turn, many people from affluent countries support these companies, if only indirectly, as consumers. Thus people often unwittingly contribute to the harm, in violation of a negative duty not to harm others. Second, these practices and their impact on poverty and health contribute to migratory flows. If people living in low- and middle-income countries had the revenue that was lost through tax gaming, they would have less reason to migrate to affluent countries. It is important for us to keep this in mind as we consider the obligations owed to newcomers.

Environmental Harms

Golam Rabbi was a student at the Genda Government Primary School in Savar, Bangladesh. The *New York Times* reported that he, his mother, and his two younger brothers lived in one room. The school was about two miles from the Rana Plaza—which had burned down in 2013. His father was a security guard at the Rana Plaza and was killed when the factory, which manufactured clothes for the American market, collapsed. The area is the world's second major clothing exporter after China, manufacturing clothes for Walmart, J. C. Penney, and H&M, among others. The garment industry was largely responsible for the disastrous air and water pollution in the area. The degree of pollution in Savar hurts agriculture and public health. Food that once grew was no longer sustainable; fish were dying and the air made people sick. Students like Golam, the top student in his grade, enjoyed a game in which they guessed the colors of the fashion season by looking at the color of the polluted canal— red, green, or purple. The color of the water in the canal changed from the dyes used by the factories. The local children got sick, complaining about the smell and the need to vomit. Golam fainted at the school, which was close to a number of factories and pharmaceutical companies. He didn't want to return to school because it was difficult for him to breathe there. In Golam's words, "The school always smells. . . . Sometimes we can't even eat there. It is making some kids sick. Sometimes my head spins. It is hard to concentrate."[41] Golam's story, like that of many children in the area, only described their current experience. It did not speak to the long-term effect of pollution on their health.

The natural environment knows no borders; pollution and global warming harm health directly and indirectly. The term "global warming" refers to increases in the temperature of the earth's atmosphere over time. Some of the consequences of global warming include severe floods, droughts, heat waves, and storms. Extreme weather events are likely to increase, and along with them, greater water shortages and food insecurity.[42]

Climate change poses a serious threat to health and public health, and, not surprisingly, it drives people from their homes to other parts of their country and to other countries. Adverse health impacts associated with the environment will be experienced most intensely by developing countries and the most vulnerable people in the world—despite the fact that rich industrialized countries are primarily responsible for global climate change. According to one study, "loss of healthy years as a result of global environmental change (including climate change) is predicted to be 500 times greater in poor African populations than in European populations."[43] The variation in impact is due to a number of factors, such as underlying susceptibilities and capacities to adapt. The 2015 heat wave in Karachi, Pakistan, killed more than eight hundred people in four days in part because of high temperatures, sometimes reaching 113 degrees Fahrenheit, but also because Karachi did not have the medical facilities, electricity, and drinking water to mitigate the casualties.[44]

Temperature has been rising around the world. Globally, 2014 was the warmest year since 1880, when record keeping began.[45] Climate change threatens health in a number of ways. Higher temperatures can have mild effects, such as increased stress due to heat, but it can also cause death from heatstroke. It can aggravate the physical harms associated with cardiovascular and respiratory disease as well.[46] Higher temperatures will also affect the reproduction of mosquitoes—as well as their population in an area. Similarly, as temperatures rise, so too will vector reproduction, parasitic development, and the frequency of bites. Diseases such as malaria, tick-borne encephalitis, and dengue fever are expected to become more prevalent because of global warming. Schistosomiasis, fascioliasis, alveolar echinococcosis, and leishmaniasis among others are also likely to increase.[47] The destruction of species because of climate change and pollution has also contributed to the movement of people and the rise in disease outbreaks.[48] Most of these problems will impact countries that are already vulnerable because of poverty and poor health. Climate change will make matters much worse for the worst off.

Because health depends on nutrition and food, and climate change threatens both, it also threatens health. The most vulnerable members of the global community are at greatest risk. Severe malnutrition, poor breast-feeding, and low birth weight are thought to kill 3.5 million mothers and young children annually.[49] Although food insecurity was a fact of life prior to 2008, it is estimated that following the rise of food prices that year between 100 million and 850 million people suffer from food insecurity.[50] Rising temperatures heat crops, threatening the world's population with evolving food insecurity.

People also depend on clean water for health. Climate change will contribute to shortages of clean water. Diarrhea and diseases associated with chemical contaminants are some of the health problems associated with a lack of clean water. Annual snowfall is expected to decrease in some places and to increase in others—both have consequences for health. In some instances, drought will impact access to drinking water and harvestable crops. In other cases, increased rainfall can be helpful, but only in countries that have the capacity to manage it appropriately.[51]

Wealthy industrial countries are largely responsible for global warming. High greenhouse emissions and the greenhouse effect have led to global warming. Industrialized nations are responsible for about 80 percent of the carbon dioxides in the atmosphere. Since 1950, the United States alone has emitted about 50.7 billion tons of carbon, China 15.7, and India 4.2.[52] Each year industrialized countries emit more than 60 percent of global industrial carbon dioxide.[53] Developing countries are in a very different position with respect to carbon emission. Although emissions are on the rise in middle-income countries such as China and India, these nations are relative latecomers to industrialization.

It is important to realize that countries that have contributed to global warming through consumption and industrialization have also benefitted economically from their high-emission activities. In addition, some of the emissions of middle-income countries, such as India, are the result of multinational corporations outsourcing their manufacturing activities to these countries. This is not to exonerate poor and middle-income nations for their role in climate change. The heart of the problem is that although poor and middle-income countries have not contributed as much as affluent countries to global warming, they nonetheless experience the burden of environmental harms caused by the activities of affluent countries, and their health is impacted by those activities.[54] People living in poor countries bear the greatest burden of climate change, have contributed less to it, and are least able to cope with it. Yet, through no fault of their own, they bear the physical and economic burden of global damage to the environment.

Environmental Migration

Climate change threatens health in countless ways, and developing countries are especially vulnerable to these threats to health. Not surprisingly, one of the consequences of global warming and the changes to the environment that it brings is that people need to relocate. Like poverty, climate change and pollution drive people from their homes to other parts of their country or the globe. Environmental migrants are people who leave their homeland because of changes in the prevailing environment. Droughts, desertification, a rise in sea levels, and extreme changes in weather, such as monsoons, can create circumstances in which people must leave their homes and relocate, whether internally, or to another country.

The International Organization for Migration defines environmental migrants in the following way:

> Environmental migrants are persons or groups of persons who, for compelling reasons of sudden or progressive changes in the environment that adversely affect their lives or living conditions, are obligated to leave their homes, or choose to do so, either temporarily or permanently, and who move either within their country, or abroad.[55]

According to the Intergovernmental Panel on Climate Change (IPCC), "millions of people" will be "displaced by shoreline erosion, coastal flooding and severe drought."[56] The IPCC also recognizes that human migration is one of the harshest consequences of climate change.[57] Although most migration is internal from one part of a country to another, climate change sometimes makes it impossible for people to remain in their home countries.

Formal international recognition of the problem of environmental migration came in 2011 with the Dhaka Ministerial Declaration of the Climate Vulnerable Forum. What has come to be known as the Dhaka Declaration was signed by nineteen countries uniquely vulnerable to climate change, including Afghanistan, Bangladesh, Bhutan, Costa Rica,

Ethiopia, Ghana, Kenya, Kiribati, Madagascar, Maldives, Nepal, the Philippines, and Rwanda.[58] The declaration recognized that migration is a "viable adaptation strategy" to the impact on the environment of climate change. Prior to the declaration, the Cancun Agreement, an agreement among the international community reached at the 2010 United Nations Climate Conference, recognized the need to reduce greenhouse gas emissions.[59] Together, the documents encouraged cooperation and coordination in the effort to reduce climate-induced displacements. The list of countries most severely affected by climate change speaks for itself. With few exceptions, these are among the poorest nations in the world.

Concerns and Responses

People emigrate to escape poverty, to find a better life for themselves, and often to send remittances home to help family members. Sometimes they migrate because of environmental challenges that make it impossible for them to remain. If migrants are seeking relief from poverty caused by the global financial structures, often migrating to countries that have contributed to the creation of that poverty, receiving nations are well positioned to remedy the wrong. This is not to say that affluent countries are only responsible to care for other people when they have harmed them, or that they only have negative duties toward other people. People also have positive duties to help others, as argued by Peter Singer.[60] But, at the minimum, there are moral responsibilities to right the harms to which one has contributed. Thomas Pogge has argued that we have a negative duty not to cause harm and that when we do cause harm we have strict moral duties of compensation to the victims of our harm. Furthermore, for Pogge, those duties are not limited to natives.[61] Rather, these moral duties are international in their scope. Other moral philosophers have also argued for cosmopolitan duties, Peter Singer, Martha Nussbaum, and Iris Young, to name a few.

If affluent countries are in part responsible for global poverty, even if unintentionally, and poverty is associated with poor health, they have additional duties for the health of the poor, including those who migrate. Consider an example. Imagine that Golam as a young adult could not support his family on the income he made in the clothes factories in

Bangladesh and left to work in NYC. While in the United States he develops debilitating respiratory problems and depression. It would not be far fetched to tie his health problems to his early childhood exposure to pollution from the factories manufacturing cheap clothes for American consumers. Under this very plausible scenario, surely, it would be morally reasonable for the United States to provide for his health needs, and not to discriminate against him because he is a "stranger." His medical problems are partly caused by the practices of American multinationals, and American consumers have had the benefit of access to inexpensive clothing as his health suffered. If global legal and financial structures contribute to poverty and poor health, and people are driven from their native countries to find ways to meet their basic needs and those of their families, arguably those who contribute to global poverty share some responsibility for the illnesses that flow from it.

Even if we were to accept that there is no strict moral duty to help strangers, because maintaining such a duty would be too great an interference in individual liberty, it is difficult to argue that people living in affluent countries have not compromised the health of people in poor countries and do not share responsibility for the health of global citizens. The liberty argument admits to an important exception. According to John Stuart Mill people are entitled to liberty with respect to their self-regarding actions.[62] Once a person's action harms another person, his or her liberty is open to restriction. This has come to be known as the harm principle. Our review shows that the actions and activities of people in affluent countries are harmful to people in poor countries. Thus their actions are "other regarding" and do not fall quite so firmly under the protective umbrella of liberty.

Ethical judgments are universal.[63] Simply put, this means that all people are equally valued and should be treated equally. Thus in the absence of a morally relevant reason the liberty of someone in Bangladesh counts as much as the liberty of someone in Canada. Liberty is universally valued. The moral principle of impartiality asks us to be mindful of the harm we cause to all people, not only the harm we cause to natives. In Jeremy Bentham's words, "Everybody to count for one, nobody for more than one."[64] Philosopher Peter Singer, in his classic book *Practical Ethics*, has referred to this as "the principle of equal consideration of interests."[65]

Consider some objections to the view developed here. First, it might be objected that in our proposal the poor in affluent countries may have to make significant sacrifices to support the health needs of newcomers and that surely that is not fair. The principle of impartiality or "equal consideration of interests" reminds us to treat all people alike and not to consider the native poor as more important than the "foreign poor." Therefore any objection to asking the poor to support the health needs of newcomers should apply similarly to asking the poor in affluent countries to support the health needs of the native poor, or native rich, for that matter. Unfortunately, asking that important, but broader, question is beyond the scope of this book. In any case, in the United States, at least in 2007, the bottom 20 percent donated 4.3 percent of their income to charity, while those in the top 20 percent gave an average of 2.1 percent of their income.[66] It would seem that the "affluent" poor are willing to help others. Nonetheless, nothing we have said commits the poor in affluent countries to supporting the health of newcomers. How these obligations to newcomers are met is a matter best left to the democratic process.

It might also be argued that the causation is too weak to impose obligations on people in one country for harms in another country when they have done little intentionally to cause the harm. Few consumers know that when they purchase cheap clothing they are complicit in violating the human rights of workers in Bangladesh. Philosopher Iris Young's concept of "structural injustice" can help us to understand why consumers, for example, might nevertheless be responsible for harms in distant countries. According to Young, we share political responsibility for structural injustice:

> Structural injustice exists when social processes put large categories of persons under a systematic threat of domination or deprivation of the means to develop and exercise their capacities, at the same time as these processes enable others to . . . have a wide range of opportunities for developing and exercising their capacities. . . . Structural injustice occurs as a consequence of many individuals and institutions acting in pursuit of their particular goals and interests, within given institutional rules and accepted norms.[67]

Young believes that injustice can result not only from individual action but also from social structures and participation in them. This insight overlaps with Pogge's explanation of the role of global institutions in the creation of poverty. Global poverty and the poor health outcomes that follow it reflect structural injustice. Global norms and practices and domestic and international law result in deprivations for some while sustaining the lives of others. How nations respond to structural injustice will be multifaceted. We will argue that the presence of structural injustice and its role in the health of newcomers supports solidarity for the health of newcomers. The densely woven ties between newcomers and natives can justify a duty to help newcomers. Natives and newcomers dwell together. In chapter 9, referring again to the work of Iris Young, we identify certain "parameters" that trigger specific responsibilities that people have to others.

Because health policy applies to all newcomers, our proposal entails that some newcomers would receive health care who have not experienced health harms because of structural injustice and the violation of negative duties. Indeed, the health of some newcomers may have improved as a result of globalization. They may have been lucky enough to receive medications that they would otherwise not have received, or that were the outcome of the considerable research and development efforts of international pharmaceutical companies. This is not an implausible scenario. As we discussed in chapter 1, many immigrants are highly educated people, leading innovation in Silicon Valley, for example. But health policy and public health are designed with communities in mind, and not specific cases. Law and policy create "bright lines" that will sometimes be overinclusive and sometimes underinclusive. Our proposed policy will be underinclusive insofar as it would not provide health care for all of those who have endured health harms because of globalization, because some have not migrated, and it would be overinclusive because some newcomers would receive health care who have not experienced health harms as a result of globalization. Whether good or bad, this is an inherent part of policy and law. Some of the concerns can be allayed if we consider the following. Meeting negative duties is only one reason for treating newcomers equally with respect to health. Another and more practical reason for so doing is that health is a global public good. It is in the interests of natives and newcomers alike when both are healthy. Disdain for the health of newcomers and, more widely, the global community, puts everyone at risk. Finally, health is a human right. At the very worst, a policy that is overinclusive will contribute to realizing the right to health. And if it is underinclusive, other policy, including the right to health, can and should be operationalized.

Our goal in this chapter has been modest. As we mentioned in chapter 1, there are numerous myths about newcomers, their health, their intentions, their skills, what they left behind when they migrated, and to what they aspire. There are also misperceptions about receiving countries, what their role in the global structure is, what they contribute to poor countries, and what they take from them. Some of these misperceptions may explain the unwillingness of receiving nations to help newcomers when they are sick, or to treat them as health equals. For example, studies show that Americans believe that they give far more in foreign aid to developing countries than they in fact do. In other words, Americans overestimate their contributions to the global poor.[68] By describing the ways that the activities of people in affluent countries impact the health of people in poor countries, we hope to dispel misperceptions about the health of newcomers. This is not to say that newcomers are a particularly sick population. As we stated in chapter 1, they are more often than not healthier than natives. Our claim is that when they are sick, receiving countries should not assume that newcomers are solely responsible for their illnesses, or that the corrupt governments of poor countries are the sole cause. In a global context, when it comes to health, there is enough blame to go around.

8

Strangers for the Sake of Health

Transnational factors, such as poverty, climate change, and tax injustice, have contributed to the current state of global health. Following a string of arguments, we also suggested that affluent nations and their organizations have played a significant role in creating the conditions that have compromised global health and the well-being of the global poor. In addition, we argued that this was in violation of the morally demanding negative duty not to harm others and could result in structural injustice, giving rise to moral responsibilities. We have suggested that fulfilling the health needs of newcomers is morally indicated given both the public-good nature of health and the violation of a negative duty.

Ironically, at the same time that people in receiving countries are reluctant to support the health needs of newcomers, they look to "strangers" to meet their health needs. In this chapter we consider three examples of how affluent countries use the health resources of poor countries: medical brain drain, medical tourism, and transplant tourism. These practices often harm the health of people in poor countries. In this respect they reflect a willingness on the part of affluent societies to subordinate the health interests of people in poor countries for the sake of the health of their own citizens. This need not reflect malevolence, nor do we wish to assert that it does. Nonetheless, basic principles of fairness, reciprocity, and justice suggest that a global scenario in which the health of the poor is sacrificed for the health of people living in affluent countries is morally unsettling. A more inclusive approach to the health of newcomers would be an important step toward health justice.

Medical Brain Drain

Carolyne Mujibi, twenty-eight years old, a nurse living in a single room in Kenya, watched her father die. She maintained that he died from nursing neglect. After working in the very same hospital in which her father died, she became frustrated with the low pay and poor working conditions. She also wanted to help support her siblings and ensure that they would receive a decent education. In 2006, Mujibi studied to take the US nursing exam, hoping to secure a job in the United States. In her words, "I love Kenya, and if I'd get a good job, I'd never go anywhere else."[1]

Mujibi's path is not unique. In fact, up to half of the nurses trained in poor countries emigrate.[2] Their migration has serious consequences for the health of those left behind. Health depends on the availability of health care workers: physicians, nurses, midwives, and nurse practitioners. Not surprisingly, there is a link between the density of health care workers and positive health outcomes.[3] The medical brain drain consists of the migration of health care workers, sometimes within their own countries, but often to other countries and often as a result of aggressive recruiting that targets people in poor countries. Just as natural resources such as oil and gas can be taken from a country, so too can its human capital, and there are both pull and push factors underlying the flow of health workers.[4] The medical brain drain takes place because of the demand for health care workers in receiving countries (pull factors), such as the United States, United Kingdom, and Canada, and because of push factors within sending countries, such as South Africa, Nigeria and the Philippines. Often, as in the case of sub-Saharan Africa, poverty drives skilled health care workers to leave countries with severe health problems for countries with far healthier populations.[5] Africa, for example, bears 25 percent of the global burden of disease, yet has only 3 percent of the global supply of health care workers and a mere 1 percent of economic resources.[6] The impact of this severe deprivation in health care workers was evident in the 2014 Ebola outbreak, in which fragile health care systems played a significant role.[7] Countries with high rates of HIV/AIDS are also vulnerable to the exodus of skilled health care workers because many of those who remain either die from HIV or have exceptionally high absenteeism. The crux of the problem is that when health care workers leave, there may not be an adequate supply of workers remaining to meet the needs of the community.

According to the WHO, 4.3 million additional health care workers (physicians, nurses, midwives, and pharmacists) are needed to meet the health Millennium Development Goals, and fifty-seven countries have critical shortages.[8] As of 2005, between 23 and 28 percent of physicians in the United States, United Kingdom, Canada, and Australia were international medical graduates, and lower-income countries supplied between 40 and 75 percent of them.[9] The leading sources of international medical graduates are India, the Philippines, and Pakistan. The United Kingdom, Canada and Australia, take a substantial number of physicians from South Africa, while the United States does from the Philippines.[10]

The situation is also dire for nurses. According to the WHO, at a minimum there should be twenty-three skilled health workers (nurses, midwives, and physicians) for every ten thousand people in order to meet basic health needs.[11] Given this minimum standard, the WHO has identified eighty-three countries with shortages. A number of countries also exceed the minimum standard. Not surprisingly, much of Africa and all of India have shortages while almost all of North America, Europe and the UK do not and indeed have more than the minimum standard.[12] According to James Johnson of the British Medical Association, "The US system regards health care professionals as a commodity to be purchased in the market and is making little provision currently to increase the number of doctors and nurses it trains at home. . . . Nurses in the US are the most highly paid in the world."[13] Populations in many developed countries are aging, and coping with chronic diseases. Their health needs will require medical attention over lifetimes. In addition, nurses undertake increasingly complex work that has expanded their relevance to health care.

It cannot be overemphasized that the need is great for health care workers in developing countries, exacerbated by diseases such as HIV, TB, and malaria. More recently, the health of the global poor has also been compromised by noncommunicable diseases following the export of unhealthy lifestyles from wealthy countries, and persistent poverty.[14] Despite the great demand for health care workers, many countries have not invested in the necessary education of health care workers to meet their needs. This is true for both rich and poor countries. When the education of health care workers is subsidized by sending countries, it would seem to be especially cost-effective for affluent countries to turn to them to supply health care workers rather than train them at home. Lawrence O. Gostin identified three factors that account for the international migration of nurses. These are globalization, supply-demand, and push-pull. In a global context, health care workers can be bought and sold.[15] A decent income is not the only pull factor for health care workers. They are also pulled by career and educational opportunities, a better working environment, and social stability.[16] Sometimes health care workers are aggressively recruited with not-to-be resisted enticements. Recruiting practices include advertising, texting, e-mailing, guaranteed earnings, reimbursed moving expenses, and assistance in immigration.[17] It is likely that given aging populations in developing countries, and the health needs that follow, the demand for health care and personal support workers will increase substantially.

Push factors also play a significant role in the migration of health care workers: outdated equipment, low wages, shortages of medical supplies, poor training, and limited advancement opportunities. Social factors such as religious tensions, human rights violations, political persecution, and war have all been cited as reasons for skilled medical workers to migrate.[18]

The effects of the medical brain drain are multifaceted and vary depending on characteristics of both sending and receiving countries. Insofar as density of health care workers is good for health, the health of receiving countries is likely better than it would be without an international workforce. At the same time, and following the same general principle, the health of those in sending countries suffers because they often experience a deprivation of health workers. Many sending countries don't have enough health care workers to serve their communities. The World Health Assembly considers the shortage in health care workers a "crisis in health," and in an effort to monitor the flow it unanimously adopted the WHO Global Code of Practice on the International Recruitment of Health Personnel in 2010.[19]

Considered from the perspective of sending countries, migrant workers and their families can benefit from the work done abroad by migrant health workers. International health workers benefit financially, in terms of skill development, enhanced professional opportunities, and pleasant working environment. Many health care workers send money (remittances) home to their families; in turn, these families enjoy a higher quality of life. But communities marked by deficits in health care workers also have higher rates of death and disability from largely preventable conditions. Countries falling below the WHO's minimum health worker–patient ratio have some of the poorest health outcomes, especially for conditions that require support, such as maternal and fetal mortality and diseases that can be prevented through vaccination.[20] A persistent shortage of health care workers can have devastating effects on the well-being and health of people whose health is already severely compromised by poverty. Sending countries not only lose skilled health care workers, they can also lose their investment in educating health workers. For example, Ghana is estimated to have lost about £35 million in its investment in health professionals while the United Kingdom is estimated to have saved £65 million as a result of recruiting from Ghana.[21]

Sending countries that experience a deficit in health care workers may also witness more people leaving the country to find care in other countries. People from Nigeria, for example, spent $1 billion a year on health care outside the country in 2003.[22] In addition, when the health care systems of sending countries have fewer qualified health care professionals, needed care may be given by less-qualified or wholly unqualified people. In some instances, the remaining qualified health workers leave the public sector because it is neglected, leaving the local poor who depend entirely on public care especially vulnerable. Remote areas suffer the most, as health workers move to urban centers.[23]

If the medical brain drain has a saving grace, it lies with remittances. Many migrant health care workers send money home to their families. These payments constitute large parts of some economies. In 2013, remittances constituted $404 billion, and they are anticipated to rise to $516 billion in 2016. In that same year, India received the most remittance money at $70 billion, China, $60 billion, the Philippines, $25 billion, Mexico, $22 billion, Nigeria, $21 billion, Egypt, $17 billion, Pakistan, $15 billion, Bangladesh, $14 billion, Vietnam, $11 billion, and Ukraine, $10 billion.[24] Very often the amount of remittances exceeds the development aid that countries receive.[25] According to Stuart Brown, "in about one-third of all developing countries remittances exceed all capital flows, . . . foreign aid and grants as well as private portfolio capital."[26] For many developing countries remittances are an integral part of the economy and help to alleviate poverty. In Nepal, they are almost double the national revenue from the exports of goods and services. In the Philippines, they are over 38 percent. In 2013, India received $70 billion in remittances, $5 billion more than the $65 billion it made from the export of software services. Uganda makes double in remittances what it makes from exporting coffee.[27] Sometimes remittances are the primary reason workers migrate. It seemed to be the driving consideration for Carolyne Mujibi as she considered a nursing career in the United States.

Career choices are often based on the potential to work abroad and send remittances home. Families may support their children's education, anticipating remittances in the future. In the Philippines, remittances are directed primarily to the families of migrant health care workers and are used to pay for housing, education, and medical care, among other expenses. For many people living in poor countries, remittances make life tolerable. According to one family: "Our families can only survive because we get money from abroad. The living conditions cannot be compared: those with relatives abroad live in houses, the others live in shacks."[28] In the Philippines a supply of nurses is trained precisely with the international market in mind.[29] Because of local poverty, many people go into nursing in order to join the international workforce and support their families at home. Despite the advantages to people in poor countries from remittances, Niamh Humphries, Ruairi Brugha, and Hannah McGee point out:

> Migration and the remittance flow that follows, could be considered to reduce pressure on national governments to provide welfare support services. Individuals migrate and remit to provide social protection for their families . . . this means that remittances become a necessary rather than an optional source of addition income.[30]

Remittances may benefit individual families and sometimes local communities as money trickles through the community. But the practice of sending trained health workers to other countries can be a burden for the countries, as states often subsidize the education of health care workers, who are unavailable to their own citizens. Although families of migrants and receiving countries benefit, the general citizenry from poor source countries are often left without an adequate supply of health care workers. This is a problem of distribution of resources. Ideally, when the state exercises its welfare duties, it does so on the basis of distributional principles that have to do with need, fairness, and democracy. Remittances, on the other hand, are blind to distributional principles. Indeed, it has been suggested that because the best and the brightest leave their native countries to practice their professions in wealthy countries, poor countries not only lose human capital, they also lose those people who stand to make the greatest contributions to their communities.[31] Another consequence of remittances may be that those who benefit from them are the families of the best and the brightest, and not necessarily those who are in greatest need.

The most obvious disadvantage of the medical brain drain is the cost to life and health for people who remain in sending countries. According to Sudhir Anand and Till Bärnighausen, the medical brain drain from some countries increases maternal and child mortality.[32] It can interfere with the effective delivery of medications in HIV-saturated countries.[33] It can also carry significant economic losses for sending countries. One study identified the financial costs of the migration of physicians from sub-Saharan countries to Australia, Canada, the United Kingdom, and the United States. The costs were significant. Across nine African countries with high HIV prevalence, estimated loss on educational investment totaled $2.17 billion. Meanwhile, the four receiving countries received a $4.55 billion net benefit.[34] In the end, the governments of poor countries subsidize the health care of people in developed countries while their own populations do without health care workers.

One response to this concern is to assert that remittances benefit the economies of developing countries enough to justify the loss in medical care workers. Remittances can reduce poverty; studies associate remittances with greater investment by households in education, entrepreneurship, and health.[35] One study, by Dilip Ratha, showed that in Sri Lanka, infants in homes receiving remittances have higher birth weights, suggesting that some remittances went to health care.[36] On the other hand, the impact of remittances on economic growth is mixed. Investment in health and education could contribute to economic growth, yet a large exodus of skilled workers can reduce it.[37] Ratha concludes, however, that it is difficult to determine the impact of remittances on growth because "the effects of remittances on human and physical capital are realized over a very long time."[38] In any case, it is worth repeating that the distribution is random and may benefit the best-off rather than the worst-off people in countries that receive remittances. What isn't controversial, however, is that wealthy nations and their patients benefit from a transnational health care workforce. The extent to which people in affluent countries rely on an international health care workforce is ironic given the suspicion with which many residents of receiving countries view newcomers. Their willingness to trust strangers as health care workers should dispel some of the concerns that have been expressed about the possibility of creating trust among diverse people.

Medical Tourism

The medical brain drain is only one way that people from wealthy countries access the health resources of other countries. Medical tourists travel from one country to another to purchase and receive care,[39] and their numbers are on the rise.[40] Patients travel from rich countries to poor countries to purchase care often because it is less expensive in a developing country. They also seek cross-border care to reduce waiting times, to access services that are otherwise unavailable to them, and to improve quality.[41]

Accurate data about medical tourism is difficult to secure. Available figures for 2011 estimate the annual value for medical tourism at $100 billion.[42] The cost of care in destination countries is often lower than in the tourist's home country because of lower labor costs and living expenses as well as lower prices for pharmaceuticals and malpractice insurance. The cost in developing countries can be a mere 10 percent of what people would pay for care in the United States, for example.[43] Medical tourists spend an enormous amount of money globally on health care. The World Travel and Tourism Council states that in 2011 medical tourism counted for 9 percent of the global GDP and for 250 million jobs.[44] Medical tourists include working-class adults who want elective surgery not covered by their insurance, patients who want procedures not covered by insurance, in fields such as cosmetic surgery, dental work, fertility treatments or gender reassignment, orthopedics, and cardiovascular medicine.[45]

Brazil is a popular destination for cosmetic surgery, and Costa Rica for dental work and cosmetic surgery.[46] Mexico, South Africa, India, Thailand, and Singapore are also important destinations for medical tourists, especially for tourists from the United States.[47] Medical tourists are concerned primarily about quality of care. Because of this, programs that cater to them typically use US-trained physicians, evidence-based medicine, affiliate with top US medical facilities, and certify medical care with the Joint Commission International (JCI).[48] As of 2008, Harvard Medical International, Johns Hopkins Medicine International, Memorial Sloan Kettering Cancer Center, and Columbia University Medical Center, among others, had international collaborations and partnerships, which assured tourists that their medical care would reach standards of excellence.[49]

The cost savings to patients who travel for care can be significant. In 2010, angioplasty was estimated at $57,000 in the United States, $17,100 in Mexico, $14,000 in Costa Rica, $10,000 in India, and $9,000 in Thailand. A facelift in the United States was $15,000, but $8,000 in Mexico and $6,500 in Costa Rica.[50] In 2013, the *New York Times* reported the case of Michael Shopenn, a sixty-seven-year-old photographer who flew to Brussels to have his hip replaced for $13,660, a price that included doctors' fees, hospital charges, medicines, crutches, and round-trip airfare from the United States. In the United States, in contrast, the artificial joint itself had a list price of $13,000, and the cost of the procedure was estimated at $65,000, not including physician's fees.[51]

Cross-border reproductive care is also on the rise. Studies in Europe show that patients who seek reproductive care in distant countries are looking for better access to care than is available in their home country, or to sidestep the legal restrictions of their homeland. For example, in the European Union people are forbidden by law from purchasing gametes under the EU Tissues and Cells Directive. Instead, member states must make an effort to provide "voluntary and unpaid donations."[52] The use of international surrogates raises concerns about the vulnerability of women and children, their exploitation, and the potential to traffic in surrogates among vulnerable women. In 1996, the British Medical Association expressed concern about the trafficking of socially and economically vulnerable women from Poland, Romania, and Hungary to Germany, Holland, and Canada, among other places.[53] Given the importance of the decision to serve as a surrogate and to give up a child for adoption, there are ethical concerns about surrogates' autonomy. The capacity to make autonomous choices can be impaired by social and economic disadvantage. It is difficult for women to make free choices when they are concerned about eating, or providing food for their families.

It could be argued that offering women an opportunity to be a surrogate by paying them for that service enhances and improves their quality of life. There is something to this. The question, however, is whether in the context of poverty and severely restricted options women are coerced to serve as surrogates for want of other viable options. There are many ways to improve the lives of people in developing countries that do not sacrifice their autonomy. It is not our intention to challenge the practice here, but only to recognize that it exists. Whether the purchase price of surrogacy is adequate compensation is difficult to determine. Using people from other countries as surrogates is another example of health's global reach. It reflects the willingness of people in developed countries to use people in poor countries for their health advantage; it also demonstrates a willingness to trust them.

International Transplantation

As we have shown, people from affluent nations use the bodies of women from poor nations as surrogates, and sometimes purchase their gametes. They also buy the organs of people in poor countries. This is known as transplant tourism. As medicine is able to transplant organs effectively, the demand for organs has increased. Although many countries have the medical skill necessary to undertake transplant surgery, people seeking organs are primarily from developed countries. The shortage in available organs from deceased donors has given rise to a market for live donors for both kidney and liver transplantation. The demand for organs is far greater than the indigenous supply in wealthy nations, fostering an international organ market.[54]

A recent study undertaken by the WHO summarizes some of the available data on transplant tourism. Typically, patients seeking organs travel to foreign destinations, often aided by health care providers, or through transplant packages. There are, however, reports of organ donors traveling from one country to another country where the transplantation surgery is done. This difference is morally important because when recipients travel to the donor's country, they not only purchase an organ from a donor, they also use the health care system of the donor's country, shifting resources from local needs to the needs of organ tourists. Heath care workers are drawn to higher-paying private-care opportunities, such as those offered to foreign patients. Thus transplant tourism can incentivize health care workers to shift their work to private care.[55]

Organ tourists travel from a number of countries. Organs Watch, based in the University of California, has identified seven countries as the primary "organ importing countries": Australia, Canada, Israel, Japan, Oman, Saudi Arabia, and the United States.[56] In some places transplant tourism is more common than local transplants. Although the data are incomplete and sometimes conflicting, there is evidence that transplants done outside a recipient's home country have worse outcomes. At the very least the studies indicate an increase in medical complications such as the transmission of HIV and hepatitis B and C viruses.[57]

The risk to donors is also great. Some countries fail to protect them from exploitation.[58] In still other cases, donors and recipients travel to a third country for the surgery. Reportedly, in South Africa at St. Augustine Hospital, more than one hundred illegal kidney transplants were done, with most of the recipients coming from Israel and most of the donors from Europe and Brazil.[59] Although there has not been extensive research on donors, the research that has been done shows that poverty and the prospect of economic improvement are the main reasons for most kidney donors. Unfortunately, studies also show that many people who have sold their organs suffer compromised health. According to one study, roughly 86 percent of those who sold a kidney were in worse health after it.[60] Poor health, of course, can make it difficult for donors to work. An early study of kidney sales in India (a number of which are to non-Indians), indicated that the overwhelming majority of sellers did so in order to pay off debts and to buy food and clothing. Many families experience a decline in income by one-third after the procedure; the number of sellers living below the poverty line increased.[61]

In some quarters, it might be argued that in a global market, the economic principles of supply and demand determine the distribution of resources. In addition, the economy of poor countries is stimulated by medical tourism, reducing an overall disadvantage to poor countries. Finally, natives of poor countries have a right to self-protection that grounds their right to assemble the resources they need to protect their lives. Denying them an opportunity to sell their organs on the open global market interferes with their liberty. Similar arguments are made about the propensity of some nations and their multinationals to exploit workers in developing countries. The argument has also been made that workers, their families, and poor countries are better off even if some of the labor practices are exploitive.

This reasoning is sufficiently problematic in relation to business, but when it is applied to health resources it is disconcerting. For one thing, health is morally special. Philosopher Norman Daniels has made the point that health is important for equal opportunity and therefore should not be subject wholly to market principles since to do so would mean that only those who could afford health care would have access to it.[62] Others, including Amartya Sen, Martha Nussbaum, and Sridhar Venkatapuram, have argued that health care is a crucial capability that should be realized.[63] It would be difficult to find anyone who is committed to the moral principle that health ought to be treated as just another commodity.

There are multiple advantages for medical tourists. Care is inexpensive, quick, and, in some instances, medical tourists may have access to care that is otherwise unavailable. The benefits to destination countries are less clear. Tourists pay for procedures, presumably at a fair market price. It could be argued that there is an economic trickle-down to the wider community. Medical tourism draws foreign currency into developing countries, which can support health and improve overall economic development.[64] The amounts can be substantial. In 2006, Thailand is estimated to have cleared $1.1 billion from cross-border patients seeking cosmetic surgery, organ transplants, dental treatment, and joint replacements. India had $480 million from cardiac surgery, joint replacements, and eye surgery, among other procedures.[65] One advantage for destination countries has been that some expatriate health care workers return to their countries of origin to continue their practices. These advantages, however, may be illusory: Ronald Labonté points out that much of the industry is foreign-owned and the revenue does not remain in the country.[66]

Medical tourism entails costs to local people, especially with respect to access to health care. Many health care resources that could be addressing the needs of poor local people are shifted to more lucrative medical tourists. Even when there is regulation intended to protect the local poor, it is often not enforced. In India, for example, private hospitals that serve both public patients and medical tourists received concessions in exchange for promising to provide 25 percent of inpatient care and 40 percent of outpatient care for free to patients who could not afford to pay. However, the hospitals simply didn't follow through. In Priya Shetty's words, "What started with a grand idea of benefiting the poor turned out to be a ground for the rich in the garb of public charitable interests."[67]

The growing trend of people from affluent countries to draw on the health resources of other countries does not reflect suspicion and distrust of strangers. Instead, it shows a high level of trust in so-called outsiders. Affluent societies buy their organs, use their bodies for reproductive purposes, and depend on their health care workers. These practices are often to the detriment of poor countries. They illustrate the extent to which health and the mechanisms for achieving it are treated as "global resources." They also demonstrate the health benefits that accrue to wealthy countries when their citizens use the health resources of other nations. Reflecting on the many ways that health interests of people in affluent nations intersect with those of other countries should help foster empathy with the health needs of others. It also manifests the many ways in which global cooperation for health prevails and can be in the health interest of all.

We need to be mindful that one of the reasons that health care is more affordable in other countries is because it is subsidized by those countries, through their governments and taxation of their citizens. In view of the willingness of people in affluent countries to use the health care resources of people in poor countries, it hardly seems appropriate to be parsimonious when it comes to the health care of newcomers. According to Iris Young, one of the main reasons people in wealthy countries have responsibilities to the victims of structural injustice is because of the connection that exists among us. "Our responsibility derives from belonging together with others in a system of interdependent processes of cooperation and competition through which we seek benefits and aim to realize projects. . . . All who dwell within the structures must take responsibility for remedying injustices they cause."[68] The abundant and multifaceted connections between people in affluent countries and people in poor countries, for the sake of health, are precisely the kind of connection that triggers responsibilities to the victims of structural injustice.

Solidarity for Newcomers, Health for All

The Story of Karim

Karim Alagha died on December 13, 2012, in Cambridge, Massachusetts. He pumped gas for more than twenty-five years at Nick's Service Station, often working from 7 a.m. to 10 p.m. He sent money home to his wife in Lebanon and put his kids through college with the money he made pumping gas. He always had a kind word for his customers, treats for their dogs (including for Sam, the Labrador retriever of one of the authors of this volume), and lollipops for their children. Unfortunately, Karim was diagnosed with lung cancer. He checked into a local hospital and underwent chemotherapy. The cancer advanced, and with only a short time to live he expressed a wish to be buried next to his father in Lebanon. Neighbors and customers came to his aid. They collected money to send back to his family in Lebanon, paid some of his bills, and bought him food. One neighbor gave him an apartment in which to live. When Karim died, the community collected still more money to ensure that he would be buried next to his father in Lebanon. There is little doubt that the people of West Cambridge "carried costs" for Karim both financially and emotionally. They acted in solidarity to provide him with the care that he needed. Together, they raised thousands of dollars for him.[1]

Health: For Citizens Only

Health, we have seen, is not a purely private good, but has public-good dimensions. As a global public good, health is determined for good or ill, by forces beyond the scope of any individual or nation. The transnational, reciprocal etiology of health gives rise to ethical duties to newcomers while also ensuring that policies that deny them health care, or discriminate against them in the development and implementation of public health, are doomed to failure. Moreover, affluent nations have contributed to global poverty and the poor health that follows it. They have done so in violation of a morally demanding duty not to harm others. We also argued that far from distancing themselves from the global poor, when it comes to health many people in affluent nations demonstrate a penchant for the health resources of poor nations. They buy their organs, recruit their doctors and nurses, and travel thousands of miles to use their hospitals and medical expertise. Although these transnational flows for health foster important social ties among diverse people, they are often detrimental to people in poor nations. Nonetheless, they show a capacity for diverse people to work together in the name of health.

Before further considering the significance of these global ties for health, it is important to ask whether the absence of citizenship or lawful immigration status is relevant to the question of how newcomers should be treated. Even if we accept the moral commitment to impartiality, that all individuals have duties to all others with respect to health—that no man is an island[2]—and that there is a right to health as a matter of international law, that does not mean that nations have the same obligations to those who are not legal members of their polity as they do to their own citizens. To put it another way, it does not mean that citizenship and legal status are irrelevant factors to the distribution of health resources or the implementation of public health policies.

Many justifications are offered for disparately treating immigrants with respect to health care resources and public health policies. Some justifications rely on empirical claims, namely, that immigrants pose a threat to a nation's economic and physical health. As we have shown, the evidence does not support these claims. Rather than protecting public health, policies that discriminate against newcomers at the border offer a dangerous illusion of protection but fail to protect the residents of a nation from health threats. These policies also divert resources from more effective health interventions while reinforcing stigma that can undermine trust in public health officials. Likewise, policies that limit newcomers' access to government-supported health care benefits impede access to preventive and primary care, increasing and shifting costs onto others in the health care system.

A different empirical argument is that disparate treatment is necessary to prevent an influx of freeloading immigrants. This argument, enshrined as US immigration policy in the Personal Responsibility and Work Opportunity Reconciliation Act of 1996, assumes that nations have a legal and moral right to limit immigration to those who will be economically productive, and posits that equal treatment regarding health will encourage unproductive immigrants to freeload on the services supported by citizens. We addressed some of these issues in chapter 4.

For present purposes, we grant that nations have a right to limit immigration to people who will be "productive," though it is important to note that many of the policies that screen for "productivity" employ and reinforce disturbing stereotypical assumptions about disease and disability. Nevertheless, as we argued in chapter 2, the claim that in the absence of exclusionary policies people will immigrate in large numbers to gain access to health resources is not supported by any empirical evidence. Nor is the assertion that immigrants are as a class freeloaders, apt to cost a health care system more than they contribute. To the contrary, because they tend to be younger and healthier than natives, immigrants as a class generally contribute more to health care systems than they extract.[3]

Although the empirical evidence does not support discriminating against newcomers regarding health, many of the arguments made in support of discrimination are conceptual rather than empirical. These arguments assert, in different ways, that citizenship and immigration status are morally relevant categories that give states legitimate grounds for distributing health-related resources. Before considering them, it may be helpful to put a few issues to the side. The first is a point noted previously: all nations, even those that do not accept a broad right to health as provided in the International Covenant on Economic, Social and Culture Rights, recognize at least some rights to health. Thus we need not ask whether nations should accept that there is a right to health, but only whether the rights that exist relating to health should apply to newcomers. Second, we need to consider whether citizenship continues to exist as a meaningful category. On the one hand, globalization, the establishment of supranational institutions such as the European Union, and the expansion of the international human rights regime have led many to argue that citizenship should no longer be tied to the nation-state; rather, citizenship should be viewed as global. On the other hand, many communitarians and others argue for the primacy of smaller, subnational entities, contending that citizenship, understood as active engagement in a political community, can only be fully realized in smaller units, such as towns, states, or even nongovernmental community groups. For our purposes, we need not consider these competing visions of citizenship, or how citizenship may evolve in the future. Rather, we can take as a given that national citizenship continues to exist and continues to be used along with other immigration statuses to distribute rights relating to health.

Second, we accept as a given that nations limit citizenship to discrete categories of persons. As Linda Bosniak reminds us, the question of what citizens are entitled to is inextricably connected to the question of who may become a citizen.[4] If citizenship or lawful immigration status were given freely to all and if everyone entering a country were accorded full citizenship, limiting health rights to citizens would have little bite. On the other hand, if access to citizenship were itself limited, the restriction of health rights to citizens would have a serious impact and require further scrutiny. In the world we live in, citizenship and immigration status are restricted. Hence we need to look carefully at the claim that health rights should be limited to citizens, or at least newcomers with legal status.

The arguments take many forms. One set of arguments, which we call *definitional*, build upon Hannah Arendt's observation that "rights and duties must be defined and limited, not only by those of his fellow citizens, but also by the boundaries of a territory."[5] In other words, legal rights, as opposed to ethical or human rights, are by their very nature created by and limited to the reach of a sovereign nation. (In this chapter, when we discuss rights, we have in mind legal rights, the enforceable rights of a given nation.) Citizens, as Michael Walzer explains, are the "member[s] of a political community entitled to whatever prerogatives and encumbered with whatever responsibilities are attached to membership."[6] In effect, legal rights come from and are limited to bounded political communities, and citizens are those lawfully within those boundaries. Hence in this view the notion of legal rights for noncitizens is oxymoronic.

Although this argument tracks many popularly held views that equate citizenship with rights, it deserves closer examination. For a start, it ignores the many rights that noncitizens actually have. Indeed, no country claims that noncitizens, even those without lawful status, are without any legal rights. Although the image of the "man without a country" devoid of all rights is a frightening one, it isn't accurate, at least when applied to newcomers living in a nation. Once within a country, newcomers, even those who are unauthorized, have all sorts of legal rights, including rights against the state, such as the right not to be tortured, or the right to asylum. But even more "ordinary" legal rights apply to noncitizens. In the United States, for example, noncitizens have a constitutionally protected right to attend public schools. They are also entitled to the full protection of the criminal law when arrested or charged, and they have the right to legal process before they are deported. They also, as we have seen, have the right to emergency medical treatment in an emergency room. Newcomers may not have the full rights of citizens, but they do have many legal rights. The fact that rights can only be binding within a sovereign nation simply provides no basis for assuming that only citizens can have rights.

Modern discourse on citizenship typically begins with a reference to T. H. Marshall's observation that citizenship is an evolving institution that has broadened over time to encompass more classes of people and more varied types of rights.[7] For example, prior to Reconstruction, African Americans were not recognized as citizens of the United States. Women, at least white women, were considered citizens, but they lacked the full rights of citizenship. Only in the twentieth century, Marshall explains, was citizenship broadened to encompass women and, in England, members of the working class. With that new inclusion came, in Marshall's view, a new set of rights, which he terms social rights, including income security and health, the rights closely associated with the welfare state. Thus, following Marshall, rights to health are closely tied, at least as a historical matter, with expanding notions of citizenship.[8]

Marshall wrote shortly after World War II, as the British welfare state was developing. Today, the meaning of citizenship is contested. Legal scholars offer two views of citizenship. One theory, the *ascriptive theory*, claims that citizenship is something that attaches to people as a result of an innate status, such as birth in a territory or membership in a distinct demographic group. For example, under the Fourteenth Amendment of the United States Constitution, anyone born within the United States becomes a citizen by virtue of being born within the country. In Germany, by contrast, citizenship is for the most part based on birth to a German citizen.[9]

A second theory of citizenship focuses on consent. This view holds that a citizen is someone who consents to be part of the polity. The clearest example of such consent occurs when a newcomer becomes a naturalized citizen, but theorists such as Peter Schuck and Rogers M. Smith argue that even native-born citizens obtain their citizenship by consent, albeit tacit consent.[10] In effect, by living and participating within a political community, they consent to be its citizens.

In practice, around the globe, citizenship arises from both status and consent.[11] Regardless, neither status nor consent provides an adequate justification for the denial of health-related rights to noncitizens, or even newcomers without legal status. Consider the status-based account of citizenship. If citizenship is based on status, the definitional defense for limiting health-based rights to citizens collapses into a mere tautology which states that only people from a certain group (nationality, race, ethnicity, religion, or ancestry) can be citizens, and only citizens can have rights as rights are by definition obligations limited to citizens. Like all tautologies, this one is true on its own terms, but it is also inadequate because it simply assumes without further explanation or analysis that the factors such as place of birth or ethnicity constitute legitimate criteria for determining the allocation of a legal right to health. But even if ascriptive factors constitute valid grounds for determining citizenship, we need to ask why they should matter for respecting the right to health. Ascriptive factors alone seem irrelevant to whether people should have their health needs met. After all, outside the context of immigration we would not say that someone should be denied health rights simply on the basis of race or ancestry. Rather, the criteria for determining whether a person receives health care should have some explanatory power relating to health, including health as a global public good.

The consensual theory of citizenship offers a stronger argument for reserving rights for citizens. If we follow social contract theory and analogize a nation to a voluntary membership association, it would seem to make sense to argue that claims against the association should only apply to its own members.[12] After all, a private club or association, for example, a noncommercial sports league, is largely free to form its own rules and limit its benefits to its own members. This analogy, however, cannot justify denying health benefits to noncitizens, because unlike participation in the sports league, citizenship is not predicated on explicit consent. It is largely based on an accident of birth (or parents' birth). Moreover, even if we were to concede that most citizens consent to citizenship implicitly, status still serves as a common basis for denying citizenship. Although many newcomers would welcome the opportunity to consent and would happily meet any and all corresponding obligations, they are often unable, simply by virtue of their place of birth or their parents' place of birth, to obtain citizenship. Thus the denial of health benefits to noncitizens is not comparable to limiting benefits to a voluntary membership organization. Rather, it is akin to the ethically dubious practice of barring racial or ethnic minorities from private associations. This suggests that the claim that rights (at least to health) by definition can only be available to citizens cannot provide a valid defense for denying health benefits to noncitizens unless and until the membership rules for citizenship are based on grounds that are ethically relevant to health. Hence, as long as nations have absolute, or plenary, authority over determining who may become a citizen, citizenship alone cannot serve as a valid normative justification for the denial of health-based rights.

As Michael Walzer has argued, the fact that an organization has the right to define the criteria for its membership, as well as the rules that apply to its own members, does not give it moral authority to make decisions that affect outsiders.[13] A sports league can decide the type of gear it will provide its members, but it has no moral right to decide what nonmembers will wear. Nor do members of the league, within the bounds of justice, have the right to engage in behaviors that harm nonmembers, for example, by committing acts of domestic violence. Indeed, as Walzer explains, the imposition of policies that harm people who are denied membership to the group constitutes subjugation.[14] It is the tyranny that Rome and pre–Civil War America exercised over their slaves, or that the whites of South Africa exercised over that nation's black population during apartheid.

Principles of democracy suggest that groups and nations do not act justly when they govern those who are denied the right to participate in their own governance. From this principle, Walzer argues that all immigrants should have the right to be citizens.[15] No one who lives within a polity should be denied the right to help set its rules. But given that nations do not grant that opportunity to many newcomers, it would seem to follow that those who are denied citizenship should not be distinctly disadvantaged by the laws and policy about which they have no voice, especially in relation to rights that are recognized for citizens. This applies especially to rights relating to health both because health is a human right and because it is a global public good. The actions and policies of citizens inevitably affect the health of the noncitizens who live and work alongside them (and those who live far away, though indirectly). As a result, lack of citizenship provides no rationale for denying rights relating to health. For Walzer, the health of noncitizens is outside the "sphere" of citizens' own self-governance.[16]

Moreover, to the extent that citizenship relies on tacit consent, the definitional argument overlooks the many ways that newcomers demonstrate their consent to membership in the nations to which they have immigrated. As has been discussed previously, for the most part, newcomers work and pay taxes in their new countries. They also contribute to their new communities in myriad other ways. For example, some join the military and others engage in volunteer work or political activism. Many work in necessary jobs, such as caretaking for the ill, that citizens abjure. As Linda Bosniak explains, "As workers, taxpayers, consumers, neighbors, [noncitizens] are part of the life of the (nationally bounded) political community—the very community that citizenship in its internal mode considers the proper domain of concern."[17] Indeed, with the exception of exercising the political rights and duties from which they are often excluded (such as the franchise and jury duty), newcomers in general demonstrate as much loyalty and consent to be a part of the community as do most citizens, many of whom, of course, also do not vote, and take their citizenship for granted.

Some argue that the situation is different for those who enter a country illegally, that by violating a nation's immigration laws, unauthorized immigrants demonstrate their lack of loyalty to the community and hence lose their claim to participate in the rights it bestows. This argument overlooks the fact that some undocumented immigrants arrive as young children and were unable to exercise any choice as to whether or not to immigrate. Hence, their entry into their new country cannot be viewed as demonstrating any disloyalty to that country. This is one reason why many immigration reform advocates in the United States have advocated that those who arrive as children should be put on a path to citizenship; although Congress has not provided for this path, President Obama suspended deportations of such immigrants as long as they did not have a criminal record. The argument also overlooks the complexity of immigration. Some immigrants who arrive without visas have legitimate claims for asylum. And some who arrive with visas accidentally overstay their status and become unauthorized. It isn't always easy to decide who is a legal and who is an unauthorized immigrant.

But even if we put these complexities to the side, as James Dwyer notes, "Nothing about access to health care follows from the mere fact that unauthorized aliens have violated a law. Many people break many different laws. Whether a violation of a law should disqualify people from public services probably depends on the nature and purpose of the services, the nature and the gravity of the violation, and many other matters."[18] In other words, there is nothing about violating an immigration law per se that entails that an immigrant has not consented to membership in the polity or has lost the right to receive health benefits.[19]

Solidarity, Defined and Explained

Citizenship's association with solidarity may provide another rationale for limiting the health-related rights of noncitizens. In Western Europe, citizenship has long been associated with solidarity, and as Marshall first suggested, it has been critical to the rise and maintenance of the welfare state.[20] Thus the argument goes that without citizenship, there may be no (or little) solidarity, and without solidarity, health cannot be secured. Either preference is given to citizens, or no one's right to health can be recognized.

In assessing this argument, it is important to consider what is meant by "solidarity." Solidarity does not have a single definition. It has been used as a call for action. In the 1980s, the Polish Solidarity movement called for social justice and democracy. Philosopher Shawn Harmon identifies three characteristics that he associates with solidarity. These are: (1) solidarity emphasizes community, recognizing that individuals are embedded in social contexts and that they share connections with other people, society, and groups; (2) it is grounded in an interest in the well-being of others and an active commitment to promote their well-being; and (3) "[s]olidarity demands common action to uphold the complex of social relationships and values that is needed to realise useful standards of decency and justice."[21] Solidarity is understood to have prescriptive qualities. It creates an obligation to act for the sake of others and creates the possibility that individual interest may need to be subordinated to community interest.[22] That is, solidarity triggers a duty to carry costs for other people.

Scholars have stressed the importance of group membership for solidarity, whether ethnic, racial, gender, or religious. "[O]ne cannot show solidarity with just anybody."[23] Rather, solidarity exists only with those within a "community to which one believes oneself to belong."[24] A common goal has also been identified as necessary for solidarity. For our purposes, however, it is important to understand that solidarity is triggered by participation in a community. Bayertz, for example, doesn't tie solidarity to citizenship per se, but to belonging to a community, potentially a far broader group.

One reason for thinking that solidarity can exist only among citizens is that solidarity may be based on feelings people have for one and another, such as feelings of mutual concern. Philosopher David Heyd says of solidarity, "One may describe solidarity as sympathy mediated by a belief in a common project. Solidarity combines personal and impersonal components: the objects of solidarity are mostly anonymous in the sense that the subject does not personally know them. . . . We care for people with whom we feel solidarity, but do so on the basis of their belonging to 'our' group, fighting for a certain goal rather than as just individual human beings."[25] An underlying assumption of the view that citizenship triggers solidarity is that people are only able to have fellow feeling toward citizens. People are surely predisposed toward people they view as in their group (in-group bias), and groups are often constituted by citizens. Studies on in-group bias show that people have a preference for those who seem to be just like them.[26] Indeed, such preferences are called *homophilous*. Nonetheless, in-group bias is more likely in some places than in other places, and at some times more than others. Today, however, groups are often constituted by diverse people, with citizens from around the world.

In some quarters, it is argued that solidarity coupled with citizenship is essential for the recognition of social rights.[27] In effect citizenship provides the glue, the common characteristic that nurtures fellow feeling and a willingness to engage in the type of redistribution required to support the right to health. Some scholars have gone further and have suggested that immigration itself, regardless of the rights conferred, weakens solidarity among citizens, thereby threatening support for the welfare state. David J. Abraham writes, "Tolerance, trust and solidarity" are needed for a "viable socio-democratic conception of justice."[28] Noting as many have that the more homogenous northern European countries are the homes of some of the most generous welfare states, he warns that greater diversity may threaten solidarity and thus the state's willingness or ability to provide social benefits. He states: "The German 'we' is thicker and more substantial than the American 'we'; it is also, and not accidentally, more exclusionary."[29]

Securing the borders and limiting immigration to those who appear to be similar is one way to respond to this perceived threat to solidarity. Such an argument can be heard frequently by nativists who bemoan the loss of national identity and homogeneity that immigration entails. Yet the argument that borders must be secured simply to maintain racial, religious, or ethnic fellowship among the majority population is in need of further justification and may be little more than a thinly veiled rationalization for invidious status-based discrimination. Although it may be true that people who discriminate on the basis of race, religion, or ethnicity feel more fellowship for members of their in-group, and as a result exhibit a greater willingness to carry costs for them, that alone is no justification for discriminating against those who seem different.

A more sophisticated argument is that citizenship can play an important role by separating an obligation to carry costs from race, religion, or ethnicity. According to this perspective, citizenship can replace kin, clan, and tribe, creating a new liberal, nonnativist national identity. Thus the French feel solidarity with other *citoyens*, and citizens of the United States feel kinship with other Americans, regardless of their race, religion, or ethnicity. To the extent that citizenship requires civic engagement with the state, as proponents of civic republicanism suggest, it can also build habits of mutual interaction in a shared enterprise—the polity—which, in turn, may foster solidarity across citizen groups. Naturally, this liberal ideal would only be possible if the criteria for achieving citizenship were similarly liberal. If citizenship depends only upon racial or ethnic categories, it would have no ability to foster solidarity across groups.

Where the attainment of citizenship is relatively open, such as in the United States and Canada, citizenship may in principle play a role in promoting solidarity across diverse groups. However, this does not mean that citizenship is necessary for solidarity, or that solidarity need be undermined by the recognition that there are duties to carry costs for noncitizens. There is good reason that neither is the case.

Solidarity with Newcomers

Realizing newcomers' right to health requires considerable solidarity between natives and newcomers, as natives would need to carry the health-related costs of newcomers. Let us look more closely at solidarity with an eye to understanding how it might be more inclusive. Barbara Prainsack and Alena Buyx explain, "solidarity signifies *shared practices reflecting a collective commitment to carry 'costs' (financial, social, emotional, or otherwise) to assist others.* . . . [I]t requires actions—motivations, feelings such as empathy etc. are not sufficient to satisfy this understanding of solidarity, unless they manifest themselves in acts."[30] Briefly, according to these authors, solidarity consists in three tiers, each reflecting different ways that it is expressed. Tier 1 solidarity exists at the interpersonal level, and Tier 2 consists of group practices among individuals who recognize a relevant similarity. As Prainsack and Buyx note, when practices among individuals become normalized at Tier 2, solidarity emerges in which solidaristic practices shift from individuals to groups. At Tier 3, solidarity is embedded in contractual and legal manifestations. In all cases, for solidarity to exist individuals must exhibit a willingness to carry costs for those similarly situated.[31]

Consider some examples. Tier 1 solidarity exists among individuals who have at least one interest in common with other people. The authors mention, as an example, the solidarity people feel toward fellow travelers who miss a connecting flight.[32] Patients who share an overcrowded hospital waiting room might also come together in solidarity. At the level of Tier 2, solidarity consists of "manifestations of a collective commitment to carry costs to assist others (who are all linked by means of a shared situation or cause)."[33] Tier 2 is the most common form of solidarity. In the case of health, people often form self-help groups and engage in activities to help others. The walk for breast cancer is one example in which people across the United States act in solidarity to find support for those with the disease. Many people come together because of their common concerns with the victims of breast cancer.

Tier 2 solidarity also exists transnationally. Ebola clinics, such as those run by International Medical Corps in Liberia to address the needs of Ebola patients, are a good example. Together 172 people—a combination of locals, internationals, and volunteers—worked as physicians, nurses, gravediggers, scientists, survivors, and university students to fight the spread of Ebola and help patients ravaged by it. One physician, Steven Hatch from Massachusetts, remarked, "I have dreams in the middle of the night waking up in the Ebola ward as a patient. I've had dreams where I am in the ward without any gear, just standing there in my pants and shirt. But I like getting up in the morning, and I like coming here, I think we're actually making a difference for these people."[34] Hatch's dream expresses a shared sense of common vulnerability, and his actions, together with those of others, demonstrate a willingness to carry costs for distant others.

Tier 1 and 2 practices typically exist before Tier 3 solidarity surfaces. From these practices norms and values emerge that can foster Tier 3 solidarity. Tier 3 solidarity involves legal mechanisms, such as contracts, treaties, and government action. State-funded health care is a good example. Health policy that is blind to immigration status would foster Tier 3 solidarity among citizens and newcomers. Recognition of shared vulnerability of health, combined with a willingness to carry costs for others, demonstrates solidarity. Prainsack and Buyx point out that according to the German government, health insurance constitutes a solidarity-based community.[35] It seems to fit the Tier 3 definition of government action with respect to a common cause and a willingness to carry costs. Tier 3 solidarity is also reflected in efforts by the US Centers for Disease Control and Prevention (CDC) to help end the spread of the Ebola virus in West Africa. Tom Frieden, director of the CDC, promised to do everything in the CDC's power to stop the outbreak. In his words, "The Ebola outbreak in West Africa is a tragic and painful reminder that global health security has a direct impact on the health of all of us here in the United States. Infectious diseases do not recognize borders. Uncontrolled disease anywhere is potentially a disease everywhere."[36] Frieden's words highlight the public-good dimension of health with the corresponding need for solidarity. Another example of Tier 3 global health solidarity can be found in France's tax on air tickets. According to the French civil aviation authority, the tax has collected more than €1 billion since its inception in 2006. The money has been used to fight TB, HIV/AIDS, and malaria worldwide helping some of the world's poorest people.[37] Nations such as Canada that have welcomed refugees from Syria and extend health care to them also demonstrate Tier 3 solidarity with newcomers.

The CDC's actions and those of other organizations and international institutions meet the criteria for Tier 3 solidarity and do so on a global scale. The CDC provided assistance to West Africa and thus was committed to carrying costs to help people through the crisis. Frieden's words also reflect a sense of shared interest with the other members of the global community. On the CDC blog, commentators encouraged the CDC to send ZMapp, an experimental drug, to West Africa to help people with Ebola, again reflecting a willingness to carry costs for distant others. In a show of solidarity, Frieden stated, "We want to do everything in our power to stop this outbreak. We will protect people around the world, including in the United States, by stopping Ebola at its source."[38]

For Prainsack and Buyx, solidarity at Tiers 1 and 2 concern people who have a sense of shared cause that bears some relationship to a situation. Thus, solidarity at Tiers 1 and 2 can exist with people one does not know. Although a sense of similarity is often present, similarities need not be based on culture, skin color, national origin, or religion. We can imagine, for example, that as diverse people fled the World Trade Center in New York City during the 9/11 terrorist attack, they experienced solidarity as individuals trying to save their own lives and the lives of others. Similarly, many of those working together in Ebola clinics in West Africa are from different nations, cultures, religions, and socioeconomic groups. They come together because of their compassion for human suffering and the desire to join in solidarity to help others. Likewise, the people of West Cambridge who came to Karim's aid understood his human vulnerability and wish to be buried near his father. Although lacking ties based on citizenship, diverse people, strangers and natives, newcomers and citizens, can share situation-based connections that can give rise to solidarity.

Many of the experiences between natives and newcomers that give rise to solidarity are focused on taking care of the sick and elderly. Solidarity can evolve from multiple interactions between immigrants who work in health care and natives who depend on them for care. In the United States, for example, roughly 45 percent of maids and housekeepers are immigrants.[39] Immigrant women are also heavily represented in the home health and private caregiving workforces in many wealthy countries.[40] Immigrants form a significant share of the professional health care workforce in receiving nations. In the United Kingdom, for example, more than one-third of physicians registered with the General Medical Council qualified outside the European Economic Area.[41] Luisa M. Pettigrew notes that "there is little doubt that the NHS would not have been sustainable" but for the "on-going contribution of health professionals from overseas."[42] The reliance on foreign-born professionals is similar in other affluent countries. In 2011 only 47.3 percent of physicians in Australia were natives, and more than 40 percent of midwives were immigrants.[43] In the United States in 2010, 14 percent of registered nurses were immigrants.[44] The daily interactions that noncitizen health care workers have with their patients, and the families of their patients, can help to create solidarity.[45]

Newcomers also work as nannies, caring for the children of natives in order to send money home to educate their own children. They share a common goal with the families who hire them, a desire to raise healthy, happy children. The elderly and the international caretakers who support them also share common goals. Out of these connections, norms of behavior are established, as shown by the story of Florence Tratar, a women in her eighties who fell and needed full-time, in-home care. She had no family close by. The help she needed was provided by Joesy Gerrish, a caregiver from Fiji. Florence and Joesy hit it off immediately, and both agreed that Joesy did everything for Florence. In Florence's words, "I don't know what I would do without Joesy. I couldn't survive."[46] Both women worked together toward Florence's survival, with Joesy often awake every two to three hours in a night to help Florence.

The relationship between Florence and Joesy was one of solidarity; both women were working toward the common goal of keeping Florence safe and maintaining her health. The interaction toward this end falls into a Tier 1 practice. What are the factors about the relationship between them that created a commitment to carry costs, and do those factors extend more broadly to newcomers? A commitment to carry costs regardless of citizenship can be justified on the basis of reciprocity and the need for cooperation.[47] Although neither family nor compatriots, Florence and Joesy needed to cooperate with each other. To be supportive, Joesy had to not only wake up every few hours but must also be kind. Florence may have had to help Joesy gain legal immigration status, perhaps by hiring an immigration attorney to help her or serving as a sponsor. Thus she may well have had to carry costs for her caretaker.

Karim, a native of Lebanon, also touched the lives of a community of people by giving their children lollipops and their dogs treats. In the end, that community acted in solidarity, bound by a deep understanding of common humanity and the need to be near loved ones at the end of life. West Cantabrigians showed solidarity with Karim when they carried a variety of costs for him. If solidarity at Tier 1 is exemplified by a common cause, interpersonal relations, and a willingness to carry costs, then from a purely descriptive point of view solidarity existed between Joesy and Florence, and among Karim and the West Cantabrigians. As these relationships illustrate, citizenship isn't necessary for people to both have fellow feelings for newcomers and be prepared to carry their costs at the interpersonal level.

Even apart from caretaking relationships, solidarity may form between citizens and newcomers because of their interdependency in relation to health. Because health is a public good, the health of citizens depends, in part, on the health of newcomers, and vice versa. Newcomers and citizens live and work together; they contract each other's diseases and use the same hospitals when they are sick. This shared fate, which is global in expanse, but especially prominent at the local level, prompts newcomers and natives to work together to improve community health services, as is evident when they establish community clinics or undertake community health initiatives. These actions are precisely the type of Tier 2 forms of solidarity that help establish shared norms, and ultimately the willingness to carry costs that are manifested through the legal system.

Despite the fact that most wealthy nations deny some newcomers full participation in their health care systems, there is a strong reason to believe that health-related solidarity does in fact exist between many citizens and newcomers. At the community level, this is most evident in the increasingly important role that NGOs are playing in providing health care to immigrant communities.[48] But there is further evidence of Tier 3 health-related solidarity between citizens and immigrants. For example, as we have seen, wealthy nations for the most part provide newcomers with access to emergency medical care, evincing a willingness to carry costs when it is critical. And perhaps in recognition of the interdependency between citizens and newcomers, receiving nations generally provide newcomers with treatment for at least some communicable diseases. Moreover, receiving nations generally grant some groups of newcomers full and equal access to their health insurance systems and often provide less-robust coverage for those immigrants who are not fully included. While the provision of less-comprehensive health care manifests a failure to fully recognize newcomers' right to health, it nonetheless reflects an obligation to carry the costs of newcomers' care. This suggests that while discrimination against newcomers persists, it does not preclude a willingness to support health care for newcomers.

Solidarity for Health

But does such solidarity go further and create a moral obligation to carry the health costs of newcomers? The presence of fellow feeling underlying solidarity is not enough in and of itself to assert that solidarity is morally required. Fellow feeling cannot be enough to trigger a moral duty to carry costs for the simple reason that sometimes fellow feeling can be in the service of immoral ends—such as the fellow feeling among ISIS members or the Ku Klux Klan. Iris Young provides a framework for distinguishing occasions when solidarity-based duties are triggered. Briefly, her answer is that generally duties of solidarity are triggered by the presence of structural injustice. We discussed this important concept in chapter 7. Recall that, according to Young, injustice exists when some people experience material disadvantage, such as poverty, through no choice of their own, and other people benefit, as a result of circumstances. Young argues that injustice is fostered not only through the acts of individuals but also through social structures.[49]

Young believes that responsibility for carrying costs can arise when there is structural injustice. People who participate by their actions in the ongoing schemes of cooperation that constitute structural injustice are responsible for them, in the sense that they are part of the process that causes them.[50] As with a violation of negative duties not to harm others, complicity in a structural injustice can give rise to a duty to help. Today, structural injustice is both local and transnational.

With her focus on structural injustice, Young gives some normative and prescriptive content to solidarity. Some of the examples discussed in chapter 7 are illustrative of structural injustice. For example, medical tourism contributes to the creation of structural injustice. Medical tourists benefit from inexpensive health care, enhancing their own opportunities, and at the same time compromising, although unintentionally, the health of people in poor countries by diverting skilled medical help away from them. The medical brain drain also exhibits characteristics of structural injustice. As people in wealthy countries recruit and hire skilled medical personnel to care for their loved ones, they deprive people in poor countries of the medical workers they need, often leaving them without an adequate health care workforce. People who hire health care workers from other countries or support workers to care for their elderly parents do not intentionally or directly harm people in poor countries. Yet they are complicit in a global structure that results in harms to others, including to some of the most vulnerable people in the world. In some cases, they recruit health care workers; in others, they hire them; and in still others, they are nursed to health by them. If we follow Young's reasoning, solidarity responsibilities are triggered by the role that people play in structural injustice. Put simply, the fact that people engage in practices that shift medical resources away from the global poor to wealthy countries can give rise to solidarity duties to poor countries and to the victims of structural injustice.

As we saw in chapter 7, affluent societies contribute to the creation and persistence of global poverty and attending health problems. The multiple mechanisms that impact global health contribute to structural injustice. Newcomers are often victims of structural injustice. To the extent that the activities of rich countries and their communities exacerbate global poverty and contribute to structural injustice, solidarity responsibilities are triggered. Those responsibilities can be met internationally, for example by funding clean water projects in the sending countries, or locally, for example by supporting the health of newcomers. Structural injustice is not only transnational. Sometimes the victims of structural injustice live next door.

Young grounds the obligation to carry costs for others, and to act in solidarity, on the presence of "social connection": "Our responsibility derives from belonging together with others in a system of interdependent processes of cooperation and competition through which we seek benefits and aim to realize projects. . . . Responsibility in relation to injustice thus derives not from living under a common constitution, but rather from participating in the diverse institutional processes that produce structural injustices."[51]

For Young what matters are the connections among people and the responsibilities that are generated by those connections. People are connected to others in countless ways, both directly and indirectly, strongly and weakly. Young identifies some parameters to determine when people ought to carry costs for others.[52]

There are four parameters that trigger solidarity responsibilities for structural injustice. These are power, privilege, interest, and collective ability.[53] The first, power, advises that efforts toward achieving structural injustice should target injustices in which the actors are able to successfully effect change. Second, when people have enjoyed privilege within a structure, they ought to carry costs. In terms of health care, people in affluent nations who have benefitted from migrant health care workers would have responsibility to the victims of structural injustice, such as HIV patients in sub-Saharan Africa who are in want of nurses and physicians. Third, having a vested interest in structural injustice triggers responsibilities to address the injustice. Thus, even the victims of structural injustice may have solidarity responsibilities with respect to the injustice because they have a strong vested interest in the injustice. Arguably, because health has public-good qualities, it would seem that *all* people have a vested interest in health and, in turn, an interest in ensuring the health of all. Fourth, the ability to act as a collective, and in solidarity, is a triggering consideration. Universities, for example, enjoy collective ability to address structural injustice in a way that a small business owner might not.[54] If we recognize duties to carry costs when there is (1) power to effect change, (2) privilege connected to the structure, (3) a vested interest, and (4) collective ability, a strong case can be made that there are solidarity-based responsibilities to carry the health care costs of newcomers. We share close ties with newcomers in a way that we do not with people across the globe. By invoking Young's parameters, we can identify which instances of structural injustice have priority. This is not to say that we are *only* responsible when the four parameters are satisfied. But they provide a place to start.

Most people are involved one way or another in a large number of structural injustices. They buy clothes made in sweatshops, eat fruit farmed by immigrants who die from pesticides, receive medical care from physicians who have left developing countries, and enjoy the leisure that is made possible through international caretakers. When it is necessary to prioritize help because of time and resources constraints, Young's parameters can be informative. When they are applied to newcomers, a strong argument can be made that there is a responsibility to carry health costs for them.

Many newcomers work in low-skill occupations: farming, domestic work, and house painting, to name a few. These occupations are especially burdensome on their health. Paint fumes, cleaning products, and nursing the sick carry health risks for those who undertake this kind of work. Exposing newcomers disproportionately to these risky jobs arguably creates an injustice.[55] Poverty is a risk factor for health, and many immigrants live in conditions of poverty. The role that social structure plays in sustaining global poverty gives rise to the push factors that drive immigrants to new countries, offering hope of relief from poverty. We also share other kinds of connections with newcomers: we eat the food they harvest, drive the cars for which they pump the gas, and are the patients for whom they care. We employ them and we fire them. We see them on a daily basis. We flood their habitats with greenhouse gas emissions. The connections people from wealthy countries have to newcomers both internationally and domestically are substantial, close, and often intimate.

Young's second criterion for triggering solidarity responsibilities is also satisfied in the case of newcomers. Providing for the health of newcomers is one sphere in which receiving countries can have an enormous impact. Of all the structural injustice to which people bear a connection, a duty to carry costs is triggered when there is a probability of effective impact. The health of newcomers is one place where clear steps can be taken that will result in good health outcomes for newcomers. Health care is available and it is possible to modify some of the social determinants of health. Laws that discriminate against newcomers can be changed, and often for little to no additional cost. Moreover, the health systems in affluent countries have the collective wherewithal to support the health needs of newcomers in a way that those in sending countries cannot. Health is often compromised in the poor countries from which newcomers originate, and good health care is more difficult to come by, because of weak infrastructure and corruption in those countries. The health care that can be given to newcomers may be more effective in receiving countries than in sending countries.

Third, being a privileged beneficiary can trigger a duty to carry costs. People who have benefitted from structural injustice may enjoy greater privileges.[56] This too would seem to require receiving countries to carry costs for newcomers. Those who hire newcomers, and often pay them under the table, benefit financially from such arrangements. They hold a privileged position with respect to others. Many newcomers also pay into Social Security, or similar national pension systems, without ever receiving benefits. Citizens who collect Social Security benefit from the contributions of newcomers who have contributed, but who will never receive Social Security. Many citizens in receiving countries are able to remain healthy because newcomers perform unhealthy work. Were it not for newcomers, many unhealthy jobs would need to be performed by natives. Public health benefits from the work that newcomers perform both because newcomers toil in many unhealthy occupations, and because they very often care for sick citizens, putting their own health at risk. Thus, citizens are privileged with respect to them. Fourth, if we consider only the responsibilities to carry health care costs, and set aside the other policies for the present, health systems in developed countries have the capacity for collective action, and are easily able to extend what exists to noncitizens. Indeed, as we suggested in chapter 2, it can be more expensive to exclude newcomers than to include them. The ability to act collectively is likely to be stronger in nations with more efficient health systems.

Wealthy nations that receive newcomers benefit enormously from them, and it would be foolhardy not to ensure that those with whom they interact and depend on a daily basis are healthy. Not only would failure to do so put the health of natives at risk, but it would also threaten the ways in which natives can cooperate with newcomers. We have argued that among those affected by structural injustice, newcomers have priority with respect to our solidarity-based duties to carry health costs. We are both connected to their health harms and to them personally. We have benefited from these connections. In addition, the role of affluent societies in structural injustice violates negative duties. Finally, because health is a global public good, it behooves receiving nations to ensure the health of all people.

The health-related responsibilities to newcomers do not seem to change when newcomers are present in large numbers, as they have been with the global migrant crisis that began in 2011. Some countries in the European Union found themselves overwhelmed by the sheer number of newcomers during the crisis. Many, but not all, newcomers are entitled, by international law, to refugee status. But not all migrants qualify as refugees; some migrate to escape poverty and find a better life.[57]

Economic migrants, those seeking a better life and escape from poverty, also constitute part of the current crisis, but they are not legal refugees and do not have a valid claim to asylum. In the absence of a legal obligation, some EU countries, such as Macedonia, Serbia, and Croatia, have turned them away.[58] It is beyond the scope of this book to provide a close review of the crisis. Nor do we address the question of what a nation's obligations are to admit migrants. From a moral point of view, however, and given the arguments of this book, the fact that there are *many* newcomers to help does not change our health obligation to help them. If anything, large numbers of newcomers may make the global public-good argument especially compelling. We have argued that *all* newcomers should be treated equally with citizens with respect to health. Because health is a public good, and nonexcludable, potential health harms of *many* newcomers may be greater than they would be if there were fewer.[59] When refugees (some who may have been more appropriately termed asylum seekers) arrived in Germany, for example, they were immediately checked for health problems and serious injuries. They were then moved to camps where they received free care from Refudocs. Refudocs founder Mathias Wendeborn reported that the health problems encountered in the refugee population most often resulted from the trip the refugees had taken—skin infections, foot injuries, and symptoms of poverty and compromised hygiene.[60] He also noted that the refugee population is overall healthy. Others have observed mental health problems that require alleviation.[61] Lawrence O. Gostin and Anna E. Roberts note that forced migrants face "profound health hazards" at each stage of the journey, beginning before departure. They have high mortality rates, many die at sea, and they face health risks caused by "people smugglers," poverty, and lack of food, water, and shelter. Women and girls are subject to sexual abuse, and refugee and internally displaced person (IDP) camps are subject to epidemics of infectious diseases: typhoid, tuberculosis, measles, cholera, and infections that accompany overcrowding.[62] Given the public-good dimension of health, and the arguments of this book, there is no moral reason to treat forced migrants differently than any other newcomers. In view of our argument, the burden of proof shifts to others to demonstrate that newcomers who are a part of the migration crisis should be treated differently.

The international response to the refugee crisis also speaks to the willingness of different nations to help strangers: nations vary over time in their willingness to show solidarity with refugees. Canada is projected to accept as many as 50,000 government- and privately sponsored refugees by the end of 2016, while in 2015, Donald Trump, then the Republican frontrunner for the party's presidential nomination, wanted to ban Muslims from entering the United States.[63] The Obama administration aspires to welcome 10,000. The United Kingdom intended to bring 20,000 refugees by 2020. France planned on 30,000 over two years. Germany had shown the greatest generosity, having taken one million refugees in one year. Sweden took in 150,000 refugees in roughly a year.[64] At the time of writing, Canada had not experienced the kind of backlash against refugees that other countries report. It has a unique program that combines private and public sponsorship of refugees.[65] Justin Trudeau welcomed refugees at the airport with the words, "You are home now." In turn, he was thanked by a Syrian man for the warm welcome. In Trudeau's words, "This is something that we are able to do in this country because we define a Canadian not by a skin color or a language or a religion or a background, but by a shared set of values, aspirations, hopes and dreams that not just Canadians but people around the world share."[66]

Far more common, however, are stories demonstrating ethnocentrism. Many people show hostility toward strangers rather than a desire to bring them into the fold. Ethnocentrism, a disposition to divide the world into in-groups and out-groups, is a fact of life. Donald Kinder and Cindy Kam found that ethnocentrism is pervasive in modern society, affects public opinion about immigration, and influences policy toward immigrants.[67]

Ethnocentrism, like racism and sexism, is a form of bias and in-group favoritism.[68] It may be a form of unconscious or implicit bias, an example of social identity theory, or an outcome of natural selection. In any case, as an expression of discrimination, it is unethical, inconsistent with principles of universality, the very heart of ethics. And, as we have argued, it makes for ineffective health policy. It is beyond the scope of this book to review the social and psychological causes of ethnocentrism. Nonetheless, it is safe to say that because ethnocentrism is unethical, it does not constitute a good foundation for health policy for newcomers. If anything, recognizing the pervasiveness of ethnocentrism and the impact it has on policy should signal a warning to create policy that is unburdened by in-group bias and discrimination against "strangers." The point of policy, law, and ethics is in large part to monitor behavior that does not come easily to human beings, and to ensure that their better selves guide their conduct.

Natives and Newcomers

Moving Forward Together

On September 25, 2014, Thomas Eric Duncan, a Liberian national who had traveled to Dallas, Texas, to reunite with his family, went to the emergency room at Texas Health Presbyterian Hospital with a high fever and gastrointestinal symptoms. Although he told health care workers that he had come from Liberia, which was in the midst of a horrific Ebola epidemic, Duncan was sent home with antibiotics, which are useless against Ebola, a viral disease. Two days later, he returned to the hospital gravely ill and was diagnosed with Ebola, the first person to have been diagnosed with the disease outside Africa. He died a few days later.[1]

Duncan's diagnosis and the subsequent discovery that two of his nurses had caught the disease, as had a New York physician who had treated patients in West Africa, and a Spanish nurse who had treated a missionary who had flown to Spain for treatment, sparked a full-scale panic in the West, as reports about Ebola came to dominate the news cycle. By October, 50 percent of Americans reported being "very" or "somewhat" concerned that there would be a large outbreak in the United States within twelve months, and 36 percent reported being "very" or "somewhat" concerned that either they or a close family member would contract Ebola.[2]

With fear in the air, anti-immigrant activists and politicians in the United States pointed to Ebola as a rationale for cracking down on immigration across the Mexican border.[3] Representative Joe Wilson, the Republican congressman from South Carolina who charged that President Obama "lied" about covering undocumented immigrants through Obamacare, asserted that terrorists might try to enter the country and spread Ebola: "Part of their creed would be to bring persons who have Ebola into our country."[4] When asked whether he supported travel restrictions for people coming from West Africa, former US senator from

Massachusetts Scott Brown, who was then running for the Senate in New Hampshire, replied, "I think it's naïve to think that people aren't going to be walking through here who have these type of diseases and/ or other types of intent, criminal or terrorist."[5]

The anger over Ebola was aimed not only at immigrants but at all travelers from West Africa. Within days of Duncan's diagnosis, there were calls in many Western nations to deny visas to people from West Africa. Although health officials repeatedly explained that such measures would be counterproductive because they would undermine efforts to stem the epidemic at its source, both Canada and Australia instituted such policies.[6] In the United States, the federal government resisted calls to shut the borders but ordered all air travelers from West Africa to land in one of five designated airports, where they would be subject to enhanced screening.

Even Western health care workers who traveled to West Africa to treat Ebola patients became targets. In the United States, for example, nurse Kaci Hickox was held in a tent outside a New Jersey hospital for several days after New Jersey's governor, Chris Christie, ordered that all health care workers who treated Ebola patients in Africa be subject to a twenty-one-day quarantine.[7] When Hickox publicly denounced her treatment, she was disparaged for being selfish and arrogant. Eventually Christie permitted her to travel to Maine, where a judge refused the state's request to quarantine her, ruling that the state had "not met its burden at this time to prove by clear and convincing evidence that limiting [Hickox's] movements to the degree requested is 'necessary to protect other individuals from the dangers of infection.'"[8]

To many in the West, the Ebola outbreak demonstrated the dangers of an interconnected world, the very risks highlighted by the outbreak narrative discussed in chapter 2. Migrants and travelers can carry dangerous emerging diseases from less-developed regions to the West, threatening catastrophic pandemics. To protect public health, the narrative suggests, borders must be closed and migration discouraged. Further, health care should be denied, so that migrants do not carry their diseases to the West in order to receive medical care, a motivation that some ascribed to Duncan.[9]

On closer inspection, however, the Ebola epidemic and the panic that erupted around it offered far different lessons. One is the risk of denying health care to newcomers. We do not know why Texas Health Presbyterian Hospital initially failed to diagnose Duncan's Ebola, an error that exposed his family, first responders, and other health care workers to the risk of infection. It is possible that the misdiagnosis was a simple medical error, the type that happens every day. Duncan's status as an uninsured newcomer (it isn't clear whether he intended to stay in the United States, but it is likely given that he planned to reunite with his family and marry the American mother of his child) may not have played any role. But it might have, given the barriers newcomers face in obtaining health insurance and the restrictions imposed on Emergency Medicaid. As a result, when a patient such as Duncan arrives in an emergency room, the hospital faces the possibility that it will not receive any compensation for the treatment that is given, even though the Emergency Medical Treatment and Active Labor Act (EMTALA) requires it to screen and stabilize the patient. These conflicting policies create a strong incentive for hospitals to provide newcomers with as little treatment as possible, an incentive that is only weakly counterbalanced by the threat of lawsuits in states such as Texas that have strict tort reform laws that make it difficult for injured plaintiffs to sue health care providers.[10] Whether economic pressures influenced Duncan's care we will never know; the hospital quickly settled a lawsuit brought by his family charging that he had received subpar treatment due to his race, preventing a full airing of what had transpired.[11] But the very possibility that immigration status might influence the care of someone who might have an infectious and deadly disease suggests the risks of denying coverage to newcomers.

More broadly, West Africa's Ebola epidemic illustrates the global public-good dimension of health and the costs of ignoring it. The Ebola virus was discovered in 1976 on the Ebola River in the Democratic Republic of the Congo. It is believed to have started with fruit bats. People who are infected can be asymptomatic for several weeks. During this period, they are not contagious. Once they develop significant symptoms, however, they are highly contagious. Broken skin, blood, vomit, feces, urine, semen, and contact with the nose and mouth can effectively transmit the virus. Bedding, clothes, and surfaces can also transmit the Ebola virus when contact is made with broken skin. Ebola is easily killed with bleach and chlorine. The initial symptoms are much like the flu: fever, fatigue, aches and pains, and sore throat. Later there is a rash, vomiting, diarrhea, and internal and external bleeding. At present, there is no cure for Ebola.[12]

The 2014 Ebola outbreak in West Africa is thought to have begun with the infection of two-year-old Emile Ouamouno, from the small village of Meliandou in Guinea. Soon after he died, both his sister Philomene and pregnant mother died. The next victims were health workers from Meliandou. At the onset of the outbreak, hospital staff did not know they were dealing with Ebola but attributed the illness to other local diseases that shared similar symptoms. The disease spread into Liberia and Sierra Leone as villagers traveled to sell their wares. Within the first few months, hospitals became "Ebola incubators." Out of the first fifteen deaths from Ebola, the first four were health care workers, who, in turn, infected others.[13] By the end of the epidemic, the Ebola virus had killed more than eleven thousand people.[14]

Ebola took such a heavy toll in West Africa because the area was already ravaged by poverty and political strife. The health care system in Guinea is among the weakest in the world. In Liberia, there are 70,000 people per one doctor, Sierra Leone, 45,000, and in Guinea, 10,000. In contrast, the United States has one doctor for every 410 people and the United Kingdom has one for every 360.[15] Traditional funeral practices exacerbated the rate of infection. The first confirmed case of Ebola in Sierra Leone, for example, was in a woman who attended the funeral of a beloved local healer who had been treating Ebola patients from nearby Guinea. According to the WHO, the burial of this beloved healer was ultimately responsible for 365 Ebola deaths among those who participated in the funeral.[16]

A simple explanation of the 2014 Ebola outbreak, thus far the worst in history, would refer to fruit bats, bush meat, and primitive burial practices. Yet this explanation ignores the role of both social determinants in laying the foundation in which disease spreads and health care systems in transmitting it. There may be disagreement about why health systems in afflicted areas are weak, but there is agreement that weak health systems played a significant role in the spread of this deadly virus both in 2014 and in earlier epidemics. Jared Jones makes the point that "the culturalist epidemiology that dominates the study of Ebola is limiting. It exoticizes the disease, and reconfigures assumptions about a vaguely monolithic African culture into causal explanations for the spread of infection. Culture becomes a 'risk factor.'"[17] Although referring to earlier outbreaks of Ebola, Jones highlighted the role of hospitalization in the transmission of Ebola. Patients received what little treatment was available but did so in hospitals that lacked running water, electricity, and appropriate waste disposal.[18] Of course, there was also an inadequate supply of health care workers.

Health care systems in West Africa are extraordinarily weak because of poverty and civil strife. Jones identifies some of the global conditions that can explain African poverty. Although some poverty in Africa has been attributed to local corruption, he argues that corruption is not a characteristic of African culture, but rather a consequence of colonialism in which colonial states ignored the demands of chiefs in exchange for profit.[19] For example, in the Democratic Republic of the Congo, the CIA, a US agency, helped assassinate Patrice Lumumba and helped Mobutu Sese Seko become president. Mobutu not only amassed great wealth at the cost of the public but was notorious for ignoring the health and well-being of the population. According to Jones, the US intervention in African politics was part of US-Soviet gamesmanship.[20] In addition, Structural Adjustment Programs (SAPs), promoted by both the International Monetary Fund (IMF) and the World Bank, advocated cutbacks in public expenditure for developing countries as a condition for trade liberalization. As a result, health care spending was cut back.[21] Philosopher Jonathan Wolff comments on the harmful effects of SAPs, noting that they required nations to cut spending on social programs, including health. Not only was health compromised by these programs, but the programs also did little in the way of eradicating poverty.[22] These global, externally imposed policies exacerbated already weak health care systems in many African countries.[23]

This weakening of health care systems made them vulnerable to Ebola in 2014. Alexander Kentikelenis and colleagues first note that Ebola spread rapidly because of the weak health systems in the region.[24] They suggest that although the IMF provided support to the affected countries in the years preceding the 2014 Ebola outbreak, the support may have been conditioned on cutbacks in health and education. In a letter to the IMF, Guinean authorities wrote, "Unfortunately, because of the reduction in spending, including on domestic investment, it was not possible to respect the indicative targets for spending in priority sectors."[25] Of course, the IMF has its own perspective on this.[26] The IMF announced $430 million to fight Ebola in Sierra Leone, Guinea, and Liberia.[27]

Settling the debate among the IMF, the World Bank, and their critics is an important conversation, but beyond the scope of this book. It is safe to say, however, that global institutions tolerated weak health care systems in vulnerable countries and that these systems were one of the many reasons for the severity of the recent Ebola outbreak. The weakness in these health care systems is multifaceted, but a shortage of health care workers was a critical part of the vulnerability. This shortage has been fostered by the medical brain drain. Eszter Kollar and Alena Buyx explain the medical brain drain in terms of the proportion of health care workers who migrate in comparison to those who remain in the country in which they received their training.[28] In these terms, in Sierra Leone, 58 percent of doctors who trained in the country leave for jobs in OECD member states, and in Liberia, it is 55 percent.[29] The expatriation rate in Guinea is just 9 percent.[30] Reports from Liberia during the 2014 outbreak confirm the shortage and its impact on the care of patients. Within weeks of the first cases, there were fewer than 170 doctors in the country, and many of those who migrated did not want to return to help. Many health care workers on the front lines died from Ebola. Some doctors and nurses went on strike, seeking a "risk bonus."[31] Although international health care workers went to West Africa to help, Liberian health care workers were reluctant to return. Prior to the outbreak there was one doctor for 90,000 people. Indeed, medical students complained about the quality of faculty and facilities in Liberia's only medical school.[32] The state of the health care system was dire in Liberia and other West African nations. Michele Barry, who partnered with a hospital in Liberia, confirmed that "[h]ealthcare workers have been stretched to the limits," and that

> the solution to this Ebola crisis is not drugs, mass quarantine, vaccines, or even airdrops of personal protective gear. The real reasons this outbreak has turned into an epidemic are weak health systems and lack of workforce; any real solution needs to address these structural issues.[33]

Barry is correct to highlight the structural problems with the Liberian health care system and the mammoth role the brain drain played in the

2014 epidemic. But the structural issues that need to be addressed are not only those that have to do with the technical wherewithal of improving weak health care systems. The role of the medical brain drain in the Ebola epidemic is also a paradigmatic case of structural injustice on a global scale. Global factors, including the push factors and pull factors discussed in chapter 8, contributed to the situation in which Ebola patients who desperately needed medical care were not able to get it, because many health workers had left for affluent countries. The result was a fragile system that was ill equipped to cope with an epidemic of the magnitude and complexity of the 2014 Ebola outbreak. As with much in global health, the 2014 Ebola outbreak derived from global structures but it was not the result of intentional wrongdoing by individuals.

The tastes of people in affluent countries for expensive medical care, with a high doctor-patient ratio, combined with a desire to secure that labor in a cost-effective manner, had consequences for West Africans who died from Ebola, and for the decimated economies of afflicted West African nations. The economic impact on these nations has been great; tourism, an important industry for Africa, has declined considerably, with bookings for safaris down throughout Africa, even in countries far from the center of the epidemic.[34] The borders of core Ebola countries, once porous, were closed. In addition to the impact at the epicenter of the crisis, the economic impact extended beyond these nations. Some of Africa's largest mining companies are located in West Africa. Vale, the largest iron ore producer in the world, evacuated its staff from an affiliate, Simandou, located in Guinea. London Mining moved some of its staff from Sierra Leone, where mining is an important source of economic growth.[35]

By the fall of 2014, 3,700 children had lost one or both parents due to Ebola and were in need of caretakers. Many of these "Ebola orphans" were shunned out of fear of contagion.[36] Food insecurity was another consequence of the Ebola epidemic. According to the World Food Programme, 1.4 million people may have been malnourished because of Ebola.[37] The World Bank estimated that by the end of 2015 the cost of the epidemic would be $30 billion.[38] The costs to West Africa were high, and to the global community as well—though in very different ways. Had there been a recognition of health's global public-good dimension, rather than stubborn adherence to the idea that health is a private good, much of the harm and global costs of the 2014 outbreak might have been avoided. Although there is currently no cure for Ebola, the spread of the virus might have been mitigated more quickly with appropriate management and more funds. Instead of approaching the Ebola outbreak as a global problem, international actors initially dragged their feet.

Global Solidarity, Norm Change

Eventually, the world responded to the Ebola epidemic. In September 2014, President Obama committed military support to coordinate epidemic control efforts and health care workers to build treatment centers. The British and French also provided support. Following this, in late September of that year, the UN Security Council in an unprecedented resolution declared Ebola a "threat to international peace and security."[39] Progress was made, and the global community came together to ensure safe burials and that patients would be placed in appropriate treatment facilities.[40] By February 2015, seventy countries had contributed $5 billion.[41] Still, as of June 2015, there was a shortfall of $1 billion. The United States contributed more than a billion dollars, and France, Germany, and the United Kingdom also contributed significant amounts. Poor countries also demonstrated solidarity with Ebola patients in West Africa.

The people of Cuba, a relatively poor island, provided health care workers. The WHO worked with Cuba to train 460 doctors and nurses in the care of Ebola patients. Cuba also took the lead role in treating cholera in Haiti in 2010, at some cost to Cuba as cholera subsequently surfaced on the island.[42] According to the editorial board of the New York Times, "It is a shame that Washington, the chief donor in the fight against Ebola, is diplomatically estranged from Havana, the boldest contributor. In this case the schism has life-or-death consequences, because American and Cuban officials are not equipped to coordinate global efforts."[43] In other words, everyone has more to gain through collaboration and solidarity than through estrangement. Indeed, it was not long after Cuba's show of solidarity with West Africa that President Obama undertook to restore full diplomatic relations with Cuba.[44] Help also came from international nongovernment organizations such as Médecins Sans Frontières (MSF), Partners in Health, and Samaritan's Purse.[45]

Solidarity comes at a cost, however. MSF lost twenty-seven staff members, mostly through their work in the community. Overall, the picture is mixed. Many countries and organizations came together to help West Africa, but the help came late.

Time magazine named the "Ebola Fighters" as its Person of the Year in 2014. The honored group consisted of an international array of health care workers and others who came together to help Ebola patients, and the afflicted nations. Among this group were Dr. Jerry Brown, from Liberia, Dr. Debbie Eisenhut, an American, Dr. Kent Brantly, also from the United States, and Ella Watson-Stryker, a public health worker from New York. Workers from Médecins Sans Frontières and Samaritan's Purse worked side by side with local doctors, nurses, and others.[46] In explaining the choice of Person of the Year, *Time* stated: "Ebola is a war, and a warning. The global health system is nowhere close to strong enough to keep us safe from infectious disease, and 'us' means everyone. . . . The rest of the world can sleep at night because a group of men and women are willing to stand and fight."[47]

The editors of *Time* seemed to understand that health is a public good when they stated that safety is difficult to come by for us, where *us* includes everyone. Although in different words, *Time* was celebrating global health solidarity, the willingness of people worldwide to come together with a diverse team of helpers in the service of caring for those with Ebola and stemming the epidemic. This remarkable group of honorees demonstrates the ability of people to come to the aid of "strangers," to carry costs for them, and to incur personal sacrifice in so doing. In this way, they fulfill the responsibilities of global solidarity and demonstrate that people are able to help those in "out-groups," despite our tendency toward in-group bias and homophily. The Ebola crisis shows that many people are willing to risk their lives for strangers. Nonetheless, although the 2014 Ebola epidemic reflected the global capacity to come together in solidarity, solidarity was slow in coming. Compassion can be challenging. The path to solidarity among strangers in the name of public health was slow, but persistent. In the end, recognition of our shared humanity and universal vulnerability to a health threat succeeded in bringing diverse people, from around the globe, together for the sake of one another. This bodes well for newcomers, and the possibility of extending to them the same health care rights enjoyed by natives. It bears witness to the fact that health has the capacity to over-ride the tendency to "hunker" in the face of strangers.

There is much to learn about how to integrate newcomers into the fabric of a community from the 2011–2015 refugee crisis. In Canada, for example, there was little opposition to welcoming 25,000 refugees by early 2016, though that target was not reached within the designated time frame. Canada's refugee program is relatively unique. It has both public- and privately sponsored programs. There is also a hybrid version, combining the two. From 2010 to 2014, between 37 percent and 52 percent of refugees resettling in Canada were privately sponsored, with an overall average of 43 percent of refugees being privately sponsored.[48] Refugees are responsible for their own travel expenses, but since most cannot afford to travel, they are eligible for a "travel loan" of CAD 10,000 from the Canadian government. Groups of five or more people can sponsor refugees. Community groups and "sponsorship agreement" holders, consisting of faith-based and secular groups, agree in advance to sponsor refugees. Private sponsorship has been available in Canada since 1979.[49] Of the 25,000 refugees expected in Canada in early 2016, officials estimated that 15,000 would be government sponsored and 10,000 privately sponsored.[50] Sponsors are responsible for helping refugees financially from the time they arrive in Canada. They also help with travel, finding homes, and arranging for children to go to school and adapt to life in Canada. Sponsors subsidize the cost of food and other expenses during the first year of a refugee's life in Canada.

In effect, Canada has systemized solidarity, using policy to enable individuals and communities to help strangers transition to their new homes. Private sponsorship by individual Canadians is a voluntary effort and sponsors are committed to carry costs for strangers. Everyone gains: the Canadian economy stands to benefit, and individual Canadians forge new ties with newcomers, helping to break down xenophobia and build social capital among diverse people.[51] According to the Canadian government, refugees who are privately sponsored become self-supporting more quickly than government-sponsored refugees.[52] Canada is not the only nation to have had private sponsorship. From 1987 to 1995, the Private Sector Initiative, launched by the US State Department, resettled about 8,000 refugees, mainly from Cuba.[53]

As the IMF has noted, countries that absorb large numbers of refugees experience short-term economic costs. But there is no reason that these countries that accept large numbers of refugees should alone bare the financial burden of settling refugees. As Christine Lagarde, managing director of IMF, noted, "No country can manage the refugee issue on their own. We need global cooperation."[54] Countries that do not, for whatever reason, welcome forced migrants may nonetheless have a responsibility to help countries that have done so. Moral theories, such as cosmopolitanism[55] and utilitarianism,[56] support such responsibilities. Furthermore, the right to health, discussed in chapter 5, specifies health-related obligations of states for the health of people in other nations and specifies that these obligations are transnational. "Economically developed state parties have a special responsibility and interest to assist people in poorer developing states."[57] There is also reason to believe that responsibilities to help people in other countries extend to nonstate actors.[58] In a global context, the benefits of healthy newcomers will not be restricted to the nations in which they settle. Rather than "beggar thy neighbor," nations ought to act in solidarity even if only by contributing to the financial costs of settling forced migrants.

Despite intermittent acts of solidarity and the hope they create for newcomers and natives, there is reason to temper our optimism and be mindful of what we might learn from recent experiences. Although Ebola had its heroes, the dictum "too little, too late" also applies. Lawrence O. Gostin and Eric A. Friedman do a good job of identifying some of the problems with the international response to Ebola.[59] As we saw, tragically weak health care systems hobbled the response to Ebola, resulting in great loss of life. The first Ebola case surfaced in December 2013. In mid-June 2014, Médecins Sans Frontières stated that Ebola was "out of control." Yet it was not until early August 2014 that the director general of the World Health Organization declared a Public Health Emergency of International Concern.[60]

The dictum "too little, too late" seems apt with respect to the international response to Ebola because solidarity was slow to emerge and was mixed with resistance to carry costs, and even once the responsibility was recognized, given the $1 billion shortfall, it appears not to have been fulfilled. There are a variety of reasons for this, but the response was ambivalent enough to suggest that there is more work to be done.

In addition, the global migrant crisis has brought a significant backlash against newcomers in Europe and the United States. Arguably, given this ambivalence, the global community may be in the midst of a dramatic shift in norms.

Newcomers, Natives, and Norm Change

The 2014 Ebola outbreak reflects the tension between those who act for the sake of health as a global public good and those who are slow to assume responsibility for stemming the epidemic. These conflicting responses represent different approaches to both public health and responsibilities to strangers in distant countries. The fact that polar opposite norms exist at the same time suggests that we are in a period of norm change. On the one hand, as Dr. Joanne Liu, international president of MSF, said, "The most appalling thing from this epidemic is that when there's a public-health emergency, no one feels responsible to tackle it or respond."[61] Reluctance to help West Africa and the failure to take responsibility, as observed by Dr. Liu, may be attributed to social norms that can be summed up in the expression "not our problem." This perspective was illustrated by Ann Coulter's comments about Dr. Kent Brantly, an American physician with Samaritan's Purse, who went to West Africa to help, contracted Ebola, and survived. Coulter stated:

> Why did Dr. Brantly have to go to Africa? . . . Can't anyone serve Christ in America anymore? . . . Your country is like your family. We're supposed to take care of our own first. . . . Right there in Texas, near where Dr. Brantly left his wife and children to fly to Liberia and get Ebola, is one of the poorest counties in the nation, Zavala County—where he wouldn't have risked making his wife a widow and his children fatherless.[62]

Coulter's words, considered together with Dr. Liu's words, illustrate competing norms about those who went to West Africa—one that celebrates them as heroic "Person[s] of the Year," and another as "idiotic" and self-seeking narcissists. Norms about what our obligations are to strangers may be in a period of change. According to Karl-Dieter Opp, norms are typically instrumental and emerge when they serve the interests of collectives.[63] Cass Sunstein has more to say about when and how norms change:

> Current social states can be far more fragile than is generally thought-small shocks to publicly endorsed norms and roles decrease the cost of displaying deviant norms and rapidly bring about large-scale changes in publicly displayed judgments and desires. Hence societies experience *norm bandwagons* and *norm cascades*. Norm bandwagons occur when the lowered cost of expressing new norms encourages an ever-increasing number of people to reject previously popular norms, to a 'tipping point' where it is adherence to the old norms that produces social disapproval. Norm cascades occur when societies experience rapid shifts toward new norms.[64]

Today, many people reject the extreme views of Ann Coulter. Although in early 2016 it appeared that nativism and xenophobia remain strong, as we discussed in chapter 1, the international response that finally emerged for Ebola suggests a willingness to help strangers. As we noted, in the end nations came together to help West Africa with both funds and human capital. Whether these norm fluctuations are a bandwagon or a cascade is not as important for our purposes as is the observation that norms are changing in favor of international solidarity for global health.

Norm change signals that the time is ripe for nations to modify their approach to the health of strangers—whether those "strangers" live in distant lands or whether they live next door. Global solidarity in support of West Africa demonstrates a willingness to carry costs for the health of strangers, even when those strangers are thousands of miles away, of a different cultural background, and very often a different skin color. If anything, the reasoning that supports solidarity for global health should be more compelling when a stranger is also a neighbor. As Iris Young explains, solidarity responsibilities may be strongest among those who dwell together.

Our arguments in support of providing for the health of newcomers apply equally to large migrations as to smaller ones. In either case, health remains a global public good, and all countries stand to benefit from healthy newcomers. Without question, rapid flows of large numbers of newcomers can strain the health and social service systems of receiving countries. This was evident in parts of Europe in 2015. Nonetheless, some countries may fare better as a result of accepting refugees. For example, it is estimated that Canada will spend CAD 1.2 billion as it settles 25,000 refugees from Syria. Some regions of Canada, like other areas or nations, have low population growth, an aging workforce, and a stagnating economy. "Without immigrants, Canada faces labour shortages, a smaller tax base, and increased strain on our medical system and pension funds," wrote Kareem El-Assal.[65] Syrian refugees tend to be middle-class and professional; they have something to contribute to communities, and various regions in Canada have made an effort to reach out to refugees, mindful of this.

Canada is not alone in recognizing the economic boost refugees can bring to a country. Germany can also benefit from increased flows of young immigrants. According to the European Commission, Germany's population is expected to decline from 81.3 million people in 2013 to 70.8 million in 2060. In contrast, the United Kingdom's population during the same period of time is expected to rise from 64.1 million to 80.1 million.[66] Moreover, 59 percent of the population in Germany is expected to be sixty-five or older by 2060. The potential for countries to benefit from refugees does not diminish the value of solidarity; rather, it underscores the value of newcomers, including those who arrive in large numbers.[67]

The IMF supports this insight. After some research, the IMF notes that the burden on member states from massive flows of refugees will be challenging in the short term, but over the long term migrants will benefit the economies of EU states.[68] The same point is made by Christine Lagarde: "Migrants can boost a country's labor force, encourage investment and boost growth." She calls for global cooperation.[69] Still, not all countries will benefit from migrants, and even those that will benefit over the long term may not have the economic wherewithal to sustain large migrant flows in the short term. In such cases when a nation cannot meet its health obligations to newcomers, it falls to the international community to help them. As we saw, cosmopolitan moral theories as well as the right to health support the idea that affluent nations have right-to-health responsibilities for people in poor nations.

Prompted in large part by the refugee crisis, the United Nations reinforced the need for a global approach to finance the needs of refugees. In the words of the report, "additional revenues from a solidarity levy on air travel or fuel could be used to support the provision of health services in camps and urban areas hosting displaced people. Ensuring the good health of people on the move is a global public good that deserves to be supported by an international funding source."[70]

Policy Recommendations

The recognition that newcomers and natives dwell together and that health is a public good creates powerful pragmatic and ethical reasons to rethink many common policies relating to immigration and health. It demands that care be taken when immigration status is used in health policy. As we have seen, immigration status often provides a fig leaf for importing racist and other identity-based forms of animus into health policy. Not only is the acceptance of such animus deeply troubling in and of itself, it interferes with a country's ability to achieve its health policy goals. And because health is a global public good, it undermines global health.

What does this mean concretely? What changes in policy are required? Space precludes discussion of all of the changes that are entailed by our analysis, but below we review some of the conclusions that emerge from prior chapters and outline some of the most pressing policy recommendations.

Health Care Access

As we have seen, nations commonly exclude one or more classes of newcomers—most frequently unauthorized migrants, but often those with legal status—from their health insurance systems. These exclusions are explained on grounds that fail to withstand scrutiny: covering immigrants encourages illegal immigration; it costs too much; it undermines solidarity; and newcomers have lost their right to health care because they have violated immigration laws. We showed that the first two claims lack empirical support, and the latter two are conceptually vulnerable. In addition, because health is a global public good, the exclusion of immigrants from health systems creates health risks for the population at large, as the health of newcomers affects the health of natives. This is most obvious in the case of communicable diseases such as Ebola and HIV, but it holds true more broadly. For example, immigrant parents with untreated chronic conditions may be less able to support and care for their children, many of whom are natives of the receiving country and often citizens. Moreover, because of network effects, depression, untreated obesity, or substance abuse disorders among immigrant populations may influence the rates of disease among natives within their network. Citizens and newcomers alike suffer when emergency departments are overcrowded and underfunded because newcomers lack other sources of care.

Excluding newcomers from national health programs adds both cost and complexity to health care systems. Because immigrant populations are in general younger and healthier than native populations, their exclusion from national health programs deprives the system of young and healthy beneficiaries who may pay more into the system than they would cost it. The common policy of limiting coverage to emergency conditions means that immigrants are less likely to receive preventive care, and their illnesses are more likely to be treated only when they become expensive emergencies. Moreover, the many exceptions that nations such as the United States and Canada make to ensure that various classes of immigrants have some, but not full, access to national health program, add enormous administrative complexity, which is both costly and unnecessary for health care providers. Since health is nonexcludable, this strategy is at risk of backfiring. Furthermore, it isn't in anyone's health interest to erode the professional ethic of health care workers from one of universalism, treating all patients alike, to one based on prejudice and market principles.

The simplest solution is to eliminate immigration-specific barriers to health insurance programs. All residents, regardless of immigration status, should be able to participate in the health programs that are available within a country, subject to non-immigration-related criteria. That would not necessarily mean that coverage must be universal, comprehensive, or unfettered. Respect for the legal right to health permits nations to organize their health insurance systems in different ways and take into account their own resources in setting benefit packages.

Hence, less wealthy countries may provide more limited access to very costly treatments than wealthier countries. And all nations can and do impose medically related criteria on coverage. Of course, we recognize that a country could both provide the same health care to natives and newcomers but violate the human right to health. What nations cannot do ethically—and should not do from a practical perspective—is limit either basic or expensive treatments to natives.

Although some nations, like the UK, finance health care through general tax revenues, other countries expect citizens to pay for some or all of the costs of their care through insurance premiums, dedicated taxes, or co-insurance. The nondiscrimination principle advocated here would not prohibit this. If a particular health insurance program is available only to those who pay employment taxes, unauthorized immigrants can be required to pay those taxes; but there must also be means for them to do so. Likewise, if citizens are expected to pay a share of their cost of care, so should noncitizen residents. On the other hand, programs that are available to assist low-income citizens who cannot afford to pay for their own care should also be available to newcomers. In effect, newcomers' access to health insurance should mirror the health policy that applies to citizens. Immigration should not distort the formulation of a nation's chosen health policy. Applying health care to newcomers in this unbiased way will ensure that they enjoy the same legal right to health as citizens. It does not, of course, speak to the question of ensuring the human right to health. We have addressed that important question elsewhere.[71] Given that health is a global public good, it would certainly be imprudent for nations not to fulfill the right to health.

Two additional points merit mention. First is the importance of culturally competent care. Because health is a public good, formal inclusion in national health programs is insufficient. Newcomers should receive meaningful access to the health care they need on a roughly equal basis to what's offered to natives and citizens. This requires the elimination (or at least reduction) of linguistic and cultural barriers, which can be as formidable as economic barriers. For this reason, the World Health Assembly in 2007 called for the development of "migrant-sensitive" health policies.[72] Such systems provide language services as well as "culturally informed health care delivery."[73] Health care workers should cultivate the ability to "acknowledge their own cultural backgrounds, biases, and professional cultural norms and to incorporate relevant knowledge and interpersonal skills related to the care of patients from different cultural backgrounds."[74]

Critics may object that the call for migrant-sensitive health systems conflicts with the nondiscrimination principle articulated earlier. It does not. Rather the call recognizes that health care is less effective for all patients when they do not feel comfortable with their providers, and their providers do not understand their needs, concerns, and health risks.[75] This applies whether patients are newcomers or natives. Indeed, culturally competent care is essential for *all* populations. However, in the case of some (but not all) newcomers, the linguistic and cultural divides between patients and providers can be especially wide, although the large numbers of newcomers in the health care workforce can narrow these divides. To this end, native health professionals may need special training to ensure that they can understand their patients' concerns and meet their needs. Likewise, translation services are often necessary to enable free and open communication between patients and physicians. When it comes to health care, "equal access" requires recognition of the unique needs and circumstances of different patient populations. This is also critical with respect to economic migrants and refugee populations, who have often experienced unimaginable trauma both in their conflict-torn native countries and on the journey to escape them.[76] In such cases, cultural competency requires knowledge not only of another religion or culture but also of trauma and suffering.

The need for culturally competent care may suggest some advantages to establishing clinics that specialize in the health needs of newcomers and offer them services in their own communities. Without question, newcomers may feel more comfortable in community clinics that also treat fellow immigrants.[77] Community clinics may be uniquely positioned to engage with newcomers primarily and respond to their concerns. Local clinics that focus on serving newcomers may also develop special expertise in treating PTSD and violence-related traumas that are common in some immigrant communities.[78] Likewise, it makes sense to put TB clinics in communities where the populations have higher than typical rates of that disease. Throughout the developed world, many such health centers exist, and they often provide outstanding, culturally competent care to newcomers.[79] Nonetheless, in terms of bringing together multicultural and diverse people, specialized clinics risk segregating communities. If one goal is to expedite the shift to more inclusive norms, segregating newcomers in distinct health care facilities may be counterproductive.

The recognition that "we're all in this together" and that when it comes to health natives and newcomers are mutually dependent is far easier to perceive when we are sitting in the same overcrowded waiting room, or sharing the same hospital room. It is thus critical that the goal of culturally competent care does not result in relegating newcomers to separate, and usually unequal, facilities. Rather, cultural competence should be an aspiration for all health care systems. Indeed, since proximity is one important mechanism to override in-group bias in favor of inclusiveness, the goals of cultural competence and inclusiveness are complementary. It is difficult to imagine one without the other.

Public Health

The public-good nature of health applies with special force to public health policies, which unlike health care focus on improving the health of populations. As we have seen, nations have long used immigration status to shape and implement their public health policies, both at their borders and within them. This only plays upon irrelevant associations between disease and outsiders, offering the mere illusion of effective public health policy. It stigmatizes newcomers, solidifies in-group bias, and fosters ethnocentrism.

Perhaps most troubling is the common practice of closing the borders to nonnationals in a futile effort to keep epidemics at bay. As noted earlier, during the autumn of 2014, Australia and Canada barred migrants and travelers from West Africa in order to prevent the importation of Ebola. But pathogens do not care about passports. Natives and citizens who had been in "the hot zone" were also at risk. From a public health perspective, the use of immigration status made little sense; it could not keep the disease out. Moreover, the policy provided a false assurance of safety, while also reinforcing the perception that newcomers and travelers threaten a nation's health.

As we have seen, conflating immigration status with public health extends beyond novel epidemics such as Ebola. Health status is a common bar to immigration. Would-be immigrants with HIV/AIDS, tuber-culosis, and a wide range of cognitive and mental disabilities are often denied entry. Yet there is no evidence that these policies protect public health. Rather, as with the Ebola bans, they offer the false promise of keeping the ill out, thereby diverting attention and resources from more effective public health policies while reinforcing the ethnocentric mes-sage that immigrants represent a danger to public health and that those who are ill are not wanted.

Nations frequently defend exclusionary policies, especially those aimed at disability, on economic grounds, as critical for preventing the migration of economically unproductive people who will burden social welfare systems. This claim assumes that the gross categories that are used to exclude newcomers constitute accurate predictions of the productivity of newcomers. But as the disability-rights move-ment has convincingly demonstrated, people with physical and mental disabilities are often highly productive members of society.[80] And in many instances, their lack of productivity results as much from social barriers, for example, a lack of accessible transportation or discrimina-tion, as from the impairments themselves. Thus by excluding would-be newcomers with illnesses and disabilities simply on the basis of their diagnosis, nations risk losing immigrants who may be highly produc-tive, as well as their family members. Equally, nations legitimatize the troubling message that people with disabilities are but a drain on soci-ety, while diverting attention from the important task of reducing the social barriers that impede the productivity and quality of life of people with disabilities.

This does not mean that nations should never require newcomers to undergo some forms of medical screening. Health screening can be use-ful in determining newcomers' medical needs and is especially critical for ensuring that the needs of refugees and asylum seekers are met both before and after entry.[81] We also do not argue here that nations must have open borders or that they cannot take factors such as education, skills, and work history into account in granting visas. Such criteria may well have a disproportionate impact on individuals with some health conditions, but they raise issues beyond the scope of this book. What our analysis makes clear is that nations should not base immigration decisions on health status.

It is also critical that domestic public health policies are not enforced in a disparate manner against newcomers. As discussed in chapter 3, public health officials often impose highly coercive measures, such as isolation and quarantine, more readily upon newcomers than upon citizens. There is no public health justification for such discrimination. Although the protection of public health may at times warrant significant restrictions of individual liberty, immigration should not be a relevant factor. Immigration status has no bearing on determining the appropriateness of coercive public health measures. Instead, the restriction of liberty is justified only when it is the least restrictive means necessary for preventing the spread of a serious disease. Moreover, the use of immigration status in the implementation of public health protections has the significant potential for alienating immigrant communities from public health officials. This can be especially dangerous during a public health emergency, when officials must rely more on trust than coercion.[82] And even with respect to chronic diseases, such as obesity and smoking, public health efforts depend upon communities trusting the counsel provided and actions undertaken by public health departments.

Public health policies should be culturally competent in order to foster trust. This is especially critical with regard to immigrant communities, who may have different perspectives on many issues. And, as suggested above, culturally competent policies may be especially important in the case of refugees who are often reeling from physical and psychological trauma. For public health efforts to be successful in improving health in immigrant communities, practitioners must understand and respect the perspectives and concerns of the populations they are serving. To this end, it would be prudent to take their guidance from the communities in which they work. Importantly, because health is a public good, and the health of immigrant populations affects the health of native populations, and vice versa, trust is important not only for the health of immigrants, but for the health of all.

More broadly, once we recognize that health is a public good, and that social and environmental factors play a critical role in determining population health, it becomes clear that public health policy, and the norms on which it is based, must shift away from isolating and stigmatizing immigrants, to those that address social determinants, domestically and globally.

Operationalizing Solidarity

It is one thing to say that policy should be changed and that immigrants should be given the same care as citizens. But ethnocentrism and its influence on policy is a significant impediment to a more generous approach to the health of newcomers. It might be argued that our proposal is either not possible or only possible with unacceptable costs to affluent countries. The combination of homophily and xenophobia make it unlikely that people will support the kinds of inclusive policies that are recommended in this volume. Some would also argue that not only is it unlikely that these policies would be embraced by natives, it would be undesirable. This view largely stems from the observation that social capital declines in the face of diversity. Furthermore, the connection between decline in social capital and diversity has been observed not only between diverse groups, but also within native communities.[83] Diminished social capital is regrettable because trust and social capital are critical for social engagement, cooperation, and the willingness to help others. According to Robert Putnam:

> Diversity does *not* produce 'bad race relations' or ethnically-defined group hostility. . . . Rather, inhabitants of diverse communities tend to withdraw from collective life, to distrust their neighbours, regardless of the colour of their skin, to withdraw even from close friends, to expect the worst from their community and its leaders. . . . Diversity, at least in the short run, seems to bring out the turtle in all of us.[84]

On a similar theme, Dora Costa and Matthew Kahn state:

> Diversity . . . imposes costs. Whether in choosing a college roommate, a residential community, or a place to pray, people tend to self-segregate. They prefer to interact with others like them because of shared interests, socialization to the same cultural norms, and greater empathy toward individuals who remind them of themselves.[85]

These observations are relevant to our proposals because we advocate extending culturally competent health care to newcomers and providing them with public health services. Doing so will require redistributing wealth from natives to newcomers in need. According to Paul Collier, it is unlikely that many people would be willing to engage in this kind of redistribution. Collier writes, "cultural diversity reduces the willingness to redistribute income," while homogeneity fosters it.[86] People appear to be more willing to help people who are similar to themselves. In other words, homophily and ethnocentrism affect the willingness of people to redistribute wealth. If Collier is right, any policy that requires redistribution to immigrants is unlikely to be welcome, even if it is a win-win.

Insofar as Collier's argument addresses questions about the desirability of immigration per se, it is beyond the scope of this book. Our focus has been on questions concerning responsibilities and policies regarding the health of immigrants who have relocated. We have not addressed the question of whether immigrants should be present. Nonetheless, to the extent that Collier's position suggests that our proposal is impossible, it needs to be addressed. There is a well-accepted principle in ethics, "ought implies can," according to which if someone is morally obligated to do something, then the action must be possible.[87]

At the outset, although diversity has been thought to challenge social capital and a willingness to redistribute, others have questioned this view. Christel Kesler and Irene Bloemraad found that "countries with an institutional or policy context promoting economic equality and recognition and accommodation of immigrant minorities experience less dramatic or no declines in collective-mindedness."[88] These scholars conclude that if immigration threatens the community, it can lead to the kind of hunkering that Putnam describes and about which Collier worries. However, social structures—including inequality and the presence of multicultural policies—can affect the level of social engagement. The combination of both decreased income inequality and multicultural policies minimizes the adverse impact of diversity on social capital.[89] Government-based programs, such as Canada's private sponsorship agreements, can help ease the transition of newcomers to their new homes and familiarize natives with newcomers. Large numbers of newcomers may require additional opportunities for private sponsorships and more culturally nuanced programs.

As we have seen in this book, there is widespread fear of immigrants as the carriers of pathogens and disease, even though for the most part they are healthier than natives. More importantly, the Kesler and Bloemraad study shows that it is possible to override the harmful effects of diversity on social capital and that immigrants per se are not the cause of the decline in social capital and in social cooperation. The social context into which immigrants arrive will influence how they are received and whether their presence will undermine social capital. Since how newcomers are perceived and the beliefs that are formed about them influence how receiving countries treat them, it is crucial that we educate native populations about immigrants, global health, and the health of immigrants. The consequence of perpetuating stereotypes, implicit bias, and false information will be harmful for natives and newcomers alike. In addition, Xavier de Souza Briggs points out that historically societies have managed coexistence through three mechanisms.[90] These are (1) boundary shifting, in which outsiders become insiders with time; (2) tolerance, in which people learn to live with difference; and (3) crosscutting obligations, according to which people with multiple identities bond on one dimension that they share, such as being a parent.[91]

Health may provide us with a significant crosscutting obligation that can be used to turn fear of and animosity toward immigrants into interaction on which to found both inclusive and compassionate health policy, as well as other kinds of policy. Regardless of cultural or ethnic heritage, all people experience pain and suffering when they are sick. Although people follow different traditions when they lose a loved one, grief and mourning are crosscutting. This was evident when the people of West Cambridge acted in solidarity to help Karim at the time of his illness. In effect health, human suffering, and grief unify people even in the face of vast cultural, economic, and ethnic differences.

Health can serve as an opportunity to bring natives and newcomers together in the interest of an important public good. To this end, it is critical that diverse people have a thorough knowledge of international health. Philosopher Martha Nussbaum has argued for the use of education as a mechanism for creating global citizens. She advocates moving toward cosmopolitanism by focusing on solving problems that require international cooperation.[92] For Nussbaum, the recognition of a "shared future" is important, as is global knowledge. She states that "to conduct this sort of global dialogue, we need knowledge not only of the geography and ecology of other nations . . . but also a great deal about their people."[93] To this end, she supports teaching students "to recognize humanity wherever they encounter it undeterred by traits that are strange to them."[94] Health not only affords an opportunity to educate people about the specifics of disease but is also a place where people can recognize their shared humanity, regardless of difference. Health has the potential to bring us together as a global community rather than tear us apart as natives and newcomers. For this to happen, people must recognize the role of health as a global public good and its inevitable role in our shared future as a global community. Newcomers should be viewed not as a burden on natives but as providing an opportunity to work together, toward health for all.

Public health will constitute one important component of this. But the professional values of medicine are also critical and can be mined for their emphasis on universalism.[95] Medical professionalism is focused on the sick and vulnerable, and not on the identity or culture of patients. These values are at the heart of *Time*'s Person of the Year choice. The Ebola workers put aside cultural difference in favor of shared humanity and a future together.

As the global responses to the Ebola epidemic and the 2015 refugee crisis demonstrate, there is enough evidence of implicit bias, ethnocentrism, and discrimination against newcomers' health interests that an approach that focuses on legal remedies alone will be inadequate. Prevention of discrimination through a due-diligence approach would both deter discrimination and bias and educate the public and foster new and inclusive norms. Due diligence and cultural competency must be embraced by both natives and newcomers. Some due-diligence efforts could focus on school curricula and on cultural competence, both within health care organizations and outside them. Monitoring health care organizations and health care workers for implicit bias both at policy and patient levels would foster change in norms from the ground up. Newcomers should also be educated about prevailing norms, and how they translate in day-to-day interactions with natives. Due-diligence assessments could be reported with an eye to scoring organizations and communities on the basis of their inclusiveness and success with respect to the health of newcomers. Transparency about the health outcomes of newcomers would be crucial. Audits should be public and available to communities in an effort to eradicate destructive norms in favor of those that support health as a global public good. Eventually, a social movement, similar to fair trade, may evolve in which natives who respect the health rights of newcomers are given preference. It may be tricky to capitalize on the window of opportunity opened by norm change to fashion health policy in the direction of inclusion. Yet in the end, we may find that natives and newcomers alike shun policies that demonstrate bias in favor of those that are inclusive, together welcoming health for all.

NOTES

CHAPTER 1. HEALTH AND MIGRATION

1 Parmet, "Public Health and Social Control: Implications for Human Rights," 44.
2 Ibid., 45; Chrisafis, "Man Guilty of Infecting Two Women with HIV."
3 Hulse, "In Lawmaker's Outburst, a Rare Breach of Protocol."
4 Reuters, "Polish Opposition Warns Refugees Could Spread Infectious Diseases"; Smith, "Fear and Xenophobia Poison Polish Polls."
5 Human Rights Watch, "Hungary: Abysmal Conditions in Border Detention."
6 Nossiter, "Marine Le Pen's Anti-Islam Message Gains Influence in France."
7 Melber and Abdullah, "Can Governors Block Syrian Refugees? Probably Not."
8 Bilefsky, "Trump's Plan to Bar Muslims Is Widely Condemned Abroad."
9 Carter, "'Potential for a Public Health Disaster.'"
10 Levitan, "Mo Brooks, Ben Carson Share False Narratives on Measles Outbreak."
11 Kaiser Family Foundation, "NPR/Kaiser/Kennedy School Immigration Survey."
12 Pew Research Center, "Most Say Illegal Immigrants Should Be Allowed to Stay, but Citizenship Is More Divisive."
13 Ipsos, "Global Views on Immigration," August 2011.
14 US Council of Economic Advisers, "The US Council of Economic Advisers on Immigration's Economic Impact," 641–646.
15 Bennhold, "From Afar, Moneymaker and Mother."
16 Ibid.
17 Hennessy-Fiske and Carcamo, "In Texas' Rio Grande Valley, a Seemingly Endless Surge of Immigrants."
18 Wheatstone, "Refugee Who Dragged Pregnant Wife and Baby Son."
19 United Nations, "232 Million International Migrants."
20 International Organization for Migration, "Irregular Migrant, Refugee Arrivals in Europe Top One Million in 2015."
21 Ibid.
22 BBC News, "Migrant Crisis: Migration to Europe Explained in Graphics."
23 United Nations, "232 Million International Migrants."
24 International Organization for Migration, "Global Migration Trends: An Overview."
25 Camarota, "A Record-Setting Decade of Immigration: 2000–2010," 13.
26 Garcia, "Canada: A Northern Refuge for Central Americans."

27 International Organization on Migration, *World Migration Report 2013*, 23.
28 Migration Policy Institute, "Rising Child Migration to the United States."
29 Passel and Taylor, "Unauthorized Immigrants and Their US-Born Children."
30 Mather, "Children in Immigrant Families Chart New Path."
31 Capps, Fortuny, and Fix, "Trends in the Low-Wage Immigrant Labor Force, 2002–2005."
32 Grieco et al., "The Foreign-Born Population in the United States: 2010," 2.
33 Keung, "Canada Faces Dramatic Drop in Citizenship."
34 Lee, "Donald Trump's False Comments Connecting Mexican Immigrants and Crime."
35 Ibid.
36 Abrams, "Terrorism Attacks since 9/11 Have Involved US Citizens, Not Immigrants."
37 Hall et al., "The Geography of Immigrant Skills," 4.
38 Ibid., 7; Institute of International Education, "A Quick Look at International Students in the U.S."
39 Hall et al., "The Geography of Immigrant Skills," 8.
40 Saxenian, "Silicon Valley's New Immigrant High-Growth Entrepreneurs," 29–30.
41 Wadhwa, Saxenian, and Siciliano, "Then and Now: America's New Immigrant Entrepreneurs, Part VII."
42 Saxenian, "Silicon Valley's New Immigrant High-Growth Entrepreneurs," 29.
43 Wadhwa et al., "Skilled Immigration," 6–14.
44 Bloomberg, "Satya Nadella."
45 Wadhwa et al., "Skilled Immigration," 9–11.
46 Saxenian, "Brain Circulation."
47 Ibid.
48 Ibid.
49 Singh and Miller, "Health, Life Expectancy, and Mortality Patterns among Immigrant Populations," I-14–I-21.
50 Chen, Ng, and Wilkins, "The Health of Canada's Immigrants in 1994–95," 33–45, and Chen, Wilkins, and Ng, "Health Expectancy by Immigrant Status, 1986 and 1991," 29–38, as cited in Singh and Miller, "Health, Life Expectancy, and Mortality Patterns among Immigrant Populations"; Kennedy, McDonald, and Biddle, "The Healthy Immigrant Effect and Immigrant Selection."
51 Gornall, "Healthcare for Syrian Refugees."
52 Singh and Miller, "Health, Life Expectancy, and Mortality Patterns among Immigrant Populations," I-17.
53 Putnam, *Bowling Alone*.
54 Singh and Miller, "Health, Life Expectancy, and Mortality Patterns among Immigrant Populations," I-15 and I-18–I-19.
55 Sampson, Morenoff, and Raudenbush, "Social Anatomy of Racial and Ethnic Disparities in Violence," 224–232.

56 Molnar et al., "A Multilevel Study of Neighborhoods and Parent-to-Child Physical Aggression," 84–97, as cited in Acevedo-Garcia and Almeida, "Special Issue Introduction: Place, Migration and Health," 2056.

57 Acevedo-Garcia and Almeida, "Special Issue Introduction: Place, Migration and Health," 2057.

58 Illingworth and Parmet, "The Right to Health," 1–14.

CHAPTER 2. KEEP OUT!

1 Clary, "Death of Refugee with AIDS Renews Controversy."

2 Ratner, "The Legacy of Guantanamo."

3 Ibid.

4 Wald, *Contagious*, 2.

5 Ibid., 2–3.

6 Barnett and Walker, "Role of Immigrants and Migrants in Emerging Infectious Diseases," 1447.

7 Siegel, "Health and Migration," 572.

8 Barnett and Walker, "Role of Immigrants in Emerging Infectious Diseases," 1447–1450.

9 Gulland, "Refugees Pose Little Health Risk, Says WHO."

10 Moeller, *Compassion Fatigue*, 62.

11 Tomes, "The Making of a Germ Panic, Then and Now," 197.

12 Keane and Gushulak, "The Medical Assessment of Migrants," 29–42.

13 Garrett, *The Coming Plague*.

14 Ungar, "Moral Panic versus the Risk Society," 271–291.

15 Washer, *Emerging Infectious Diseases and Society*; Tomes, "The Making of a Germ Panic," 192; Parmet, "Public Health and Social Control," 11.

16 Haidt, *The Righteous Mind*, 173.

17 Nagan and Haddad, "The Holocaust and Mass Atrocity," 359 (for the Jews); Molina, *Fit to Be Citizens?*, 61–63 and 121 (for the Mexicans); Kraut, *Silent Travelers*, 33–34 and 109 (for the Italians and Irish); Batlan, "Law in the Time of Cholera," 105–107 (for the Chinese).

18 Dolgin and Dieterich, "When Others Get Too Close," 329.

19 Boerma, "Republican Congressman: Immigrant Children Might Carry Ebola"; Richinick, "GOP Congressman: Ebola Could Spread across the Border."

20 Reuters, "Polish Opposition Warns Refugees Could Spread Infectious Diseases"; Smith, "Fear and Xenophobia Poison Polish Polls."

21 Batlan, "Law in the Time of Cholera," 63.

22 World Health Organization, "Nonpharmaceutical Interventions," 84–85.

23 Parmet, "Public Health and Social Control," 43.

24 Associated Press and Gayle, "Soldiers Spill Blood in Liberian Ebola Slum."

25 Kraut, *Silent Travelers*, 30.

26 Ibid.

27 Neuman, "The Lost Century of American Immigration Law," 1834.

28 Gibbons v. Ogden, 203.

29 Ibid.

30 Mayor of New York v. Miln, 142–143. The Supreme Court's views about the breadth of state power over immigrants evolved over the course of the nineteenth century. Even before the Court concluded that immigration belonged to the federal government, the Chinese Exclusion Cases, Chae Chan Ping v. United States, 589, placed some limits on state power.

31 Neuman, "The Lost Century of American Immigration Law," 1891–1892.

32 Act of Feb. 15, 1893, 27 Stat. 449 (1893); Neuman, "The Lost Century of American Immigration Law," 1865.

33 Neuman, "The Lost Century of American Immigration Law," 1862–1863.

34 Ibid., 1863.

35 Ibid., 1861, citing Act of Mar. 30, 1797, ch. 67, § 5, 1797 N.Y. Laws 93 (1797).

36 Passenger Cases, Smith v. Turner, 409.

37 Compagnie Francaise de Navigation a Vapeur v. Louisiana State Board of Health, 399.

38 Price, "Can U.S. Immigration Law Be Reconciled with the Protection of Public Health?," 14.

39 Act of Feb. 15, 1893, 27 Stat. 449, 450 (1893).

40 Ibid., 405–451.

41 Chae Chan Ping v. United States, 604.

42 Ibid., 608.

43 Immigration Act of 1891, 26 Stat. 1084, 1084 (1891).

44 Ibid., 1085.

45 Ibid., 1086; see also Fairchild, Science at the Borders, 58.

46 Ibid., 59.

47 Ibid., 15 and 59.

48 Ibid., 64.

49 Fairchild, "Policies of Inclusion," 528–539.

50 Immigration Act of 1903, Pub. L. No. 57–162, 32 Stat. 1213 (1903).

51 Kraut, Silent Travelers, 67, citing US Public Health Service, Book of Instructions.

52 Kraut, Silent Travelers, 273–274.

53 Ibid., 273.

54 Ibid., 66.

55 Ibid.

56 Ibid.

57 Ibid., 66–67.

58 Molina, Fit to Be Citizens?, 73; Fairchild, Science at the Borders, 42.

59 Fairchild, Science at the Borders, 65–67.

60 Linder and Grove, Vital Statistics Rates in the United States.

61 Schlosser, "Trachoma through History."

62 Ibid.

63 *Ex parte* Mitchell, 230.

64 Fairchild, *Science at the Borders*, 47–48.

65 Baynton, "Defectives in the Land," 34.

66 Ibid., 37.

67 Kraut, *Silent Travelers*, 74.

68 Price, "Can U.S. Immigration Law Be Reconciled," 10.

69 8 U.S.C. § 1182(a)(1) (2012).

70 US Department of Health and Human Services, Medical Examination of Aliens (AIDS), 51 Fed. Reg. 15354 (proposed Apr. 23, 1986) (to be codified at 14 C.F.R. pt. 34).

71 Urgent Relief for the Homeless Supplemental Appropriations Act of 1987, Pub. L. No. 100–71, 101 Stat. 468 (1987).

72 Watkins et al., *Report of the Presidential Commission on the Human Immunodeficiency Virus Epidemic.*

73 Ibid., 156.

74 Ibid., 165.

75 AIDS 2012, "International AIDS Conference Opens in the U.S. for the First Time in 22 Years at Defining Moment in the History of the AIDS Epidemic"; see also Centers for Disease Control and Prevention, "Medical Examination of Aliens."

76 Haitian Refugee Center, Inc. v. Baker. The forced repatriations were eventually upheld in Sale v. Haitian Centers Council, Inc.

77 Haitian Centers Council v. Sale, vacated by Stipulated Order Approving Class Action Settlement Agreement (Feb. 22, 1994).

78 Ibid., 1045.

79 Ibid., 1049.

80 "Declaration of Commitment on HIV/AIDS."

81 Centers for Disease Control and Prevention, "Medical Examination of Aliens."

82 Joint United Nations Programme on HIV/AIDS (UNAIDS), "HIV-Related Restrictions on Entry, Stay, and Residence."

83 Joint United Nations Programme on HIV/AIDS (UNAIDS), *Mapping of Restrictions on the Entry, Stay and Residence of People Living with HIV*, 9.

84 Todrys, "Returned to Risk," 16.

85 Ibid., 17, citing US Department of State, "2008 Human Rights Report: United Arab Emirates."

86 Todrys, "Returned to Risk," 1.

87 Joint United Nations Programme on HIV/AIDS (UNAIDS), *Report of the International Task Team on HIV-Related Travel Restrictions.*

88 Ibid., 18.

89 Parmet, "Dangerous Perspectives," 83–108.

90 Horner, Wood, and Kelly, "Public Health in/as 'National Security,'" 418–431.

91 World Health Organization, "Update 42."

92 Parmet, "Public Health and Social Control," 23.

93 World Health Organization, "International Health Regulations," Art. 23.

94 Ibid., Art. 32.

95 Parmet, "Dangerous Perspectives," 98.

96 US Homeland Security Council, "National Strategy for Pandemic Influenza."

97 Parmet, "Dangerous Perspectives," 98.

98 Washington, "Immigration Foes Link Flu to Mexican Threat Claims."

99 Abcarian, "Obama News Conference: President Says Swine Flu No Reason to Close Border with Mexico."

100 Browne, "China Forces Dozens of Mexican Travelers into Quarantine."

101 Parmet, "Public Health and Social Control," 31.

102 Priest et al., "Effectiveness of Border Screening for Detecting," 1412–1418.

103 Markel et al., "Nonpharmaceutical Influenza Mitigation Strategies," 1961–1964.

104 Wood et al., "Effects of Internal Border Control on Spread of Pandemic Influenza," 1038–1045.

105 Sahara Reporters, "Ebola"; Branswell, "Feds and WHO Discuss Canadian Ebola-Related Travel Restrictions."

106 Centers for Disease Control and Prevention, "Update," October 27, 2014. The guidance has been updated several times since, most recently on October 9, 2015: Centers for Disease Control and Prevention, "Interim U.S. Guidance for Monitoring and Movement of Persons with Potential Ebola Virus Exposure."

107 Centers for Disease Control and Prevention, "State Ebola Protocols."

108 Epstein et al., "Controlling Pandemic Flu," e401.

109 Di Costanzo, "Autistic Son Denied Entry."

110 Hill v. United States Immigration and Naturalization Serv., 1472; National Immigration Project of the National Lawyers Guild, "Immigration Law and Defense Database," chapter 5.

111 8 U.S.C. §§ 1182(a)(1)(A)(I); 1182(a)(1)(A)(II) (2012).

112 Ibid. § 1182(a)(1)(A)(v) (2012).

113 Ibid. § 1182(a)(4) (2012).

114 Ibid. § 1182(a)(4)(B) (2012).

115 Solomon, "Shameful Profiling of the Mentally Ill."

116 42 C.F.R. § 34.1(a) (2015).

117 Ibid. § 34.1(d) (2015).

118 Maloney, Ortega, and Cetron, "Overseas Medical Screening for Immigrants and Refugees," 115.

119 Centers for Disease Control and Prevention, "DGMQ's Asia Field Program in Thailand."

120 Cochran, O'Fallon, and Geltman, "US Medical Screening for Immigrants and Refugees: Public Health Issues," 124.

121 Immigration and Refugee Protection Regulations, SOR/2002–227, § 29 (Can.).

122 Immigration and Refugee Protection Act, 2001 S.C., ch. 27, § 38(1) (Can.).

123 Immigration and Refugee Protection Regulations, SOR/2002–227, §1(1) (Can.).

124 UK Border Agency, "Entry Clearance Guidance, Medical Issues (MED)."

125 Migration Regulations, sch. 4, item 4005(1)(ab)(b) (Austl.).

126 Ibid., sch. 4, item 4005(1)(ab)(c) (Austl.).

127 Jean, "SA Police Recruit Denied Entry."

128 Department of Immigration and Citizenship, "Inquiry into Immigration Treatment of Disability."

129 Australian Government, "Response to the Joint Standing Committee on Migration Report," 6.

130 Joint Standing Committee on Migration, "Enabling Australia: Inquiry into Immigration Treatment of Disability," 47.

131 Convention on the Rights of Persons with Disabilities, art. 3, Mar. 30, 2007, 2515 U.N.T.S. 3.

132 Ibid., art. 18.

133 United Nations, Convention on the Rights of Persons with Disabilities.

134 WHO, "International Health Regulations," Art. 31.1.

135 Americans with Disabilities Act, Pub. L. 101–336, 104 Stat. 328 (1990).

136 Council of Canadians with Disabilities, "Immigration and Disability."

137 Price, "Can U.S. Immigration Law Be Reconciled," 47.

CHAPTER 3. BLAMING THE VICTIM

1 Leavitt, "Typhoid Mary: Villain or Victim."

2 Tyson, "In Her Own Words."

3 Tobey, "Public Health and the Police Power," 126.

4 International Covenant on Economic, Social and Cultural Rights (ICESCR), art. 12, Dec. 16, 1966, 993 U.N.T.S. 3.

5 Ibid.

6 Burris and Anderson, "Legal Regulation of Health-Related Behavior," 97.

7 Ibid., 96–98.

8 Jacobson v. Massachusetts, 26–28.

9 International Covenant on Civil and Political Rights, art. 4, Dec. 19, 1966, 999 U.N.T.S. 171.

10 Kraut, *Silent Travelers*, 107.

11 Ibid., 79.

12 Molina, *Fit to Be Citizens?*, 2.

13 Nayan Shah, *Contagious Divides*, 121.

14 Barbier v. Connolly.

15 Ibid., 31.

16 Ibid., 32.

17 Ibid., 30.

18 Soon Hing v. Crowley.

19 Ibid., 710.

20 Ibid.

21 Ibid., 711.

22 Yick Wo. v. Hopkins.

23 Ibid., 374.

24 Ibid., 369.

25 Ibid., 370–373.

26 Ibid., 373–374.

27 Nayan Shah, *Contagious Divides*, 120.

28 Ibid., 130.

29 Ibid.

30 Ibid., 129.

31 Wong Wai v. Williamson.

32 Ibid., 9.

33 Ibid.

34 Jew Ho v. Williamson.

35 Ibid., 20.

36 Ibid., 26.

37 Graham v. Richardson.

38 Arizona v. U.S.

39 Nayan Shah, *Contagious Divides*, 134.

40 Ibid., 130.

41 Willrich, *Pox*.

42 *Boston Herald*, "Workmen Vaccinated."

43 Willrich, *Pox*.

44 Jacobson v. Massachusetts.

45 Ibid., 27.

46 Ibid., 28.

47 Ibid., 38.

48 Knox, "Arizona TB Patient Jailed as a Public Health Menace."

49 Ibid.

50 Chong, "Diagnosis Changed for TB Patient."

51 Parmet, "Dangerous Perspectives."

52 UN Commission on Human Rights, "Siracusa Principles."

53 World Health Organization, *Global Tuberculosis Report 2015*, 1.

54 Ibid., 2.

55 Ibid.

56 Ibid.

57 Ibid.

58 Ibid., 16.

59 Ibid., 13.

60 Neel, "Screening Immigrants for TB Pays Dividends in U.S."

61 Alvarez et al., "A Comparative Examination of Tuberculosis Immigration Medical Screening Programs," 3.

62 Ibid.

63 Ricks et al., "Estimating the Burden of Tuberculosis among Foreign-Born Persons," e27405.

64 Centers for Disease Control and Prevention, "Fact Sheets: The Difference between Latent TB Infection and TB Disease."

65 Greenaway et al., "Tuberculosis," e939.

66 Alami et al., "Trends in Tuberculosis."

67 Thomas and Gushulak, "Screening and Treatment of Immigrants and Refugees to Canada for Tuberculosis," 247.

68 Cousins, "Experts Sound Alarm."

69 Gilbert et al., "The Impact of Immigration on Tuberculosis Rates," 645.

70 Ibid.

71 Svensson et al., "Impact of Immigration on Tuberculosis Epidemiology," 881–887.

72 Ibid.

73 Kenyon et al., "Immigration and Tuberculosis," 103.

74 Menzies, Chan, and Vissandjée, "Impact of Immigration on Tuberculosis Infection," 1915–1921.

75 Sandgren et al., "Tuberculosis Transmission between Foreign- and Native-Born Populations," 1159–1171.

76 Greenwood and Warriner, "Immigrants and the Spread of Tuberculosis in the United States," 839–859; Martínez-Lirola et al., "Advanced Survey of Tuberculosis," 8–14.

77 Alvarez et al., "Comparative Examination of Screening Programs."

78 Hirsch-Moverman et al., "Adherence to Treatment for Latent Tuberculosis Infection," 1235–1254.

79 Horner, Wood, and Kelly, "Public Health in/as 'National Security.'"

80 Munro et al., "Patient Adherence to Tuberculosis Treatment," 1230–1245.

81 Ibid.

82 Centers for Disease Control and Prevention, "Self-Study Modules on Tuberculosis."

83 Pasipanodya and Gumbo, "A Meta-Analysis of Self-Administered vs. Directly Observed Therapy Effect," 21–31.

84 World Health Organization, Global Tuberculosis Report 2013.

85 World Health Organization, "The Patients' Charter for Tuberculosis Care."

86 Coker, From Chaos to Coercion, 47–81.

87 Ibid., 122–129.

88 IRIN News, "South Africa."

89 Shin-Rou Lin, "A Costly Illusion?," 107–166.

90 Frieden et al., "Tuberculosis in New York City," 229–233.

91 Lerner, "Catching Patients," 236–241.

92 Ibid.

93 Coker, From Chaos to Coercion, 47–81.

94 Gostin, Public Health Law, 416–417.

95 Ibid., 417.

96 World Health Organization, "WHO Guidance on Human Rights and Involuntary Detention."

97 City of Newark v. J. S.; *In re* City of New York v. Antoinette R.

98 Greene v. Edwards (holding that TB patient subject to isolation order is entitled to due process protections).

99 Horner, Wood, and Kelly, "Public Health in/as 'National Security.'"

100 Ibid.

101 Blaas et al., "Extensively Drug Resistant Tuberculosis in a High Income Country," 60.

102 Ibid.

103 Parmet, "Pandemics, Populism and the Role of Law," 143.

104 Onishi, "Clashes Erupt"; *Telegraph*, "Riots in China over SARS Quarantine."

105 World Health Organization, *Global Tuberculosis Report 2013*.

CHAPTER 4. A NATION OF UNINSURED IMMIGRANTS

1 Kiefer, "Lawyers Confer on Patient's Fate."

2 Sontag, "Deported, by U.S. Hospitals."

3 Pew Research Center, "Statistical Portrait of the Foreign-Born Population in the United States."

4 Graham v. Richardson.

5 Kaiser Family Foundation, "Key Facts about the Uninsured Population."

6 For a discussion of anti-immigrant rhetoric in the debates over the Affordable Care Act, see Dolgin and Dieterich, "When Others Get Too Close."

7 Donathan L. Brown, "Manufacturing Fear, Creating the Threat," 59.

8 Initiative Statute, Illegal Aliens—Public Services, Verification, and Reporting, 1994 Cal. Legis. Serv. Prop. 187 (West) (preempted by federal law in the case of League of United Latin American Citizens v. Wilson).

9 Ibid.

10 Martinez, "Illegal Immigrants' Tab for Emergency Care: $61 Million."

11 Ibid.

12 League of United Latin American Citizens v. Wilson, 908 F. Supp. 755, 763; Dolgin and Dieterich, "When Others Get Too Close," 283.

13 Personal Responsibility and Work Opportunity Reconciliation Act (PRWORA), Pub. L. No. 104–193, 110 Stat. 2105 (1996) (codified as amended primarily in scattered sections of 42 U.S.C.).

14 8 U.S.C. § 1601 (1) (2016).

15 Fortuny and Chaudry, "A Comprehensive Review of Immigrant Access to Health and Human Services."

16 King, "Immigrants in the U.S. Health Care System"; Riosmena, "Policy Shocks," 270.

17 Zallman et al., "Immigrants Contributed an Estimated $115.2 Billion More to the Medicare," 1158. ("Encouraging a steady flow of young immigrants would help offset the aging of the US population and the health care financing challenges that it presents.")

18 Pylypchuk and Hudson, "Immigrants and the Use of Preventive Care in the United States," 783–806; Park, *Entitled to Nothing*, 5; Akresh, "Health Service

Utilization," 785–815 (reviewing literature showing immigrant populations are healthier than natives when they arrive, but that immigrant health declines over time); Derose, Escarce, and Lurie, "Immigrants and Health Care," 1258–1268.

19 Derose et al., "Immigrants and Health Care Access, Quality, and Cost," 355–408.

20 Ibid., 355.

21 Kaiser Family Foundation, "Key Facts."

22 DeNavas-Walt, Proctor, and Smith, "Income, Poverty, and Health Insurance Coverage in the United States: 2010"; Kaiser Commission on Medicaid and the Uninsured, "Five Basic Facts on Immigrants and Their Health Care."

23 Cortez, "Embracing the New Geography of Health Care," 867–872; Clemans-Cope et al., "The Affordable Care Act's Coverage Expansions," 923; Zuckerman, Waidmann, and Lawton, "Undocumented Immigrants, 1997–2004" (focusing specifically on undocumented immigrants, stating that they are likely to form an increasingly large share of the uninsured, up to 25 percent).

24 Derose et al., "Immigrants and Health Care Access, Quality, and Cost," 355–362; Capps et al., "A Demographic, Socioeconomic, and Health Coverage Profile of Unauthorized Immigrants in the United States."

25 Derose, Escarce, and Lurie, "Immigrants and Health Care," 1260.

26 Kaiser Commission on Medicaid and the Uninsured, "How Race/Ethnicity, Immigration Status and Language Affect Health Insurance Coverage"; Fortuny and Chaudry, "Comprehensive Review," 1–2. ("U.S.-born children with immigrant parents also have lower rates of use relative to children in native-born families.").

27 Kaiser Commission on Medicaid and the Uninsured, "Immigrants' Health Coverage and Health Reform."

28 Derose et al., "Immigrants and Health Care Access, Quality, and Cost," 362–363.

29 Finch v. Commonwealth Health Ins. Connector Auth., 946, N.E.2d 1275, 1275; City of Chicago v. Shalala, 607.

30 Mathews v. Diaz, 79.

31 8 U.S.C. § 1641(b) (2016).

32 Ibid. § 1611 (2016).

33 Ibid. § 1611(b)(1) (2016).

34 Ibid. § 1621(d) (2016).

35 Ibid. § 1613(a) (2016).

36 Ibid. § 1622 (2016).

37 Fortuny and Chaudry, "Comprehensive Review," 13–14.

38 Okie, "Immigrants and Health Care," 525–529.

39 Reuters, "California Senate Approves Bill."

40 Graham v. Richardson, 378.

41 Compare Soskin v. Reinertson, 1257; Hong Pham v. Starkowski, 431; Aliessa ex rel. Fayad v. Novello, 1098; Ehrlich v. Perez, 1244; Finch v. Commonwealth Health Ins. Connector Auth., 959, N.E.2d, 970, 976.

42 Pew Charitable Trusts, "Mapping Public Benefits," 7.

43 Fortuny and Chaudry, "A Comprehensive Review," 14.

44 Pew Charitable Trusts, "Mapping Public Benefits," 7.

45 Children's Health Insurance Program Reauthorization Act, 42 U.S.C. § 1397ll (2015).

46 Kaiser Family Foundation, "Medicaid/CHIP Coverage of Lawfully-Residing Immigrant Children and Pregnant Women."

47 Hammel, "Prenatal Care a 'Magnet.'"

48 For example, a study in the respected journal *Health Services Research* was based on a misreading of PRWORA that assumed that all qualified aliens were eligible and the five-year bar applied only to unqualified aliens. See Kandula et al., "The Unintended Impact of Welfare Reform," 1509–1526.

49 Derose et al., "Immigrants and Health Care Access, Quality, and Cost," 365.

50 Ibid., 366.

51 8 U.S.C. § 1183a (2016).

52 Park, *Entitled to Nothing*.

53 Ibid., 1.

54 Ibid., 27.

55 Kaiser Commission on Medicaid and the Uninsured, "Immigrants' Health Coverage and Health Reform."

56 Reyes, "Infants Caught in Political Crossfire."

57 Sec. 211, Children's Health Insurance Program Reauthorization Act of 2009, Pub. L. 111–3, 123 Stat. 8 (2009).

58 Kaiser Commission on Medicaid and the Uninsured, "Immigrants' Access to Health Care after Welfare Reform."

59 Ben-Asher, "Obligatory Health," 2.

60 Parmet, "The Individual Mandate," 410.

61 Diamond, "Legal Triage for Healthcare Reform," 265.

62 42 U.S.C. § 18071 (2016).

63 Nat'l Fed'n of Indep. Bus. v. Sebelius, 2607.

64 Galewitz, "States Balk at Expanding Medicaid."

65 Kaiser Commission on Medicaid and the Uninsured, "Immigrants' Health Coverage and Health Reform."

66 42 U.S.C. § 18081(b)(2) (2016).

67 Goldstein, "Administration Warns Some Could Lose Health-Care."

68 Sontag, "Deported, by U.S. Hospitals."

69 Ibid.

70 O'Connell, "Note: Return to Sender," 1429.

71 Sontag, "Deported, by U.S. Hospitals."

72 Montejo v. Martin Mem'l Med. Ctr., 874 So.2d 654, 657.

73 Montejo v. Martin Mem'l Med. Ctr., Inc., 935 So.2d 1266, 1272.

74 42 U.S.C. § 1395dd(a) (2011).

75 Ibid. § 1395dd(b) (2011).

76 Ibid. § 1396b(v) (2011).

77 Ibid., § 1396b(v)(3) (2011).

78 Ibid., § 1396b(v) (2011).

79 DuBard and Massing, "Trends in Emergency Medicaid," 1088.

80 Diaz v. Division of Social Services, 386.

81 Ibid., 391.

82 Ibid.

83 Ibid., quoting PRWORA at 8 U.S.C. § 1601(6) (2016).

84 Spring Creek Mgmt., L.P. v. Dep't of Pub. Welfare, 475.

85 Ibid., 479 (quoting Scottsdale Healthcare, Inc. v. Arizona Health Care Cost Containment Admin., 97) (italics omitted).

86 See, for example, Arellano v. DHS, 677–678 (saying that there is no sudden-onset requirement for Emergency Medicaid).

87 See also Greenery Rehab Group, Inc. v. Hammon, 232.

88 Center for Social Justice at Seton Hall Law School (CSJ) and Health Justice Program at New York Lawyers for the Public Interest (NYLPI), "Discharge, Deportation, and Dangerous Journeys."

89 Sontag, "Deported, by U.S. Hospitals."

90 Mexcare, accessed November 23, 2012.

91 Cruz v. Central Iowa Hospital Corp.

92 Sontag, "Deported in a Coma."

93 Ibid.

94 Ibid.

95 Ibid.

96 Ibid.

97 Sack, "Immigrants Cling to Fragile Lifeline."

98 42 U.S.C. § 1395rr (2016).

99 Ibid. § 1396b(v) (2016); Linden, Cano, and Coritsidis, "Kidney Transplantation in Undocumented Immigrants," 354–359.

100 Linden, Cano, and Coritsidis, "Kidney Transplantation in Undocumented Immigrants."

101 Ibid.

102 Hurley et al., "Care of Undocumented Individuals," 940–949.

103 Sheikh-Hamad et al., "Care for Immigrants with End-Stage Renal Disease in Houston," 54–57.

104 Sack, "Judge Rules That Hospital Can Close Dialysis Unit."

105 Sack, Agren, and Einhorn, "Ailing Immigrants Find No Relief Back Home."

106 Ibid.

107 Ibid.

108 Sack, "Deal Reached on Dialysis for Immigrants."

109 Ibid.

110 Institute of Medicine, Care without Coverage, 162.

111 Wilper et al., "Health Insurance and Mortality in US Adults," 2292.

112 Pylypchuk and Hudson, "Immigrants and Preventive Care," 783–806; Antecol and Bedard, "Unhealthy Assimilation," 337–360; Mohanty et al., "Health Care Expenditures of Immigrants in the United States," 1431–1438.

113 Antecol and Bedard, "Unhealthy Assimilation," 338.

114 Pylypchuk and Hudson, "Immigrants and Preventive Care."

115 Derose et al., "Immigrants and Health Care Access, Quality, and Cost," 363.

116 Ibid.

117 Ibid.

118 Mohanty et al., "Health Care Expenditures."

119 Ibid.

120 Stimpson et al., "Persistent Disparities in Cholesterol Screening."

121 Derose et al., "Immigrants and Health Care Access, Quality, and Cost," 364.

122 Ibid., 368.

123 Portes, Light, and Fernández-Kelly, "The U.S. Health Care System and Immigration," 502.

124 Derose et al., "Immigrants and Health Care Access, Quality, and Cost," 363–365.

125 See, for example, Pavlish, Noor, and Brandt, "Somali Immigrant Women and the American Health Care System," 353–361; Potocky-Tripodi, Dodge, and Greene, "Bridging Cultural Chasms," 105–117; Kim et al., "The Use of Traditional and Western Medicine among Korean American Elderly," 109–120; Vu, "Cultural Barriers between Obstetrician-Gynecologists and Vietnamese/Chinese Immigrant Women," 47–52.

126 Derose, Escarce, and Lurie, "Immigrants and Health Care," 1262.

127 Ibid.

128 Park, Entitled to Nothing.

129 McDonnell, "Health Clinics Report Declines After Prop. 18."

130 Ibid.

131 Romney, Brazil, and Miller, "Child Cited as Prop. 187 Casualty Had Leukemia."

132 Cortez, "Embracing the New Geography of Health Care," 884.

133 US General Accounting Office, "Undocumented Aliens."

134 Okie, "Immigrants and Health Care."

135 Mitchell et al., "Who Will Cover the Cost of Undocumented Immigrant Trauma Care?," 609–613.

136 Ibid.

137 Institute of Medicine, A Shared Destiny; see also Hsia, Kellermann, and Shen, "Factors Associated with Closures of Emergency Departments in the United States," 1978–1985.

138 Nissen, "Health Care Disparities, the Uninsured, and the Role of Cardiologists in the National Debate," 249–251.

139 Pauly and Pagán, "Spillovers and Vulnerability," 1304–1314.

140 Portes, Light, and Fernández-Kelly, "U.S. Health Care System and Immigration," 494.

141 California Medical Association House of Delegates, "Forced Deportation of Patients."

142 American Medical Association, "Physician Responsibilities for Safe Patient Discharge," 90.

143 Ibid., 91.

144 Ibid., 92.

145 Ibid., 94.

146 Hurley et al., "Care of Undocumented Individuals."

147 Ibid.

148 Raghavan and Nuila, "Survivors—Dialysis, Immigration, and U.S. Law," 2183–2185.

149 Ibid., 2184.

150 Ibid., 2184–2185.

151 Pauly and Pagán, "Spillovers and Vulnerability."

152 Ibid.

153 Pauly and Pagán, "Spillovers of Uninsurance in Communities."

154 Ibid.

155 Nandi, Loue, and Galea, "Expanding the Universe of Universal Coverage," 433–436.

156 Ibid., 435.

157 Anderson et al., "It's the Prices, Stupid," 90.

158 Knoll and Shewmaker, "It's Not Just Immigration Anymore."

CHAPTER 5. DENYING THE RIGHT TO HEALTH

1 Caulford and D'Andrade, "Health Care for Canada's Medically Uninsured Immigrants and Refugees," 725–726.

2 Ibid.

3 G.A. Res. 217 (III) A, Universal Declaration of Human Rights, art. 25 (Dec. 10, 1948).

4 International Covenant on Economic, Social, and Cultural Rights, art. 12.1, Dec. 16, 1966, 993 U.N.T.S. 3.

5 Björngren-Cuadra, "Policy towards Undocumented Migrants of the EU 27," 112.

6 Comm. on Econ., Soc. and Cultural Rights, General Comment No. 14, The Right to the Highest Attainable Standard of Health, ¶ 4, U.N. Doc. E/C 12/2000/4 (Aug. 11, 2000).

7 International Covenant on Economic, Social, and Cultural Rights, art. 12.2(d), Dec. 16, 1966, 993 U.N.T.S. 3.

8 Björngren-Cuadra, "Policy towards Undocumented Migrants," 112.

9 International Covenant on Economic, Social, and Cultural Rights, art. 2.1, Dec. 16, 1966, 993 U.N.T.S. 3.

10 Comm. on Econ., Soc. and Cultural Rights, General Comment No. 14, The Right to the Highest Attainable Standard of Health, ¶ 30, U.N. Doc. E/C 12/2000/4 (Aug. 11, 2000).

11 Office of the United Nations High Commissioner for Human Rights (OHCHR), "The Right to Health," 4.

12 Ibid., 7.

13 Comm. on Econ., Soc. and Cultural Rights, General Comment No. 14, The Right to the Highest Attainable Standard of Health, ¶ 34, U.N. Doc. E/C 12/2000/4 (Aug. 11, 2000).

14 Comm. on Econ., Soc. and Cultural Rights, General Comment No. 19, The Right to Social Security, ¶ 37, U.N. Doc. E/C 12/GC/19 (Nov. 23, 2007).

15 United Nations Declaration on the Human Rights of Individuals Who Are Not Nationals of the Country in Which They Live, G.A. Res. 40/144, art. 8.1(c) (Dec. 13, 1985).

16 World Health Organization, "Health of Migrants," 24.

17 International Organization for Migration (IOM), World Health Organization (WHO), and Office of the United Nations High Commissioner for Human Rights (OHCHR), *International Migration, Health and Human Rights*, 16–18.

18 Organization of American States, Additional Protocol to the American Convention on Human Rights in the Area of Economic, Social, and Cultural Rights (Protocol of San Salvador), art. 3, Nov. 17, 1988, 28 I.L.M. 156.

19 Eur. Consult, *Bratislava Declaration on Health, Human Rights and Migration*, 3 (Nov. 23, 2007).

20 International Organization for Migration, World Health Organization, and Office of the United Nations High Commissioner for Human Rights, *International Migration*, 41.

21 International Convention on the Protection of the Rights of All Migrant Workers and Members of their Families, art. X, Dec. 18, 1990, 2220 U.N.T.S. 3.

22 Eur. Consult, *Recommendation CM/Rec 13 of the Committee of Ministers to Member States on Mobility, Migration and Access to Health Care*, preamble iv (Nov. 16, 2011).

23 Organisation for Economic Co-operation and Development, *International Migration Outlook 2013*, 131.

24 Canada Health Act, S.C. 1984, c. 6, s. 3 (Can.).

25 Lebrun and Dubay, "Access to Primary and Preventive Care," 1694.

26 Ibid., 1701.

27 Mowat and Chambers, "Producing More Relevant Evidence," 308; McDonald and Kennedy, "Insights into the 'Healthy Immigrant Effect,'" 1623–1624.

28 Lebrun and Dubay, "Access to Primary and Preventive Care," 1708; Siddiqi, Zuberi, and Nguyen, "The Role of Health Insurance in Explaining Immigrant versus Non-Immigrant Disparities," 1458–1459.

29 Elgersma, "Immigration Status and Legal Entitlement to Insured Health Services," 2–4.

30 Ibid., 3n10.

31 Ibid., 3.

32 Barnes, "The Real Cost of Cutting Refugee Health Benefits," 2.

33 Canadian Doctors for Refugee Care v. Attorney General of Canada.

34 Ibid., para. 83.

35 Ibid., para. 571.

36 Ibid., para. 474.

37 Ibid., para. 691.

38 Ibid., paras. 646, 654.

39 Citizenship and Immigration Canada (CIC), "Interim Federal Health Program."

40 Citizenship and Immigration Canada (CIC), "Determine Your Eligibility and Coverage Type."

41 Zilio, "Liberals Restore Refugee Health Benefits."

42 Canadian Doctors for Refugee Care v. Attorney General of Canada, para. 148.

43 Biffl, "Access to Health Care in the European Union," 7.

44 Convention Relating to the Status of Refugees, art. 23, Jul. 28, 1951, 189 U.N.T.S. 150.

45 Pace, "The Right to Health of Migrants in Europe," 61.

46 Gulland, "The Refugee Crisis."

47 Ibid.

48 Stanciole and Huber, "Access to Health Care for Migrants, Ethnic Minorities and Asylum Seekers in Europe."

49 Björngren-Cuadra, "Policy towards Undocumented Migrants," 122–123.

50 Ibid., 123.

51 Ibid., 115–116.

52 Ibid., 117.

53 Ibid., 117–119.

54 Ibid., 117.

55 Grit, den Otter, and Spreij, "Access to Health Care for Undocumented Migrants," 47.

56 Ibid.

57 Ibid.

58 Ibid., 57; Thomas, Aggleton, and Anderson, "'If I Cannot Access Services, Then There Is No Reason for Me to Test,'" 526–531.

59 Björngren-Cuadra, "Policy towards Undocumented Migrants," 118.

60 Ibid.

61 Arie, "Are Migrant Patients Really a Drain on European Health Systems?," 2.

62 Björngren-Cuadra, "Policy towards Undocumented Migrants," 119–121.

63 Arie, "How Europe Keeps Migrants Out of Its Health System."

64 Björngren-Cuadra, "Policy towards Undocumented Migrants," 121.

65 Ibid.

66 Grit, den Otter, and Spreij, "Access to Health Care," 48.

67 Ibid., 50.

68 Ibid.

69 Steele et al., "The Immigration Bill," 132–133.

70 Arie, "Are Migrant Patients Really a Drain on European Health Systems?"

71 International Organization for Migration, World Health Organization, and Office of the United Nations High Commissioner for Human Rights, *International Migration*, 44.

72 Messina, "Asylum, Residency and Citizenship Policies and Models of Migrant Incorporation," 43.

73 Ibid., 47.

74 Ibid.

75 Ibid., 43–45.

76 Gray and Ginneken, "Health Care for Undocumented Migrants," 3.

77 Ibid.

78 Grit, den Otter, and Spreij, "Access to Health Care," 39.

79 N. v. United Kingdom, ¶ 44.

80 Ibid.

81 MM (Zimbabwe) v. Sec'y of State for the Home Dept.

82 Sec'y of State for the Home Dept. v. Roseline Onoshoagbe Akhalu.

83 Ibid.

84 R (on the application of) SQ (Pakistan) & Anor v. The Upper Tribunal Immigration and Asylum Chamber & Anor.

85 Agudelo-Suárez, Ronda-Pérez, and Benavides, "Occupational Health," 159.

86 Rechel et al., "Migration and Health in an Increasingly Diverse Europe," 1238.

87 Reeske and Razum, "Maternal and Child Health," 141.

88 Rechel et al., "Migration and Health," 1238.

89 Nørredam and Krasnik, "Migrants' Access to Health Services," 69.

90 Reeske and Razum, "Maternal and Child Health," 147.

91 Delamothe, "Migrant Healthcare."

92 Torres-Cantero et al., "Health Care Provision for Illegal Migrants," 483–485.

93 Ibid.

94 Biffl, "Access to Health Care," 92–93.

95 Nørredam and Krasnik, "Migrants' Access to Health Services," 71.

96 Ibid.

97 Biffl, "Access to Health Care," 77–93.

98 Thomas, Aggleton, and Anderson, "'If I Cannot Access Services,'" 528.

99 Ibid., 529.

100 Ibid., 528.

101 Ibid., 530.

102 Delamothe, "Migrant Healthcare," 1–2.

103 International Organization for Migration, World Health Organization, and Office of the United Nations High Commissioner for Human Rights, *International Migration*, 19.

104 Ibid., 40.

105 Ibid., 12.

106 Grit, den Otter, and Spreij, "Access to Health Care," 47 and 51.

107 International Organization for Migration, World Health Organization, and Office of the United Nations High Commissioner for Human Rights, *International Migration*, 51.

CHAPTER 6. HEALTH AS A GLOBAL PUBLIC GOOD

1 World Health Organization, "Smallpox."
2 Chen, Evans, and Cash, "Health as a Global Public Good," 298.
3 Woodward and Smith, "Global Public Goods and Health," 4.
4 Kaul, Grunberg, and Stern, "Defining Global Public Goods," 3.
5 Outterson, "Fair Followers," 164–178.
6 Ibid.
7 Illingworth, *Us before Me*, 50.
8 Kaul, Grunberg, and Stern, "Defining Global Public Goods," 3.
9 Ibid., 3–4.
10 Ibid., 10–11.
11 Ibid., 11.
12 Ibid., 2–3.
13 Woodward and Smith, "Global Public Goods and Health," 10.
14 Ibid., 11.
15 Ibid., 10.
16 Ibid.
17 O'Neill, "Broadening Bioethics."
18 Christakis and Fowler, *Connected*, 108.
19 Ibid., 115.
20 Rosenquist, Fowler, and Christakis, "Social Network Determinants of Depression," 273–281.
21 Iacoboni, *Mirroring People*, 126.
22 Joint United Nations Programme on HIV/AIDS (UNAIDS) and World Health Organization (WHO), *AIDS Epidemic Update*.
23 Ibid., 11.
24 Lopez, "The Subversive Links between HIV/AIDS and the Forest Sector," 230.
25 Rosen et al., "The Impact of AIDS on Government Service Delivery," S53–S59.
26 Bosma et al., "Low Job Control and Risk of Coronary Heart Disease," 558–565.
27 Bollyky, "Developing Symptoms," 135.
28 Thaler and Sunstein, *Nudge*.
29 Fried, "Longevity and Aging," 213.
30 Woodward and Smith, "Global Public Goods and Health," 12.
31 World Health Organization, "Social Determinants of Health."
32 Wilkinson and Pickett, *Spirit Level*.
33 Ibid.
34 Bosma et al., "Low Job Control."
35 Rabin, "Unemployment May Be Hazardous to Your Health."

36 World Health Organization, "Social Determinants of Health."

37 Wilkinson and Pickett, *Spirit Level*, 73–77.

38 World Health Organization, "What Are Social Determinants of Health?"

39 Marmot, "Social Determinants of Health Inequalities," 1099–1104.

40 Wilkinson and Pickett, *Spirit Level*.

41 Mill, *Utilitarianism*, 40.

42 Iacoboni, *Mirroring People*.

43 Woodward and Smith, "Global Public Goods and Health."

44 Cowell and Cumming-Bruce, "U.N. Agency Calls Ebola Outbreak an International Health Emergency."

45 Centers for Disease Control and Prevention, "Global Smoking."

46 Chen, Evans, and Cash, "Health as a Global Public Good," 288.

47 "World Health Organization Framework Convention on Tobacco Control," *open for signature June 16, 2003*, 2302 U.N.T.S. 166.

48 Chen, Evans, and Cash, "Health as a Global Public Good," 288–289; Kaufman and Nichter, "The Marketing of Tobacco to Women."

49 Christakis and Fowler, "The Collective Dynamics of Smoking in a Large Social Network," 2249–2258.

50 Barboza, "Another Death at Electronics Supplier in China."

CHAPTER 7. CREATING GLOBAL HEALTH

1 Heyd, *Supererogation*, 1.

2 Couch, "Bill Gates' Foundation Gives Its Largest Gift Ever to Combat Ebola Crisis."

3 Foundations do have strict legal obligations to donate once established, but there is no obligation to establish the foundation.

4 GoFundMe, "Your Donation Can Save Funke's Life."

5 Pogge, "Severe Poverty as a Violation of Negative Duties," 55–83.

6 World Health Organization, *Closing the Gap in a Generation*, 1.

7 Dodd and Cassels, "Health, Development, and the Millennium Development Goals," 379–387.

8 GiveWell, "Against Malaria Foundation (AMF)."

9 World Health Organization, "What Are Social Determinants of Health?"

10 Prüss-Üstün and Corvalán, *Preventing Disease through Healthy Environments*.

11 World Health Organization, "Health in the Post-2015 Development Agenda."

12 Ibid., 3.

13 *Economist*, "Not Always with Us," 23.

14 Ibid.

15 Pogge, "Severe Poverty as Violation."

16 Ibid.

17 Pogge, "Are We Violating?," 25.

18 Simons and Goodman, "Ex-Liberian Leader Gets 50 Years for War Crimes"; Pogge, "Are We Violating?," 29; Wenar, "Clean Trade in Natural Resources," 6.

19 Pogge, "Are We Violating?," 29.

20 Heggstad and Fjeldstad, "How Banks Assist Capital Flight from Africa."

21 Pogge, "Are We Violating?," 29.

22 World Trade Organization, "Agreement on Trade-Related Aspects of Intellectual Property Rights."

23 Outterson, "Fair Followers."

24 Prats, *Hunger*, 10; Sumner, "Where Will the World's Poor Live?: Global Poverty Projections for 2020 and 2030."

25 Prats, *Hunger*, 10.

26 United Nations Development Programme, "What Will It Take to Achieve the Millennium Development Goals?" Civil society organizations have shown that countries collecting more than 20 percent of GDP will meet most Millennium Development Goal targets. Chipunza, "Taxation and the MDGs," 1–3; Kohonen, "Tax Justice Is the Missing Ingredient in Achieving the MDGs," 3–4.

27 Prats, *Hunger*, 10.

28 Ibid.

29 Ibid.

30 Ibid.

31 Ibid.

32 Ibid., 11.

33 "Tax in Developing Countries: Increasing Resources for Development," 17.

34 Mathiason, "Western Bankers and Lawyers 'Rob Africa of $150bn Every Year.'"

35 Prats, *Hunger*, 11.

36 Ibid., 18.

37 Ibid.

38 World Bank, "Poverty and Equity: India."

39 Top 10 Companies in India, "Top 10 Multinational Companies in India."

40 Sikarwar, "Multinational Companies Rush to Seal Tax Pacts in Advance."

41 Yardley, "Bangladesh Pollution."

42 Vector-borne diseases are also expected to increase, especially among the elderly, as heat waves increase. Costello et al., "Managing the Health Effects of Climate Change," 1693.

43 Ibid., 1701.

44 Imtiaz and Ur-Rehman, "Death Toll From Karachi, Pakistan, Heat Wave Tops 800."

45 Gills, "2014 Breaks Heat Record."

46 Costello et al., "Managing the Health Effects of Climate Change," 1702.

47 Ibid., 1702–1703.

48 Ibid., 1703.

49 Ibid., 1704.

50 Ibid.

51 Ibid., 1705.

52 Anup Shah, "Climate Change and Global Warming."

53 Ibid.

54 Ibid.

55 Warner and Laczko, "Migration, Environment and Development," 239.

56 Ibid., 235 and 239.

57 Intergovernmental Panel on Climate Change, *Climate Change 2014.*

58 Climate Vulnerable Forum, "Dhaka Ministerial Declaration."

59 United Nations Framework Convention on Climate Change, "The Cancun Agreements."

60 Singer, *One World*; Singer, *The Most Good You Can Do.*

61 Pogge, "Severe Poverty as Violation."

62 Mill, *On Liberty*, 100.

63 Singer, *Practical Ethics.*

64 Bentham, quoted in Mill, *Utilitarianism*, 76.

65 Singer, *Practical Ethics*, 21.

66 Stern, *With Charity for All*, 236n13.

67 Young, "Responsibility and Global Justice," 114.

68 Murphy, "Do Americans Support Global Health Spending?"

CHAPTER 8. STRANGERS FOR THE SAKE OF HEALTH

1 NBC, "African Nurses Head to U.S. for Better Pay."

2 Gostin, "The International Migration and Recruitment of Nurses," 1828.

3 World Health Organization, *The World Health Report 2006.*

4 Gostin, "International Migration and Recruitment," 1827–1829.

5 Mills et al., "The Financial Cost of Doctors Emigrating from Sub-Saharan Africa."

6 World Health Organization, *World Health Report 2006.*

7 Kentikelenis et al., "The International Monetary Fund and the Ebola Outbreak," e69–e70.

8 Gostin, "International Migration and Recruitment," 1827–1829.

9 Mullan, "The Metrics of the Physician Brain Drain," 1810.

10 Ibid.

11 World Health Organization, "Global Health Workforce Shortage to Reach 12.9 Million in Coming Decades."

12 Ibid.

13 Johnson, "Stopping Africa's Medical Brain Drain," 2–3.

14 Gostin, "International Migration and Recruitment," 1828.

15 Ibid.

16 Ibid.

17 Ibid., 1827.

18 Ahmad, "Managing Medical Migration from Poor Countries," 43–45.

19 World Health Organization, "The WHO Global Code of Practice on the International Recruitment of Health Personnel."

20 Chu, Ford, and Trelles, "Operative Mortality in Resource-Limited Settings," 721–725; World Health Organization, *World Health Report 2006*, 9–10.

21 Save the Children, "Whose Charity?"; Martineau, Decker, and Bundred, "Briefing Note on International Migration of Health Professionals."

22 Connell et al., "Sub-Saharan Africa," 1883; Neelakantan, "India's Global Ambitions," 52–54.

23 Connell et al., "Sub-Saharan Africa," 1885.

24 World Bank, "Remittances to Developing Countries to Stay Robust."

25 Stilwell et al., "Migration of Health-Care Workers from Developing," 595–600.

26 Stuart S. Brown, "Can Remittances Spur Development?," 55–75.

27 World Bank, "Remittances to Developing Countries."

28 King, Dalipaj, and Mai, "Gendering Migration and Remittances," 409–434.

29 Stilwell et al., "Migration of Health-Care Workers," 598.

30 Humphries, Brugha, and McGee, "Sending Money Home."

31 Stilwell et al., "Migration of Health-Care Workers," 595.

32 Anand and Bärnighausen, "Human Resources and Health Outcomes," 1609.

33 Miles et al., "Antiretroviral Treatment Roll-Out in a Resource-Constrained Setting," 555–560.

34 Mills et al., "Financial Cost of Doctors Emigrating."

35 Ratha, "Leveraging Remittances for Development," 6.

36 Ibid.

37 Ibid., 7.

38 Ibid.

39 Horowitz and Rosensweig, "Medical Tourism," 24.

40 Grout, "Medical Tourism."

41 Labonté, "Overview: Medical Tourism Today," 8.

42 Chambers, "Thai Embrace of Medical Tourism Divides Professionals."

43 Labonté, "Overview: Medical Tourism Today," 11.

44 Grout, "Medical Tourism."

45 Labonté, "Overview: Medical Tourism Today," 11.

46 Grout, "Medical Tourism."

47 Labonté, "Overview: Medical Tourism Today," 18–20.

48 Ibid., 12.

49 Deloitte Center for Health Solutions, "Medical Tourism: Consumers in Search of Value," 10.

50 Labonté, "Overview: Medical Tourism Today," 12.

51 Rosenthal, "In Need of a New Hip, but Priced Out of the U.S."

52 Biggs and Jones, "Tourism: A Matter of Life and Death in the United Kingdom," 165.

53 British Medical Association, *Changing Conceptions of Motherhood*, 3.

54 Shimazono, "The State of the International Organ Trade," 955–962.

55 Ibid.

56 Scheper-Hughes, "Organs without Borders," 26–27.
57 Shimazono, "International Organ Trade," 958.
58 Ibid.
59 Ibid., 957.
60 Goyal et al., "Economic and Health Consequences of Selling a Kidney in India," 1589–1593.
61 Ibid., 1589.
62 Daniels, *Just Health*.
63 Sen, *Commodities and Capabilities*; Nussbaum and Sen, eds., *Quality of Life*; Nussbaum, *Women and Human Development*; and Venkatapuram, *Health Justice*.
64 Labonté, "Overview: Medical Tourism Today," 29.
65 Ibid., 30.
66 Ibid.
67 Shetty, "Medical Tourism Booms in India," 671–672.
68 Young, *Responsibility for Justice*, 105.

CHAPTER 9. SOLIDARITY FOR NEWCOMERS, HEALTH FOR ALL
1 McGrory, "A Life Filled Up with Love."
2 Donne, "Meditation XVII."
3 Rechel et al., "Migration and Health"; Zallman et al., "Immigrants Contributed."
4 Bosniak, "Citizenship Denationalized," 447–509.
5 Arendt, *Men in Dark Times*, 81, quoted in Bosniak, "Citizenship Denationalized," 448.
6 Walzer, "Citizenship," 211.
7 Marshall, *Citizenship and Social Class*, 20–21.
8 Ibid., 56–58.
9 German Missions in the United States, "Obtaining Citizenship."
10 Schuck and Smith, *Citizenship without Consent*, 130–132.
11 Schwartz, "The Amorality of Consent," 2143–2171.
12 Walzer, *Spheres of Justice*, 35–36.
13 Ibid., 61–63.
14 Ibid.
15 Ibid., 60.
16 Ibid., 60–61.
17 Bosniak, "Universal Citizenship and the Problem of Alienage," 973–974.
18 Dwyer, "Illegal Immigrants, Health Care, and Social Responsibility," 36.
19 Ibid.
20 Marshall, *Citizenship and Social Class*.
21 Harmon, "Solidarity," 218.
22 Ibid.
23 Gunson, "Solidarity and the Universal Declaration on Bioethics and Human Rights," 245.

24 Bayertz, "Four Uses of 'Solidarity,'" quoted in Gunson, "Solidarity and the Universal Declaration," 245.

25 Heyd, "Justice and Solidarity," 120.

26 Tajfel and Billic, "Familiarity and Categorization in Intergroup Behavior," 149–178.

27 Newdick, "Citizenship, Free Movement and Health Care," 1647.

28 Abraham, "Recognizing the Problem of Solidarity," 1645.

29 Ibid.

30 Prainsack and Buyx, "Solidarity in Contemporary Bioethics," 346.

31 Ibid., 347.

32 Ibid., 346.

33 Ibid., 347 (emphasis omitted).

34 Berehulak, "Braving Ebola."

35 Prainsack and Buyx, "Solidarity in Contemporary Bioethics," 347.

36 Frieden, "CDC Director on Ebola Crisis."

37 Manufacturing Chemist, "Air Ticket Tax in France."

38 Frieden, "CDC Director on Ebola Crisis."

39 Camarota and Jensenius, "Jobs Americans Won't Do."

40 Eckenwiler, Long-Term Care, Globalization, and Justice, 40.

41 Moberly, "Minority Report."

42 Pettigrew, "The NHS and International Medical Graduates," 71.

43 Negin et al., "Foreign-Born Health Workers in Australia."

44 Cortés and Pan, "Foreign Nurse Importation to the United States and the Supply of Native Registered Nurses," 6.

45 Eckenwiler, Straehle, and Chung, "Global Solidarity, Migration and Global Health Inequity," 382–390.

46 Campbell, "Invisible Workforce."

47 Collier, Exodus.

48 Biffl and Altenburg, Migration and Health in Nowhereland.

49 Young, Responsibility for Justice, 29.

50 Young, "Responsibility and Global Justice."

51 Young, Responsibility for Justice, 105.

52 Ibid., 121.

53 Ibid., 144–147.

54 Ibid., 146–147.

55 Arguably, occupations that are especially risky should be distributed fairly.

56 Young, Responsibility for Justice, 146.

57 Economist, "How Many Migrants to Europe Are Refugees?"

58 Stojanovic, "Thousands Stranded as EU Countries Close Borders."

59 Parekh, Refugees and the Ethics of Forced Displacement.

60 Gulland, "Refugee Crisis."

61 Abou-Saleh and Hughes, "Mental Health of Syrian Refugees," 870–871.

62 Gostin and Roberts, "Forced Migration," 2125–2126.

63 Pedwell, "Canada to Get up to 50,000 Refugees by End of 2016"; Trump, "Donald J. Trump Statement on Preventing Muslim Immigration"; Healy and Barbaro, "Donald Trump Calls for Barring Muslims."

64 Ibbitson, "How Does Canada Compare When It Comes to Resettling Refugees?"

65 Lum, "John Sewell, Former Toronto Mayor, Explains."

66 *New York Times*, editorial, "Canada's Warm Embrace of Refugees."

67 Kinder and Kam, *Us against Them*.

68 Ibid., 21.

CHAPTER 10. NATIVES AND NEWCOMERS

1 Berman and Brown, "Thomas Duncan, the Texas Ebola Patient, Has Died."

2 US Presidential Commission for the Study of Bioethical Issues, "Ethics and Ebola."

3 Jacobson, "Rep. Phil Gingrey Says Migrants May Be Bringing Ebola Virus."

4 Shain, "Rep. Wilson."

5 Sargent, "Scott Brown."

6 BBC News, "Ebola Crisis."

7 Robbins, Barbaro, and Santora, "Unapologetic, Christie Frees Nurse from Ebola Quarantine."

8 Mayhew v. Hickox.

9 Conservative Treehouse, "Confirmed Suspicions."

10 Associated Press, "10 Years of Tort Reform in Texas."

11 Moyer, "Ebola Victim Thomas Eric Duncan's Family Has Settled."

12 BBC News, "Ebola Basics: What You Need to Know."

13 Stylianou, "How World's Worst Ebola Outbreak Began."

14 Ibid.; Centers for Disease Control and Prevention, "2014 Ebola Outbreak in West Africa."

15 Stoddard and Fletcher, "Surviving Ebola: Africa Cries Out for Healthcare Boost"; *Economist*, "The Toll of a Tragedy."

16 World Health Organization, "Sierra Leone."

17 Jones, "Ebola, Emerging," 5.

18 Skinner, "7,000 People, One Clinic, No Running Water."

19 Jones, "Ebola, Emerging," 4.

20 Ibid.

21 Wolff, *The Human Right to Health*.

22 Ibid., 96.

23 Jones, "Ebola, Emerging," 4.

24 Kentikelenis et al., "IMF and Ebola."

25 Ibid., e69.

26 Gupta, "Response to 'The International Monetary Fund and the Ebola Outbreak,'" e78.

27 Kentikelenis et al., "IMF and Ebola," e69.

28 Kollar and Buyx, "Ethics and Policy of Medical Brain Drain."

29 Ibid.

30 Organisation for Economic Co-operation and Development, "Immigrant Health Workers," 213.

31 Collins, "Liberia's 'Brain Drain.'"

32 Ibid.

33 Barry, "Why This Ebola Outbreak Is Different."

34 *Economist*, "The Ignorance Epidemic."

35 Hamilton, "Ebola Crisis."

36 BBC News, "Ebola Outbreak."

37 Guerrero, "Ebola: How to Prevent a Lethal Legacy for Food Security."

38 World Bank, "The Economic Impact of the 2014 Ebola Epidemic."

39 Gostin and Friedman, "A Retrospective and Prospective Analysis," 1903.

40 Ibid.

41 Ibid.

42 *New York Times*, "Cuba's Impressive Role on Ebola."

43 Ibid.

44 *New York Times*, "Mr. Obama's Historic Move on Cuba."

45 Gostin and Friedman, "A Retrospective and Prospective Analysis," 1905.

46 Von Drehle, "The Ebola Fighters."

47 Gibbs, "The Choice."

48 Lum, "Ron Atkey's Advice to Liberals."

49 Friesen, "Refugee Sponsorship Can Be a Long, Complex Process."

50 Lum, "Ron Atkey's Advice to Liberals."

51 Illingworth, *Us before Me*.

52 La Corte, "An Alternative Way to Resettle the Refugees."

53 Ibid.

54 Lagarde, "Migration."

55 Pogge, "Severe Poverty as Violation."

56 Singer, *One World*.

57 Comm. on Econ., Soc. and Cultural Rights, General Comment No. 14, The Right to the Highest Attainable Standard of Health, ¶ 42, U.N. Doc. E/C 12/2000/4 (Aug. 11, 2000).

58 Hunt, "Report of the Special Rapporteur"; Ruggie, "Guiding Principles on Business and Human Rights."

59 Gostin and Friedman, "A Retrospective and Prospective Analysis."

60 Ibid., 1902.

61 *Time*, "The Directors: The Ebola Fighters in Their Own Words."

62 Coulter, "Ebola Doc's Condition Downgraded to 'Idiotic.'"

63 Opp, "Norms," 10714–10720.

64 Sunstein, "Social Norms and Social Roles," 903–968.

65 El-Assal, "Why Canada Needs a National Immigration Action Plan," as cited in Tencer, "Syrian Refugees Will Boost Economy."

66 Peston, "Why Germany Needs Migrants."

67 Ibid.

68 EU Business, "IMF Sees Silver Lining."

69 Lagarde, "Migration."

70 High-Level Panel on Humanitarian Financing, *Report to the [United Nations] Secretary General: Too Important to Fail—Addressing the Humanitarian Financial Gap* (Jan. 17, 2016), 11.

71 Illingworth and Parmet, "Right to Health."

72 World Health Organization, "Health of Migrants."

73 Fortier et al., "Migrant-Sensitive Health Systems," 5.

74 Ibid.

75 Ibid., 8.

76 Gostin and Roberts, "Forced Migration."

77 Adashi, Geiger, and Fine, "Health Care Reform and Primary Care," 2047–2050; Seo, "Justice Not for All," 143–163.

78 Sheikh et al., "The Epidemiology of Health Conditions of Newly Arrived Refugee Children," 509–513; Johnson-Agbakwu et al., "Mental Health Screening among Newly Arrived Refugees," 470–476.

79 Adashi, Geiger, and Fine, "Health Care Reform and Primary Care."

80 Gottlieb, Myhill, and Blank, "Employment of People with Disabilities," 4.

81 Maloney, Ortega, and Cetron, "Overseas Medical Screening for Immigrants and Refugees," 115–119.

82 Mariner, Annas, and Parmet, "Pandemic Preparedness," 341–382.

83 Putnam, "*E Pluribus Unum*," 150–151.

84 Ibid.

85 Costa and Kahn, "Civic Engagement and Community Heterogeneity," 104.

86 Collier, *Exodus*, 85.

87 Kant, *Critique of Pure Reason*, 473.

88 Kesler and Bloemraad, "Does Immigration Erode Social Capital?," 320.

89 Ibid., 336.

90 De Souza Briggs, "On Half-Blind Men and Elephants," 225.

91 Ibid., 226.

92 Nussbaum, "Patriotism and Cosmopolitanism," 12.

93 Ibid.

94 Ibid., 9.

95 Wynia et al., "Medical Professionalism in Society," 1612–1616.

BIBLIOGRAPHY

Abcarian, Robin. "Obama News Conference: President Says Swine Flu No Reason to Close Border with Mexico." *Top of the Ticket* (blog), *Los Angeles Times*, April 29, 2009. http://latimesblogs.latimes.com.

Abou-Saleh, Mohammed T., and Peter Hughes. "Mental Health of Syrian Refugees: Looking Backwards and Forwards." *Lancet Psychiatry* 2, no. 10 (October 2015): 870–871. doi: 10.1016/S2215-0366(15)00419-8.

Abraham, David. "Recognizing the Problem of Solidarity: Immigration in the Post-Welfare State." *Wayne Law Review* 55, no. 4 (Winter 2009): 1641–1650.

Abrams, Abigail. "Terrorism Attacks since 9/11 Have Involved US Citizens, Not Immigrants, Despite GOP Debate Claim." *International Business Times*, December 16, 2015. http://www.ibtimes.com.

Acevedo-Garcia, Dolores, and Joanna Almeida. "Special Issue Introduction: Place, Migration and Health." *Social Science and Medicine* 75, no. 12 (December 2012): 2055–2059. doi: 10.1016/j.socscimed.2012.09.008.

Adashi, Eli Y., H. Jack Geiger, and Michael D. Fine. "Health Care Reform and Primary Care: The Growing Importance of the Community Health Center." *New England Journal of Medicine* 362, no. 22 (June 3, 2010): 2047–2050. doi: 10.1056/NEJMp1003729.

Agudelo-Suárez, Andrés A., Elena Ronda-Pérez, and Fernando G. Benavides. "Occupational Health." In Rechel et al., *Migration and Health in the European Union*, 155–168.

Ahmad, Omar B. "Managing Medical Migration from Poor Countries." *BMJ* 331, no. 7507 (July 2, 2005): 43–45. doi: 10.1136/bmj.331.7507.43.

AIDS 2012. "International AIDS Conference Opens in the U.S. for the First Time in 22 Years at Defining Moment in the History of the AIDS Epidemic." July 22, 2012. http://www.aids2012.org.

Akresh, Ilana Redstone. "Health Service Utilization among Immigrants to the United States." *Population Research and Policy Review* 28, no. 6 (December 2009): 785–815. doi: 10.1007/s11113-009-9129-6.

Alami, Negar Niki, Courtney M. Yuen, Roque Miramontes, Robert Pratt, Sandy F. Price, and Thomas R. Navin. "Trends in Tuberculosis—United States, 2013." *Morbidity and Mortality Weekly Report* 63, no. 11 (March 21, 2014).

Alvarez, Gonzalo G., Brian Gushulak, Khaled Abu Rumman, Ekkehardt Altpeter, Daniel Chemtob, Paul Douglas, Connie Erkens, et al. "A Comparative Examination of Tuberculosis Immigration Medical Screening Programs from Selected Countries with High Immigration and Low Tuberculosis Incidence Rates." *BMC Infectious Diseases* 11 (2011). doi: 10.1186/1471-2334-11-3.

American Medical Association. "Physician Responsibilities for Safe Patient Discharge." Opinions and Reports of the Council on Ethical and Judicial Affairs, 2009 Interim Meeting.

Anand, Sudhir, and Till Bärnighausen. "Human Resources and Health Outcomes: Cross-Country Econometric Study." *Lancet* 364, no. 9445 (October 30, 2004): 1603–1609. doi: 10.1016/S0140-6736(04)17313-3.

Anderson, Gerard F., Uwe E. Reinhardt, Peter S. Hussey, and Varduhi Petrosyan. "It's the Prices, Stupid: Why the United States Is So Different from Other Countries." *Health Affairs* 22, no. 3 (May 2003): 89–105. doi: 10.1377/hlthaff.22.3.89.

Antecol, Heather, and Kelly Bedard. "Unhealthy Assimilation: Why Do Immigrants Converge to American Health Status Levels?" *Demography* 43, no. 2 (May 2006): 337–360.

Arendt, Hannah. *Men in Dark Times.* New York: Harcourt, Brace and World, 1968.

Arie, Sophie. "Are Migrant Patients Really a Drain on European Health Systems?" *BMJ* 347, no. f6444 (October 29, 2013). doi: 10.1136/bmj.f6444.

———. "How Europe Keeps Migrants Out of Its Health System." *BMJ* 350 (April 24, 2015). doi: 10.1136/bmj.h2216.

Assal, Kareem el-. "Why Canada Needs a National Immigration Action Plan." Conference Board of Canada, April 8, 2015. http://www.conferenceboard.ca.

Associated Press. "10 Years of Tort Reform in Texas Bring Fewer Suits, Lower Payouts." *Insurance Journal*, September 3, 2013. http://www.insurancejournal.com.

Associated Press and Damien Gayle. "Soldiers Spill Blood in Liberian Ebola Slum as Riot Breaks Out over Quarantine of 50,000 Residents." *Daily Mail*, August 21, 2014. http://www.dailymail.co.uk.

Barboza, David. "Another Death at Electronics Supplier in China." *New York Times*, May 22, 2010. http://www.nytimes.com.

Barnes, Steve. "The Real Cost of Cutting Refugee Health Benefits: A Health Equity Impact Assessment." Wellesley Institute, May 2012. http://www.wellesleyinstitute.com.

Barnett, Elizabeth D., and Patricia F. Walker. "Role of Immigrants and Migrants in Emerging Infectious Diseases." *Medical Clinics of North America* 92, no. 6 (November 2008): 1447–1458. doi: 10.1016/j.mcna.2008.07.001.

Barry, Michele. "Why This Ebola Outbreak Is Different." *Boston Review*, October 31, 2014. http://bostonreview.net.

Batlan, Felice. "Law in the Time of Cholera: Disease, State Power, and Quarantines Past and Future." *Temple Law Review* 80, no. 1 (Spring 2007): 53–122.

Bayertz, Kurt. "Four Uses of 'Solidarity.'" In *Solidarity*, edited by Kurt Bayertz, 3–28. Dordrecht, Netherlands: Kluwer, 1999.

Baynton, Douglas C. "Defectives in the Land: Disability and American Immigration Policy, 1882–1924." *Journal of American Ethnic History* 24, no. 3 (Spring 2005): 31–44.

BBC News. "Ebola Basics: What You Need to Know." December 30, 2014. http://www.bbc.com.

———. "Ebola Crisis: Canada Visa Ban Hits West Africa States." November 1, 2014. http://www.bbc.com.

———. "Ebola Outbreak: 'Thousands of Orphans Shunned.'" September 30, 2014. http://www.bbc.com.

———. "Migrant Crisis: Migration to Europe Explained in Graphics." December 22, 2015. http://www.bbc.com.

Ben-Asher, Noa. "Obligatory Health." *Yale Human Rights and Development Law Journal* 15 (2012): 1–18.

Bennhold, Katrin. "From Afar, Moneymaker and Mother." *New York Times*, March 7, 2011. http://www.nytimes.com.

Berehulak, Daniel. "Braving Ebola." *New York Times*, October 31, 2014. http://www.nytimes.com.

Berman, Mark, and DeNeen L. Brown. "Thomas Duncan, the Texas Ebola Patient, Has Died." *Washington Post*, October 8, 2014. http://www.washingtonpost.com.

Biffl, Gudrun. "Access to Health Care in the European Union." In Biffl and Altenburg, *Migration and Health in Nowhereland*, 77–97.

Biffl, Gudrun, and Friedrich Altenburg, eds. *Migration and Health in Nowhereland: Access of Undocumented Migrants to Work and Health Care in Europe*. Bad Vöslau, Austria: Omninum, 2012. http://ec.europa.eu.

Biggs, Hazel, and Caroline Jones. "Tourism: A Matter of Life and Death in the United Kingdom." In *The Globalization of Health Care: Legal and Ethical Issues*, edited by I. Glenn Cohen, 164–181. New York: Oxford University Press, 2013.

Bilefsky, Dan. "Trump's Plan to Bar Muslims Is Widely Condemned Abroad." *New York Times*, December 8, 2015. http://www.nytimes.com.

Björngren-Cuadra, Carin. "Policy towards Undocumented Migrants of the EU 27." In Biffl and Altenburg, *Migration and Health in Nowhereland*, 109–128.

Blaas, Stefan H., Ralf Mütterlein, Johannes Weig, Albert Neher, Bernd Salzberger, Norbert Lehn, and Ludmila Naumann. "Extensively Drug Resistant Tuberculosis in a High Income Country: A Report of Four Unrelated Cases." *BMC Infectious Diseases* 8 (2008). doi: 10.1186/1471-2334-8-60.

Bloomberg. "Satya Nadella: Executive Profile and Biography." Accessed July 2015. http://www.bloomberg.com.

Boerma, Lindsey. "Republican Congressman: Immigrant Children Might Carry Ebola." CBS News, August 5, 2014. http://www.cbsnews.com.

Bollyky, Thomas J. "Developing Symptoms: Noncommunicable Diseases Go Global." *Foreign Affairs* 91, no. 3 (May–June 2012): 134–144.

Bosma, Hans, Michael G. Marmot, Harry Hemingway, Amanda C. Nicholson, Eric Brunner, and Stephen A. Stansfeld. "Low Job Control and Risk of Coronary Heart Disease in Whitehall II (Prospective Cohort) Study." *BMJ* 314, no. 7080 (February 22, 1997): 558–565. doi: 10.1136/bmj.314.7080.558.

Bosniak, Linda. "Citizenship Denationalized." *Indiana Journal of Global Legal Studies* 7, no. 2 (Spring 2000): 447–509.

———. "Universal Citizenship and the Problem of Alienage." *Northwestern University Law Review* 94, no. 3 (Spring 2000): 963–982.

Boston Herald. "Workmen Vaccinated." March 16, 1902, 10.

Branswell, Helen. "Feds and WHO Discuss Canadian Ebola-Related Travel Restrictions." *Globe and Mail* (Toronto), November 7, 2014. http://www.theglobeandmail.com.

British Medical Association. *Changing Conceptions of Motherhood: The Practice of Surrogacy in Britain.* London: BMA Publications, 1996.

Brown, Donathan L. "Manufacturing Fear, Creating the Threat: The State of American Immigration Policy." *Journal of Latino–Latin American Studies* 5, no. 1 (2013): 57–67.

Brown, Stuart S. "Can Remittances Spur Development?: A Critical Survey." *International Studies Review* 8, no. 1 (March 2006): 55–75. doi: 10.1111/j.1468-2486.2006.00553.x.

Browne, Andrew. "China Forces Dozens of Mexican Travelers into Quarantine." *Wall Street Journal*, May 4, 2009. http://www.wsj.com.

Burris, Scott, and Evan Anderson. "Legal Regulation of Health-Related Behavior: A Half Century of Public Health Law Research." *Annual Review of Law and Social Science* 9 (2013): 95–117. doi: 10.1146/annurev-lawsocsci-102612-134011.

California Medical Association House of Delegates. "Forced Deportation of Patients" (Res. 105–08a). October 6, 2008.

Camarota, Steven A. "A Record-Setting Decade of Immigration: 2000–2010." Center for Immigration Studies, October 2011. http://www.cis.org.

Camarota, Steven A., and Karen Jensenius. "Jobs Americans Won't Do?: A Detailed Look at Immigrant Employment by Occupation." Center for Immigration Studies, August 2009. http://www.cis.org.

Campbell, Monica. "Invisible Workforce: An Undocumented Immigrant Caregiver Shares Her Story." *North Dallas Gazette*, May 27, 2013. http://northdallasgazette.com.

Capps, Randolph, Karina Fortuny, and Michael E. Fix. "Trends in the Low-Wage Immigrant Labor Force, 2002–2005." Urban Institute, March 2007. http://www.urban.org.

Capps, Randolph, Michael Fix, Jennifer Van Hook, and James D. Bachmeier. "A Demographic, Socioeconomic, and Health Coverage Profile of Unauthorized Immigrants in the United States." Migration Policy Institute, May 2013. http://www.migrationpolicy.org.

Carter, Sara. "'Potential for a Public Health Disaster': Illegal Immigrant Surge Leaves Officials with 'No Idea' Which Diseases Are Coming Across." *Blaze*, June 24, 2014. http://www.theblaze.com.

Caulford, Paul, and Jennifer D'Andrade. "Health Care for Canada's Medically Uninsured Immigrants and Refugees: Whose Problem Is It?" *Canadian Family Physician* 58, no. 7 (July 2012): 725–727.

Center for Social Justice at Seton Hall Law School (CSJ) and Health Justice Program at New York Lawyers for the Public Interest (NYLPI). "Discharge, Deportation, and Dangerous Journeys: A Study on the Practice of Medical Repatriation." December 2012. http://law.shu.edu.

Centers for Disease Control and Prevention. "DGMQ's Asia Field Program in Thailand." Division of Global Migration and Quarantine. June 2013. http://www.cdc.gov.

———. "Fact Sheets: The Difference between Latent TB Infection and TB Disease." Accessed April 22, 2014. http://www.cdc.gov.

———. "Global Smoking." Last modified February 8, 2011. http://www.cdc.gov.

———. "Interim U.S. Guidance for Monitoring and Movement of Persons with Potential Ebola Virus Exposure." October 9, 2015. http://www.cdc.gov.

———. "Medical Examination of Aliens—Removal of Human Immunodeficiency Virus (HIV) Infection from Definition of Communicable Disease of Public Health Significance." 74 Fed. Reg. 56547 (November 2, 2009).

———. "Self-Study Modules on Tuberculosis." Last modified February 13, 2014. http://www.cdc.gov.

———. "State Ebola Protocols." Accessed 2014. http://www.cdc.gov.

———. "2014 Ebola Outbreak in West Africa: Case Counts." Accessed January 2016. http://www.cdc.gov.

———. "Update: CDC Ebola Response and Interim Guidance." October 27, 2014. http://www.cdc.gov.

Chambers, Andrew. "Thai Embrace of Medical Tourism Divides Professionals." *Guardian* (Manchester), April 26, 2011. http://www.theguardian.com.

Chen, Jiajian, Edward Ng, and Russell Wilkins. "The Health of Canada's Immigrants in 1994–95." *Health Reports* 7, no. 4 (Spring 1996): 33–45.

Chen, Jiajian, Russell Wilkins, and Edward Ng. "Health Expectancy by Immigrant Status, 1986 and 1991." *Health Reports* 8, no. 3 (Winter 1996): 29–38.

Chen, Lincoln C., Tim G. Evans, and Richard A. Cash. "Health as a Global Public Good." In Kaul, Grunberg, and Stern, *Global Public Goods*, 284–304.

Chipunza, Fiona. "Taxation and the MDGs." *Africa Tax Spotlight* (Tax Justice Network Africa) no. 4 (2010): 1–3. http://www.taxjusticeafrica.net.

Chong, Jai-Rui. "Diagnosis Changed for TB Patient." *Los Angeles Times*, July 20, 2007. http://articles.latimes.com.

Chrisafis, Angelique. "Man Guilty of Infecting Two Women with HIV." *Guardian* (Manchester), October 14, 2003. http://www.theguardian.com.

Christakis, Nicholas A., and James H. Fowler. "The Collective Dynamics of Smoking in a Large Social Network." *New England Journal of Medicine* 358, no. 21 (May 22, 2008): 2249–2258. doi: 10.1056/NEJMsa0706154.

———. *Connected: The Surprising Power of Our Social Networks and How They Shape Our Lives.* New York: Little, Brown, 2009.

Chu, Kathryn M., Nathan Ford, and Miguel Trelles. "Operative Mortality in Resource-Limited Settings: The Experience of Médecins Sans Frontières in 13 Countries." *Archives of Surgery* 145, no. 8 (August 2010): 721–725. doi: 10.1001/archsurg.2010.137.

Citizenship and Immigration Canada (CIC). "Determine Your Eligibility and Coverage Type: Interim Federal Health Program." Accessed January 21, 2015. http://www.cic.gc.ca.

———. "Interim Federal Health Program: Summary of Benefits." Accessed January 21, 2015. http://www.cic.gc.ca.

Clary, Mike. "Death of Refugee with AIDS Renews Controversy: Immigration: Haitian's Case Sets Off New Criticism of Clinton's Policy of Refusing to Parole Sick Migrants. Guantanamo Is Called 'a Potential Waco.'" *Los Angeles Times*, April 30, 1993. http://articles.latimes.com.

Clemans-Cope, Lisa, Genevieve M. Kenney, Matthew Buettgens, Caitlin Carroll, and Fredric Blavin. "The Affordable Care Act's Coverage Expansions Will Reduce Differences in Uninsurance Rates by Race and Ethnicity." *Health Affairs* 31, no. 5 (May 2012): 920–930. doi: 10.1377/hlthaff.2011.1086.

Climate Vulnerable Forum. "Dhaka Ministerial Declaration of the Climate Vulnerable Forum." November 14, 2011. http://www.thecvf.org.

Cochran, Jennifer, Ann O'Fallon, and Paul L. Geltman. "US Medical Screening for Immigrants and Refugees: Public Health Issues." In Walker and Barnett, *Immigrant Medicine*, 123–134.

Coker, Richard. *From Chaos to Coercion: Detention and the Control of Tuberculosis.* New York: St. Martin's, 2000.

Collier, Paul. *Exodus: How Migration Is Changing Our World.* New York: Oxford University Press, 2013.

Collins, Sam P. K. "Liberia's 'Brain Drain' Is Thwarting Its Efforts to Stop Ebola." Think Progress, October 20, 2014. http://thinkprogress.org.

Connell, John, Pascal Zurn, Barbara Stilwell, Magda Awases, and Jean-Marc Braichet. "Sub-Saharan Africa: Beyond the Health Worker Migration Crisis?" *Social Science and Medicine* 64, no. 9 (May 2007): 1876–1891. doi: 10.1016/j.socscimed.2006.12.013.

Conservative Treehouse. "Confirmed Suspicions—Patient Zero, Thomas Eric Duncan, Came to U.S. to Get Treatment for His Ebola Exposure." October 1, 2014. http://theconservativetreehouse.com.

Cortés, Patricia, and Jessica Pan. "Foreign Nurse Importation to the United States and the Supply of Native Registered Nurses." Working Paper No. 14-7, Federal Reserve Bank of Boston, July 31, 2014. http://www.bostonfed.org.

Cortez, Nathan. "Embracing the New Geography of Health Care: A Novel Way to Cover Those Left Out of Health Reform." *Southern California Law Review* 84, no. 4 (May 2011): 859–932.

Costa, Dora L., and Matthew E. Kahn. "Civic Engagement and Community Heterogeneity: An Economist's Perspective." *Perspectives on Politics* 1, no. 1 (March 2003): 103–111. doi: 10.1017/S1537592703000082.

Costello, Anthony, Mustafa Abbas, Adriana Allen, Sarah Ball, Sarah Bell, Richard Bellamy, Sharon Friel, et al. "Managing the Health Effects of Climate Change." *Lancet* 373, no. 9676 (May 16–22, 2009): 1693–1733. doi: 10.1016/S0140-6736(09)60935-1.

Couch, Robbie. "Bill Gates' Foundation Gives Its Largest Gift Ever to Combat Ebola Crisis." *Huffington Post*, September 12, 2014. http://www.huffingtonpost.com.

Coulter, Ann. "Ebola Doc's Condition Downgraded to 'Idiotic.'" AnnCoulter.com, August 6, 2014. http://www.anncoulter.com.

Council of Canadians with Disabilities. "Immigration and Disability: Stephen Hawking Could Never Become a Canadian." 2013. http://www.ccdonline.ca.

Cousins, Sophie. "Experts Sound Alarm as Syrian Crisis Fuels Spread of Tuberculosis." *BMJ* 349 (December 3, 2014). doi: 10.1136/bmj.g7397.

Cowell, Alan, and Nick Cumming-Bruce. "U.N. Agency Calls Ebola Outbreak an International Health Emergency." *New York Times*, August 8, 2014. http://www.nytimes.com.

Daniels, Norman. *Just Health: Meeting Health Needs Fairly*. New York: Cambridge University Press, 2008.

De Souza Briggs, Xavier. "On Half-Blind Men and Elephants: Understanding Greater Ethnic Diversity and Responding to 'Good-Enough' Evidence." *Housing Policy Debate* 19, no. 1 (2008): 218–229. doi: 10.1080/10511482.2008.9521632.

Delamothe, Tony. "Migrant Healthcare: Public Health versus Politics." *BMJ* 344, no. e924 (February 8, 2012). doi: 10.1136/bmj.e924.

Deloitte Center for Health Solutions. "Medical Tourism: Consumers in Search of Value." 2008.

DeNavas-Walt, Carmen, Bernadette D. Proctor, and Jessica C. Smith. "Income, Poverty, and Health Insurance Coverage in the United States: 2010." Report P60-239, Current Population Reports, US Census Bureau, September 2011. http://www.census.gov.

Derose, Kathryn Pitkin, Benjamin W. Bahney, Nicole Lurie, and José J. Escarce. "Immigrants and Health Care Access, Quality, and Cost." *Medical Care Research and Review* 66, no. 4 (August 2009): 355–408. doi: 10.1177/1077558708330425.

Derose, Kathryn Pitkin, José J. Escarce, and Nicole Lurie. "Immigrants and Health Care: Sources of Vulnerability." *Health Affairs* 26, no. 5 (September 2007): 1258–1268. doi: 10.1377/hlthaff.26.5.1258.

Di Costanzo, Melissa. "Autistic Son Denied Entry." *Cornwall Standard Freeholder*, May 5, 2011. http://www.standard-freeholder.com.

Diamond, Michelle Nicole. "Legal Triage for Healthcare Reform: The Conflict between the ACA and EMTALA." *Columbia Human Rights Law Review* 43, no. 1 (Fall 2011): 255–299.

Dodd, Rebecca, and Andrew Cassels. "Health, Development, and the Millennium Development Goals." *Annals of Tropical Medicine and Parasitology* 100, no. 5–6 (August 2006): 379–387. doi: 10.1179/136485906X97471.

Dolgin, Janet L., and Katherine R. Dieterich. "When Others Get Too Close: Immigrants, Class, and the Health Care Debate." *Cornell Journal of Law and Public Policy* 19, no. 2 (Spring 2010): 283–334.

Donne, John. "Meditation XVII." In *Devotions upon Emergent Occasions*. 1624.

DuBard, C. Annette, and Mark W. Massing. "Trends in Emergency Medicaid Expenditures for Recent and Undocumented Immigrants." *Journal of the American Medical Association* 297, no. 10 (March 14, 2007): 1085–1092. doi: 10.1001/jama.297.10.1085.

Dwyer, James. "Illegal Immigrants, Health Care, and Social Responsibility." *Hastings Center Report* 34, no. 1 (January–February 2004): 36–43. doi: 10.2307/3528249.

Eckenwiler, Lisa. *Long-Term Care, Globalization, and Justice*. Baltimore: John Hopkins University Press, 2012.

Eckenwiler, Lisa, Christine Straehle, and Ryoa Chung. "Global Solidarity, Migration and Global Health Inequity." *Bioethics* 26, no. 7 (September 2012): 382–390. doi: 10.1111/j.1467-8519.2012.01991.x.

Economist. "How Many Migrants to Europe Are Refugees?" September 7, 2015. http://www.economist.com.

———. "The Ignorance Epidemic." November 15, 2014. http://www.economist.com.

———. "Not Always with Us." June 1, 2013. http://www.economist.com.

———. "The Toll of a Tragedy." July 8, 2015. http://www.economist.com.

Elgersma, Sandra. "Immigration Status and Legal Entitlement to Insured Health Services" (PRB 08-28E). Political and Social Affairs Division, Parliamentary Information and Research Service, Library of Parliament (Canada). October 28, 2008. http://www.parl.gc.ca.

Epstein, Joshua M., D. Michael Goedecke, Feng Yu, Robert J. Morris, Diane K. Wagener, and Georgiy V. Bobashev. "Controlling Pandemic Flu: The Value of International Air Travel Restrictions." *PLoS ONE* 2, no. 5 (2007): e401. doi: 10.1371/journal.pone.0000401.

EU Business. "IMF Sees Silver Lining in EU Migrant Crisis." October 6, 2015. http://www.eubusiness.com.

Fairchild, Amy L. "Policies of Inclusion: Immigrants, Disease, Dependency, and American Immigration Policy at the Dawn and Dusk of the 20th Century." *American Journal of Public Health* 94, no. 4 (April 2004): 528–539. doi: 10.2105/AJPH.94.4.528.

———. *Science at the Borders: Immigrant Medical Inspection and the Shaping of the Modern Industrial Labor Force*. Baltimore: Johns Hopkins University Press, 2003.

Fortier, Julia Puebla, et al. "Migrant-Sensitive Health Systems." Global Consultation on Migrant Health, National School of Public Health, Madrid, March 3–5, 2010. http://www.who.int.

Fortuny, Karina, and Ajay Chaudry. "A Comprehensive Review of Immigrant Access to Health and Human Services." Urban Institute, June 2011. http://www.urban.org.

Fried, Linda P. "Longevity and Aging: The Success of Global Public Health." In *Routledge Handbook of Global Public Health*, edited by Richard Parker and Marni Sommer. New York: Routledge, 2011.

Frieden, Thomas R. "CDC Director on Ebola Crisis: Why I Am Going to Africa." *CDC Director Blog* (blog), Centers for Disease Control and Prevention, August 22, 2014. http://blogs.cdc.gov.

Frieden, Thomas R., Paula I. Fujiwara, Rita M. Washko, and Margaret A. Hamburg. "Tuberculosis in New York City—Turning the Tide." *New England Journal of Medicine* 333, no. 4 (July 27, 1995): 229–233. doi: 10.1056/NEJM199507273330406.

Friesen, Joe. "Refugee Sponsorship Can Be a Long, Complex Process—Here's How It Works." *Globe and Mail* (Toronto), September 10, 2015. http://www.theglobeandmail.com.

Galewitz, Phil. "States Balk at Expanding Medicaid." Kaiser Health News, July 2, 2012. http://kaiserhealthnews.org.

Garcia, Maria Cristina. "Canada: A Northern Refuge for Central Americans." Migration Policy Institute, April 2006. http://www.migrationpolicy.org.

Garrett, Laurie. *The Coming Plague: Newly Emerging Diseases in a World out of Balance*. New York: Penguin, 1994.

German Missions in the United States. "Obtaining Citizenship." Accessed January 23, 2015. http://www.germany.info.

Gibbs, Nancy. "The Choice." *Time*, December 10, 2014. http://time.com.

Gilbert, Ruth L., D. Antoine, C. E. French, I. Abubakar, J. M. Watson, and J. A. Jones. "The Impact of Immigration on Tuberculosis Rates in the United Kingdom Compared with Other European Countries." *International Journal of Tuberculosis and Lung Disease* 13, no. 5 (May 2009): 645–651.

Gills, Justin. "2014 Breaks Heat Record, Challenging Global Warming Skeptics." *New York Times*, January 16, 2015. http://www.nytimes.com.

GiveWell. "Against Malaria Foundation (AMF)." Accessed July 2015. http://www.givewell.org.

GoFundMe. "Your Donation Can Save Funke's Life." Accessed June 2015. http://www.gofundme.com.

Goldstein, Amy. "Administration Warns Some Could Lose Health-Care Coverage on Federal Exchanges." *Washington Post*, August 12, 2014. http://www.washingtonpost.com.

Gornall, Jonathan. "Healthcare for Syrian Refugees." *BMJ* 351 (August 4, 2015). doi: 10.1136/bmj.h4150.

Gostin, Lawrence O. "The International Migration and Recruitment of Nurses: Human Rights and Global Justice." *Journal of the American Medical Association* 299, no. 15 (April 16, 2008): 1827–1829. doi: 10.1001/jama.299.15.1827.

———. *Public Health Law: Power, Duty, Restraint*. 2nd ed. Berkeley: University of California Press, 2008.

Gostin, Lawrence O., and Eric A. Friedman. "A Retrospective and Prospective Analysis of the West African Ebola Virus Disease Epidemic: Robust National Health Systems at the Foundation and an Empowered WHO at the Apex." *Lancet* 385, no. 9980 (May 9, 2015): 1902–1909. doi: 10.1016/S0140-6736(15)60644-4.

Gostin, Lawrence O., and Anna E. Roberts. "Forced Migration: The Human Face of a Health Crisis." *Journal of the American Medical Association* 314, no. 20 (November 24, 2015): 2125–2126. doi: 10.1001/jama.2015.14906.

Gottlieb, Aaron, William N. Myhill, and Peter Blanck. "Employment of People with Disabilities." *International Encyclopedia of Rehabilitation*. 2010. http://bbi.syr.edu.

Goyal, Madhav, Ravindra L. Mehta, Lawrence J. Schneiderman, and Ashwini R. Sehgal. "Economic and Health Consequences of Selling a Kidney in India." *Journal of the American Medical Association* 288, no. 13 (October 2, 2002): 1589–1593. doi: 10.1001/jama.288.13.1589.

Gray, Bradford H., and Ewout van Ginneken. "Health Care for Undocumented Migrants: European Approaches." Publication 1650, Commonwealth Fund, December 6, 2012. http://www.commonwealthfund.org.

Greenaway, Christina, Amelia Sandoe, Bilkis Vissandjee, Ian Kitai, Doug Gruner, Wendy Wobeser, Kevin Pottie, Erin Ueffing, Dick Menzies, and Kevin Schwartzman. "Tuberculosis: Evidence Review for Newly Arriving Immigrants and Refugees." *Canadian Medical Association Journal* 183, no. 12 (September 6, 2011): E939–E951. doi: 10.1503/cmaj.090302.

Greenwood, Michael J., and Watson R. Warriner. "Immigrants and the Spread of Tuberculosis in the United States: A Hidden Cost of Immigration." *Population Research and Policy Review* 30, no. 6 (December 2011): 839–859. doi: 10.1007/s11113-011-9213-6.

Grieco, Elizabeth M., Yesenia D. Acosta, G. Patricia de la Cruz, Christine Gambino, Thomas Gryn, Luke J. Larsen, Edward N. Trevelyan, and Nathan P. Walters. "The Foreign-Born Population in the United States: 2010." US Census Bureau, May 2012. http://www.census.gov.

Grit, Kor, Joost J. den Otter, and Anneke Spreij. "Access to Health Care for Undocumented Migrants: A Comparative Policy Analysis of England and the Netherlands." *Journal of Health Politics, Policy and Law* 37, no. 1 (February 2012): 37–67. doi: 10.1215/03616878-1496011.

Grout, Pam. "Medical Tourism: A Global Stampede for Affordable Care." CNN Travel, March 22, 2013. http://travel.cnn.com.

Guerrero, Saul. "Ebola: How to Prevent a Lethal Legacy for Food Security." *Guardian* (Manchester), February 23, 2015. http://www.theguardian.com.

Gulland, Anne. "The Refugee Crisis: What Care Is Needed and How Can Doctors Help?" *BMJ* 351 (September 10, 2015). doi: 10.1136/bmj.h4881.

———. "Refugees Pose Little Health Risk, Says WHO." *BMJ* 351 (September 8, 2015). doi: 10.1136/bmj.h4808.

Gunson, Darryl. "Solidarity and the Universal Declaration on Bioethics and Human Rights." *Journal of Medicine and Philosophy* 34, no. 3 (June 2009): 241–260. doi: 10.1093/jmp/jhp022.

Gupta, Sanjeev. "Response to 'The International Monetary Fund and the Ebola Outbreak.'" *Lancet Global Health* 3, no. 2 (February 2015): e78. doi: 10.1016/S2214-109X(14)70345-6.

Haidt, Jonathan. *The Righteous Mind: Why Good People Are Divided by Politics and Religion*. New York: Pantheon, 2012.

Hall, Matthew, Audrey Singer, Gordon F. De Jong, and Deborah Roempke Graefe. "The Geography of Immigrant Skills: Educational Profiles of Metropolitan Areas." Metropolitan Policy Program, Brookings Institution, June 2011. http://www.brookings.edu.

Hamilton, Richard. "Ebola Crisis: The Economic Impact." BBC News, August 21, 2014. http://www.bbc.com.

Hammel, Paul. "Prenatal Care a 'Magnet' for Illegal Immigrants?" *Omaha (NE) World-Herald*, April 10, 2012. Accessed September 30, 2012. http://www.omaha.com.

Harmon, Shawn H. E. "Solidarity: A (New) Ethic for Global Health Policy." *Health Care Analysis* 14, no. 4 (December 2006): 215–236. doi: 10.1007/s10728-006-0030-8.

Healy, Patrick, and Michael Barbaro. "Donald Trump Calls for Barring Muslims From Entering U.S." *First Draft* (blog), *New York Times*, December 7, 2015. http://www.nytimes.com.

Heggstad, Kari, and Odd-Helge Fjeldstad. "How Banks Assist Capital Flight from Africa: A Literature Review" (R2010:6). Chr. Michelsen Institute, 2010. http://www.cmi.no.

Hennessy-Fiske, Molly, and Cindy Carcamo. "In Texas' Rio Grande Valley, a Seemingly Endless Surge of Immigrants." *Los Angeles Times*, June 13, 2014. http://www.latimes.com.

Heyd, David. "Justice and Solidarity: The Contractarian Case against Global Justice." *Journal of Social Philosophy* 38, no. 1 (Spring 2007): 112–130. doi: 10.1111/j.1467-9833.2007.00369.x.

———. *Supererogation: Its Status in Ethical Theory*. Cambridge: Cambridge University Press, 1982.

High-Level Panel on Humanitarian Financing. "Report to the [United Nations] Secretary General: Too Important to Fail—Addressing the Humanitarian Financial Gap." January 2016. http://reliefweb.int.

Hirsch-Moverman, Yael, A. Daftary, J. Franks, and P. W. Colson. "Adherence to Treatment for Latent Tuberculosis Infection: Systematic Review of Studies in the US and Canada." *International Journal of Tuberculosis and Lung Disease* 12, no. 11 (November 2008): 1235–1254.

Horner, Jed, James G. Wood, and Angela Kelly. "Public Health in/as 'National Security': Tuberculosis and the Contemporary Regime of Border Control in Australia." *Critical Public Health* 23, no. 4 (December 2013): 418–431. doi: 10.1080/09581596.2013.824068.

Horowitz, Michael D., and Jeffrey A. Rosensweig. "Medical Tourism: Health Care in the Global Economy." *Physician Executive* 33, no. 6 (November–December 2007): 24–30.

Hsia, Renee Y., Arthur L. Kellermann, and Yu-Chu Shen. "Factors Associated with Closures of Emergency Departments in the United States." *Journal of the American Medical Association* 305, no. 19 (May 18, 2011): 1978–1985. doi: 10.1001/jama.2011.620.

Hulse, Carl. "In Lawmaker's Outburst, a Rare Breach of Protocol." *New York Times*, September 9, 2009. http://www.nytimes.com.

Human Rights Watch. "Hungary: Abysmal Conditions in Border Detention." September 11, 2015. http://www.hrw.org.

Humphries, Niamh, Ruairí Brugha, and Hannah McGee. "Sending Money Home: A Mixed-Methods Study of Remittances by Migrant Nurses in Ireland." *Human Resources for Health* 7, no. 66 (July 2009). doi: 10.1186/1478-4491-7-66.

Hunt, Paul. "Report of the Special Rapporteur on the Right of Everyone to the Enjoyment of the Highest Attainable Standard of Physical and Mental Health: Annex;

Mission to GlaxoSmithKlein," UN Doc. A/HRC/11/12/Add.2 (2009). http://www. refworld.org.

Hurley, Laura, Allison Kempe, Lori A. Crane, Arthur Davidson, Katherine Pratte, Stuart Linas, L. Miriam Dickinson, and Tomas Berl. "Care of Undocumented Individuals with ESRD: A National Survey of US Nephrologists." *American Journal of Kidney Diseases* 53, no. 6 (June 2009): 940–949. doi: 10.1053/j. ajkd.2008.12.029.

Iacoboni, Marco. *Mirroring People: The Science of Empathy and How We Connect with Others.* New York: Picador, 2009.

Ibbitson, John. "How Does Canada Compare When It Comes to Resettling Refugees?" *Globe and Mail* (Toronto), December 31, 2015. http://www.theglobeandmail. com.

Illingworth, Patricia. *Us before Me: Ethics and Social Capital for Global Well-Being.* New York: Palgrave Macmillan, 2012.

Illingworth, Patricia, and Wendy E. Parmet. "The Right to Health: Why It Should Apply to Immigrants." *Public Health Ethics* 8, no. 1 (April 2015): 1–14. doi: 10.1093/phe/ phv007.

Imtiaz, Saba, and Zia Ur-Rehman. "Death Toll From Karachi, Pakistan, Heat Wave Tops 800." *New York Times,* June 24, 2015. http://www.nytimes.com.

Institute of International Education. "A Quick Look at International Students in the U.S." Last modified 2014. http://www.iie.org.

Institute of Medicine. *Care without Coverage: Too Little, Too Late.* Washington, DC: National Academies Press, 2002.

———. *A Shared Destiny: Community Effects of Uninsurance.* Washington, DC: National Academies Press, 2003.

Intergovernmental Panel on Climate Change. *Climate Change 2014: Synthesis Report.* Geneva: IPCC, 2014. http://www.ipcc.ch.

International Organization for Migration. "Global Migration Trends: An Overview." December 2014. http://missingmigrants.iom.int.

———. "Irregular Migrant, Refugee Arrivals in Europe Top One Million in 2015: IOM." December 22, 2015. http://www.iom.int.

———. *World Migration Report 2013: Migrant Well-Being and Development.* Geneva: International Organization for Migration, 2013. http://publications.iom.int.

International Organization for Migration (IOM), World Health Organization (WHO), and Office of the United Nations High Commissioner for Human Rights (OHCHR). *International Migration, Health and Human Rights.* Geneva: IOM, 2013. http://publications.iom.int.

Ipsos. "Global Views on Immigration." August 2011. http://www.ipsos.fr.

IRIN News. "South Africa: Prison-Like Hospitals for Drug-Resistant TB Patients." March 25, 2008. http://www.irinnews.org.

Jacobson, Louis. "Rep. Phil Gingrey Says Migrants May Be Bringing Ebola Virus through the U.S.-Mexico Border." *PolitiFact* (blog), *Tampa Bay Times,* July 18, 2014. http://www.politifact.com.

Jean, David. "SA Police Recruit Denied Entry." *Advertiser* (Adelaide), June 12, 2012. http://www.adelaidenow.com.au.

Johnson, James. "Stopping Africa's Medical Brain Drain: The Rich Countries of the North Must Stop Looting Doctors and Nurses from Developing Countries." *BMJ* 331, no. 7507 (July 2, 2005): 2–3. doi: 10.1136/bmj.331.7507.2.

Johnson-Agbakwu, Crista E., Jennifer Allen, Jeanne F. Nizigiyimana, Glenda Ramirez, and Michael Hollifield. "Mental Health Screening among Newly Arrived Refugees Seeking Routine Obstetric and Gynecologic Care." *Psychological Services* 11, no. 4 (November 2014): 470–476. doi: 10.1037/a0036400.

Joint United Nations Programme on HIV/AIDS (UNAIDS). "HIV-Related Restrictions on Entry, Stay, and Residence." Last modified January 2013. http://www.unaids.org.

———. *Mapping of Restrictions on the Entry, Stay and Residence of People Living with HIV.* Geneva: UNAIDS, 2009. http://www.unaids.org.

———. *Report of the International Task Team on HIV-Related Travel Restrictions: Findings and Recommendations, December 2008.* Geneva: UNAIDS, 2008. http://www.unaids.org.

Joint United Nations Programme on HIV/AIDS (UNAIDS) and World Health Organization (WHO). *AIDS Epidemic Update: December 2009.* Geneva: UNAIDS, 2009. http://data.unaids.org.

Jones, Jared. "Ebola, Emerging: The Limitations of Culturalist Discourses in Epidemiology." *Journal of Global Health* (Columbia University) 1, no. 1 (Spring 2011): 1–6. http://www.ghjournal.org.

Kaiser Commission on Medicaid and the Uninsured. "Five Basic Facts on Immigrants and Their Health Care." Kaiser Family Foundation, March 2008. http://kaiserfamilyfoundation.files.wordpress.com.

———. "How Race/Ethnicity, Immigration Status and Language Affect Health Insurance Coverage, Access to Care and Quality of Care among the Low-Income Population." Kaiser Family Foundation, August 2003. http://kaiserfamilyfoundation.files.wordpress.com.

———. "Immigrants' Access to Health Care after Welfare Reform: Findings from Focus Groups in Four Cities." Kaiser Family Foundation, 2000. Accessed September 15, 2012. http://kaiserfamilyfoundation.files.wordpress.com.

———. "Immigrants' Health Coverage and Health Reform: Key Questions and Answers." Kaiser Family Foundation, December 2009. http://kaiserfamilyfoundation.files.wordpress.com.

Kaiser Family Foundation. "Key Facts about the Uninsured Population." October 5, 2015. http://kff.org.

———. "Medicaid/CHIP Coverage of Lawfully-Residing Immigrant Children and Pregnant Women." January 1, 2015. http://kff.org.

———. "NPR/Kaiser/Kennedy School Immigration Survey." September 29, 2004. http://kaiserfamilyfoundation.files.wordpress.com.

Kandula, Namratha R., Colleen M. Grogan, Paul J. Rathouz, and Diane S. Lauderdale. "The Unintended Impact of Welfare Reform on the Medicaid Enrollment of Eligible

Immigrants." *Health Services Research* 39, no. 5 (October 2004): 1509–1526. doi: 10.1111/j.1475-6773.2004.00301.x.

Kant, Immanuel. *Critique of Pure Reason.* Translated by Norman Kemp Smith. London: Macmillan, 1933.

Kaufman, Nancy J., and Mimi Nichter. "The Marketing of Tobacco to Women: Global Perspectives." In *Gender, Women, and the Tobacco Epidemic,* edited by Jonathan M. Samet and Soon-Young Yoon, 105–136. Geneva: World Health Organization, 2010. http://www.who.int.

Kaul, Inge, Isabelle Grunberg, and Marc A. Stern. "Defining Global Public Goods." In Kaul, Grunberg, and Stern, *Global Public Goods,* 2–19.

———, eds. *Global Public Goods: International Cooperation in the 21st Century.* New York: Oxford University Press, 1999.

Keane, V. P., and B. D. Gushulak. "The Medical Assessment of Migrants: Current Limitations and Future Potential." *International Migration* 39, no. 2 (June 2001): 29–42. doi: 10.1111/1468-2435.00148.

Kennedy, Steven, James Ted McDonald, and Nicholas Biddle. "The Healthy Immigrant Effect and Immigrant Selection: Evidence from Four Countries." SEDAP Research Paper No. 164, McMaster University, Hamilton, ON, Canada, December 2006.

Kentikelenis, Alexander, Lawrence King, Martin McKee, and David Stuckler. "The International Monetary Fund and the Ebola Outbreak." *Lancet Global Health* 3, no. 2 (February 2015): e69–e70. doi: 10.1016/S2214-109X(14)70377-8.

Kenyon, Thomas, Cynthia Driver, Elisabeth Haas, Sarah E. Valway, Kathleen S. Moser, and Ida M. Onorato. "Immigration and Tuberculosis among Children on the United States–Mexico Border, County of San Diego, California." *Pediatrics* 104, no. 1 (July 1999): 103.

Kesler, Christel, and Irene Bloemraad. "Does Immigration Erode Social Capital?: The Conditional Effects of Immigration-Generated Diversity on Trust, Membership, and Participation across 19 Countries, 1981–2000." *Canadian Journal of Political Science* 43, no. 2 (June 2010): 319–347. doi: 10.1017oS0008423910000077.

Keung, Nicholas. "Canada Faces Dramatic Drop in Citizenship, Prompting Concerns about Disengaged Immigrants." *Toronto Star,* March 24, 2015. http://www.thestar.com.

Kiefer, Michael. "Lawyers Confer on Patient's Fate." *Arizona Republic,* May 18, 2008.

Kim, Miyong, Hae-Ra Han, Kim B. Kim, and Diep N. Duong. "The Use of Traditional and Western Medicine among Korean American Elderly." *Journal of Community Health* 27, no. 2 (April 2002): 109–120. doi: 10.1023/A:1014509200352.

Kinder, Donald R., and Cindy D. Kam. *Us against Them: Ethnocentric Foundations of American Opinion.* Chicago: University of Chicago Press, 2009.

King, Meredith L. "Immigrants in the U.S. Health Care System: Five Myths That Misinform the American Public." Center for American Progress, June 7, 2007. http://cdn.americanprogress.org.

King, Russell, Mirela Dalipaj, and Nicola Mai. "Gendering Migration and Remittances: Evidence from London and Northern Albania." *Population, Space and Place* 12, no. 6 (2006): 409–434. doi: 10.1002/psp.439.

Knoll, Benjamin R., and Jordan Shewmaker. "It's Not Just Immigration Anymore: Nativism and Support for Health Care Reform." Paper presented at the American Political Science Association Conference, New Orleans, LA, August 30–September 2, 2012.

Knox, Richard. "Arizona TB Patient Jailed as a Public Health Menace." *Morning Edition*, National Public Radio, June 11, 2007. http://www.npr.org.

Kohonen, Matti. "Tax Justice is the Missing Ingredient in Achieving the MDGs." *Africa Tax Spotlight* (Tax Justice Network Africa) no. 4 (2010): 3–4. http://www.taxjusticeafrica.net.

Kollar, Eszter, and Alena Buyx. "Ethics and Policy of Medical Brain Drain: A Review." *Swiss Medical Weekly* 143 (2013). doi: 10.4414/smw.2013.13845.

Kraut, Alan M. *Silent Travelers: Germs, Genes, and the "Immigrant Menace."* Baltimore: Johns Hopkins University Press, 1995.

Labonté, Ronald. "Overview: Medical Tourism Today; What, Who, Why and Where?" In *Travelling Well: Essays in Medical Tourism* (Transdisciplinary Studies in Population Health 4, no. 1), edited by Ronald Labonté, Vivien Runnels, Corinne Packer, and Raywat Deonandan, 6–42. Ottawa: Institute of Population Health, University of Ottawa, 2013. http://www.ruor.uottawa.ca.

La Corte, Matthew. "An Alternative Way to Resettle the Refugees." *Wall Street Journal*, September 10, 2015. http://www.wsj.com.

Lagarde, Christine. "Migration: A Global Issue in Need of a Global Solution." *IMF Direct* (blog), International Monetary Fund, November 11, 2015. http://blog-imfdirect.imf.org.

Leavitt, Judith Walzer. "Typhoid Mary: Villain or Victim?" *Nova*, PBS. October 12, 2004. http://www.pbs.org.

Lebrun, Lydie A., and Lisa C. Dubay. "Access to Primary and Preventive Care among Foreign-Born Adults in Canada and the United States." *Health Services Research* 45, no. 6 (December 2010): 1693–1719. doi: 10.1111/j.1475-6773.2010.01163.x.

Lee, Michelle Ye Hee. "Donald Trump's False Comments Connecting Mexican Immigrants and Crime." *Fact Checker* (blog), *Washington Post*, July 8, 2015. http://www.washingtonpost.com.

Lerner, Barron II. "Catching Patients: Tuberculosis and Detention in the 1990s." *Chest* 115, no. 1 (January 1999): 236–241. doi: 10.1378/chest.115.1.236.

Levitan, Dave. "Mo Brooks, Ben Carson Share False Narratives on Measles Outbreak." *Huffington Post*, February 5, 2015. http://www.huffingtonpost.com.

Lin, Shin-Rou. "A Costly Illusion?: An Empirical Study of Taiwan's Use of Isolation to Control Tuberculosis Transmission and Its Implications for Public Health Law and Policymaking." *Asian-Pacific Law and Policy Journal* 14, no. 3 (2013): 107–166.

Linden, Ellena A., Jeannette Cano, and George N. Coritsidis. "Kidney Transplantation in Undocumented Immigrants With ESRD: A Policy Whose Time Has Come?" *American Journal of Kidney Diseases* 60, no. 3 (September 2012): 354–359. doi: 10.1053/j.ajkd.2012.05.016.

Linder, Forrest E., and Robert D. Grove. *Vital Statistics Rates in the United States, 1900–1940.* Washington, DC: US Government Printing Office, 1947. http://www.cdc.gov.

Lopez, Pascal. "The Subversive Links between HIV/AIDS and the Forest Sector." In *Human Health and Forests: A Global Overview of Issues, Practice and Policy*, edited by Carol J. Pierce Colfer, 221–237. London: Earthscan, 2008.

Lum, Zi-Ann. "John Sewell, Former Toronto Mayor, Explains Why Canada's Refugee Policy Is 'Absolutely Brilliant.'" *Huffington Post*, December 18, 2015. http://www. huffingtonpost.ca.

———. "Ron Atkey's Advice to Liberals on Syrian Refugee Resettlement: 'Move Quickly.'" *Huffington Post*, December 21, 2015. http://www.huffingtonpost.ca.

Maloney, Susan A., Luis S. Ortega, and Martin S. Cetron. "Overseas Medical Screening for Immigrants and Refugees." In Walker and Barnett, *Immigrant Medicine*, 111–121.

Manufacturing Chemist. "Air Ticket Tax in France Helps Fight HIV/AIDS, TB and Malaria." January 29, 2013. http://www.manufacturingchemist.com.

Mariner, Wendy K., George J. Annas, and Wendy E. Parmet. "Pandemic Preparedness: A Return to the Rule of Law." *Drexel Law Review* 1, no. 2 (Spring–Summer 2009): 341–382.

Markel, Howard, Alexandra M. Stern, J. Alexander Navarro, Joseph R. Michalsen, Arnold S. Monto, and Cleto DiGiovanni. "Nonpharmaceutical Influenza Mitigation Strategies, US Communities, 1918–1920 Pandemic." *Emerging Infectious Diseases* 12, no. 12 (December 2006): 1961–1964. doi: 10.3201/eid1212.060506.

Marmot, Michael. "Social Determinants of Health Inequalities." *Lancet* 365, no. 9464 (March 19, 2005): 1099–1104. doi: 10.1016/S0140-6736(05)71146-6.

Marshall, T. H. *Citizenship and Social Class*. Cambridge: University Press, 1950.

Martineau, Tim, Karola Decker, and Peter Bundred. "Briefing Note on International Migration of Health Professionals: Levelling the Playing Field for Developing Country Health Systems." Working paper, Liverpool School of Tropical Medicine, Liverpool, 2002. http://www.aspeninstitute.org.

Martínez-Lirola, Miguel, Noelia Alonso-Rodriguez, Luisa Sánchez, Marta Herranz, Sandra Andrés, Teresa Peñafiel, Cruz Rogado, et al. "Advanced Survey of Tuberculosis Transmission in a Complex Socioepidemiologic Scenario with a High Proportion of Cases in Immigrants." *Clinical Infectious Diseases* 47, no. 1 (July 2008): 8–14. doi: 10.1086/588785.

Martinez, Gebe. "Illegal Immigrants' Tab for Emergency Care: $61 Million." *Los Angeles Times*, November 2, 1994, Orange County edition, B7.

Mather, Mark. "Children in Immigrant Families Chart New Path." Population Reference Bureau, *Reports on America*, February 2009. http://www.prb.org.

Mathiason, Nick. "Western Bankers and Lawyers 'Rob Africa of $150bn Every Year.'" *Guardian* (Manchester), January 20, 2007. http://www.theguardian.com.

McDonald, James Ted, and Steven Kennedy. "Insights into the 'Healthy Immigrant Effect': Health Status and Health Service Use of Immigrants to Canada." *Social Science and Medicine* 59, no. 8 (October 2004): 1613–1627. doi: 10.1016/j. socscimed.2004.02.004.

McDonnell, Patrick J. "Health Clinics Report Declines After Prop. 187; Health: Doctors Say Fear Is Scaring Patients Away. Many Immigrants Are Unaware that Enforcement Is on Hold." *Los Angeles Times*, November 26, 1994, A1.

McGrory, Brian. "A Life Filled Up with Love." *Boston Globe*, November 14, 2012. http://www.bostonglobe.com.

Melber, Ari, and Halimah Abdullah. "Can Governors Block Syrian Refugees? Probably Not." NBC News, November 17, 2015. http://www.nbcnews.com.

Menzies, Dick, Chun Ho Chan, and Bilkis Vissandjée. "Impact of Immigration on Tuberculosis Infection among Canadian-Born Schoolchildren and Young Adults in Montreal." *American Journal of Respiratory and Critical Care Medicine* 156, no. 6 (December 1997): 1915–1921. doi: 10.1164/ajrccm.156.6.9704017.

Messina, Anthony M. "Asylum, Residency and Citizenship Policies and Models of Migrant Incorporation." In Rechel et al., *Migration and Health in the European Union*, 37–51.

MexCare. Accessed November 23, 2012. http://www.mexcare.com.

Migration Policy Institute. "Rising Child Migration to the United States." Accessed December 2015. http://www.migrationpolicy.org.

Miles, Kevin, D. J. Clutterbuck, O. Seitio, M. Sebegod, and A. Riley. "Antiretroviral Treatment Roll-Out in a Resource-Constrained Setting: Capitalizing on Nursing Resources in Botswana." *Bulletin of the World Health Organization* 85, no. 7 (July 2007): 555–560. doi: 10.2471/BLT.06.033076. http://www.who.int.

Mill, John Stuart. *On Liberty*. In *Three Essays*. Oxford: Oxford University Press, 1975.

———. *Utilitarianism*. Edited by Oskar Piest. Indianapolis: Bobbs-Merrill, 1957.

Mills, Edward J., Steve Kanters, Amy Hagopian, Nick Bansback, Jean Nachega, Mark Alberton, Christopher G. Au-Yeung, et al. "The Financial Cost of Doctors Emigrating from Sub-Saharan Africa: Human Capital Analysis." *BMJ* 343 (2011). doi: 10.1136/bmj.d7031.

Mitchell, Christopher D., Michael S. Truitt, Vanessa K. Shifflette, Van Johnson, Alicia J. Mangram, and Ernest L. Dunn. "Who Will Cover the Cost of Undocumented Immigrant Trauma Care?" *Journal of Trauma and Acute Care Surgery* 72, no. 3 (March 2012): 609–613. doi: 10.1097/TA.0b013e31824765de.

Moberly, Tom. "Minority Report: How the UK's Treatment of Foreign and Ethnic Minority Doctors Needs to Change." *BMJ* 348, no. 7955 (April 26, 2014). doi: 10.1136/bmj.g2838.

Moeller, Susan D. *Compassion Fatigue: How the Media Sell Disease, Famine, War and Death*. New York: Routledge, 1999.

Mohanty, Sarita A., Steffie Woolhandler, David U. Himmelstein, Susmita Pati, Olveen Carrasquillo, and David H. Bor. "Health Care Expenditures of Immigrants in the United States: A Nationally Representative Analysis." *American Journal of Public Health* 95, no. 8 (August 2005): 1431–1438. doi: 10.2105/AJPH.2004.044602.

Molina, Natalia. *Fit to Be Citizens?: Public Health and Race in Los Angeles, 1879–1939*. Berkeley: University of California Press, 2006.

Molnar, Beth E., Stephen L. Buka, Robert T. Brennan, John K. Holton, and Felton Earls. "A Multilevel Study of Neighborhoods and Parent-to-Child Physical Aggression: Results from the Project on Human Development in Chicago Neighborhoods." *Child Maltreatment* 8, no. 2 (May 2003): 84–97. doi: 10.1177/1077559502250822.

Mowat, David, and Catharine Chambers. "Producing More Relevant Evidence: Applying a Social Epidemiology Research Agenda to Public Health Practice." In *Rethinking Social Epidemiology: Towards a Science of Change*, edited by Patricia O'Campo and James R. Dunn, 305–326. New York: Springer, 2012.

Moyer, Justin Wm. "Ebola Victim Thomas Eric Duncan's Family Has Settled with Dallas Hospital." *Washington Post*, November 12, 2014. http://www.washingtonpost.com.

Mullan, Fitzhugh. "The Metrics of the Physician Brain Drain." *New England Journal of Medicine* 353, no. 17 (October 27, 2005): 1810–1818. doi: 10.1056/NEJMsa050004.

Munro, Salla A., Simon A. Lewin, Helen J. Smith, Mark E. Engel, Atle Fretheim, and Jimmy Volmink. "Patient Adherence to Tuberculosis Treatment: A Systematic Review of Qualitative Research." *PLoS Medicine* 4, no. 7 (July 2007): 1230–1245. doi 10.1371/journal.pmed.0040238.

Murphy, Tom. "Do Americans Support Global Health Spending?" PSI Impact, May 21, 2012. http://psiimpact.com.

Nagan, Winston P., and Aitza M. Haddad. "The Holocaust and Mass Atrocity: The Continuing Challenge for Decision." *Michigan State University College of Law International Law Review* 21, no. 2 (Spring 2013): 337–442.

Nandi, Arijit, Sana Loue, and Sandro Galea. "Expanding the Universe of Universal Coverage: The Population Health Argument for Increasing Coverage for Immigrants." *Journal of Immigrant and Minority Health* 11, no. 6 (December 2009): 433–436. doi: 10.1007/s10903-009-9267-2.

National Immigration Project of the National Lawyers Guild. "Immigration Law and Defense Database." March 2003.

NBC. "African Nurses Head to U.S. for Better Pay." June 29, 2006. http://www.nbcnews.com.

Neel, Joe. "Screening Immigrants for TB Pays Dividends in U.S." National Public Radio, March 20, 2014. http://www.npr.org.

Neelakantan, Shailaja. "India's Global Ambitions." *Far Eastern Economic Review* 166, no. 4 (November 6, 2003): 52–54.

Negin, Joel, Aneuryn Rozea, Ben Cloyd, and Alexandra L. C. Martiniuk. "Foreign-Born Health Workers in Australia: An Analysis of Census Data." *Human Resources for Health* 11, no. 69 (December 2013). doi: 10.1186/1478-4491-11-69.

Neuman, Gerald L. "The Lost Century of American Immigration Law (1776–1875)." *Columbia Law Review* 93, no. 8 (December 1993): 1833–1901.

New York Times. "Canada's Warm Embrace of Refugees." December 11, 2015. http://www.nytimes.com.

———. "Cuba's Impressive Role on Ebola." October 19, 2014. http://www.nytimes.com.

———. "Mr. Obama's Historic Move on Cuba." December 17, 2014. http://www.nytimes.com.

Newdick, Christopher. "Citizenship, Free Movement and Health Care: Cementing Individual Rights by Corroding Social Solidarity." *Common Market Law Review* 43, no. 6 (December 2006): 1645–1668.

Nissen, Steven E. "Health Care Disparities, the Uninsured, and the Role of Cardiologists in the National Debate." *Current Cardiology Reports* 9, no. 4 (July 2007): 249–251. doi: 10.1007/BF02938371.

Nossiter, Adam. "Marine Le Pen's Anti-Islam Message Gains Influence in France." *New York Times*, November 17, 2015. http://www.nytimes.com.

Nørredam, Marie, and Allan Krasnik. "Migrants' Access to Health Services." In Rechel et al., *Migration and Health in the European Union*, 67–78.

Nussbaum, Martha. "Patriotism and Cosmopolitanism." In *For Love of Country?: Debating the Limits of Patriotism*, edited by Joshua Cohen, 2–17. Boston: Beacon Press, 1996.

———. *Women and Human Development: The Capabilities Approach.* New York: Cambridge University Press, 2000.

Nussbaum, Martha, and Amartya Sen, eds. *The Quality of Life.* New York: Oxford University Press, 1993.

O'Connell, Caitlin. "Note: Return to Sender: Evaluating the Medical Repatriations of Uninsured Immigrants." *Washington University Law Review* 87, no. 6 (2010): 1429–1459.

O'Neill, Onora. "Broadening Bioethics: Clinical Ethics, Public Health and Global Health." Nuffield Council on Bioethics Lecture, Royal Society of Arts, London, May 2011. http://nuffieldbioethics.org.

Office of the United Nations High Commissioner for Human Rights (OHCHR). "The Right to Health." Fact Sheet No. 31, Human Rights Fact Sheets, June 2008. http://www.who.int.

Okie, Susan. "Immigrants and Health Care—At the Intersection of Two Broken Systems." *New England Journal of Medicine* 357, no. 6 (August 9, 2007): 525–529. doi: 10.1056/NEJMp078113.

Onishi, Norimitsu. "Clashes Erupt as Liberia Sets an Ebola Quarantine." *New York Times*, August 20, 2014. http://www.nytimes.com.

Ontario Medical Association. "Reviewing the OHIP Three-Month Wait: An Unreasonable Barrier to Accessing Health Care." *Ontario Medical Review* (April 2011). http://www.oma.org.

Opp, Karl-Dieter. "Norms." In *International Encyclopedia of the Social and Behavioral Sciences*, edited by Neil J. Smelser and Paul B. Baltes, 10714–10720. Oxford: Pergamon, 2001.

Organisation for Economic Co-operation and Development. "Immigrant Health Workers in OECD Countries in the Broader Context of Highly Skilled Migration." Part III in *International Migration Outlook 2007*. Paris: OECD, 2007. http://www.oecd.org.

———. *International Migration Outlook 2013.* Paris: OECD, 2013. doi: 10.1787/migr_outlook-2013-en.

Outterson, Kevin. "Fair Followers: Expanding Access to Generic Pharmaceuticals for Low- and Middle-Income Populations." In *The Power of Pills: Social, Ethical and Legal Issues in Drug Development, Marketing, and Pricing*, edited by Jillian Clare Cohen, Patricia Illingworth, and Udo Schüklenk, 164–178. London: Pluto, 2006.

Pace, Paola. "The Right to Health of Migrants in Europe." In Rechel et al., *Migration and Health in the European Union*, 55–66.

Parekh, Serena. *Refugees and the Ethics of Forced Displacement*. New York: Routledge, 2016.

Park, Lisa Sun-Hee. *Entitled to Nothing: The Struggle for Immigrant Health Care in the Age of Welfare Reform*. New York: New York University Press, 2011.

Parmet, Wendy E. "Dangerous Perspectives: The Perils of Individualizing Public Health Problems." *Journal of Legal Medicine* 30, no. 1 (2009): 83–108. doi: 10.1080/01947640802694593.

———. "The Individual Mandate: Implications for Public Health Law." *Journal of Law, Medicine and Ethics* 39, no. 3 (Fall 2011): 401–413.

———. "Pandemics, Populism and the Role of Law in the H1N1 Vaccine Campaign." *Saint Louis University Journal of Health Law and Policy* 4, no. 1 (2010): 113–153.

———. "Public Health and Social Control: Implications for Human Rights." Working paper, Project on Social Control and Human Rights, International Council on Human Rights Policy, 2009. http://www.ichrp.org.

Pasipanodya, Jotam G., and Tawanda Gumbo. "A Meta-Analysis of Self-Administered vs. Directly Observed Therapy Effect on Microbiologic Failure, Relapse, and Acquired Drug Resistance in Tuberculosis Patients." *Clinical Infectious Diseases* 57, no. 1 (July 2013): 21–31. doi: 10.1093/cid/cit167.

Passel, Jeffrey S., and Paul Taylor. "Unauthorized Immigrants and Their US-Born Children." Pew Research Center, August 11, 2010. http://www.pewhispanic.org.

Pauly, Mark V., and José A. Pagán. "Spillovers and Vulnerability: The Case of Community Uninsurance." *Health Affairs* 26, no. 5 (September 2007): 1304–1314. doi: 10.1377/hlthaff.26.5.1304.

———. "Spillovers of Uninsurance in Communities." Report submitted to the Committee on Health Insurance Status and Its Consequences, Institute of Medicine, 2009. http://www.iom.edu.

Pavlish, Carol Lynn, Sahra Noor, and Joan Brandt. "Somali Immigrant Women and the American Health Care System: Discordant Beliefs, Divergent Expectations, and Silent Worries." *Social Science and Medicine* 71, no. 2 (July 2010): 353–361. doi: 10.1016/j.socscimed.2010.04.010.

Pedwell, Terry. "Canada to Get up to 50,000 Refugees by End of 2016." *Toronto Star*, December 2, 2015. http://www.thestar.com.

Peston, Robert. "Why Germany Needs Migrants More Than UK." BBC News, September 7, 2015. http://www.bbc.com.

Pettigrew, Luisa M. "The NHS and International Medical Graduates." *Education for Primary Care* 25, no. 2 (March 2014): 71–75.

Pew Charitable Trusts. "Mapping Public Benefits for Immigrants." September 2014. http://www.pewtrusts.org.

Pew Research Center. "Most Say Illegal Immigrants Should Be Allowed to Stay, but Citizenship Is More Divisive." March 28, 2013. http://www.people-press.org.

———. "Statistical Portrait of the Foreign-Born Population in the United States." April 19, 2016. http://www.pewhispanic.org.

Pogge, Thomas. "Are We Violating the Human Rights of the World's Poor?" *Yale Human Rights and Development Law Journal* 14, no. 2 (2011): 1–33.

———. "Severe Poverty as a Violation of Negative Duties." *Ethics and International Affairs* 19, no. 1 (March 2005): 55–83. doi: 10.1111/j.1747-7093.2005.tb00490.x.

Portes, Alejandro, Donald Light, and Patricia Fernández-Kelly. "The U.S. Health Care System and Immigration: An Institutional Interpretation." *Sociological Forum* 24, no. 3 (September 2009): 487–514.

Potocky-Tripodi, Miriam, Karen Dodge, and Michael Greene. "Bridging Cultural Chasms between Providers and HIV-Positive Haitians in Palm Beach County, Florida." *Journal of Health Care for the Poor and Underserved* 18, no. S3 (2007): 105–117. doi: 10.1353/hpu.2007.0087.

Prainsack, Barbara, and Alena Buyx. "Solidarity in Contemporary Bioethics: Towards a New Approach." *Bioethics* 26, no. 7 (September 2012): 343–350. doi: 10.1111/j.1467-8519.2012.01987.x.

Prats, Alex. *Hunger: The Hidden Cost of Tax Injustice.* London: Christian Aid, 2013. http://www.christianaid.org.uk.

Preston, Richard. *The Hot Zone: A Terrifying True Story.* New York: Random House, 1994.

Price, Polly J. "Can U.S. Immigration Law Be Reconciled with the Protection of Public Health?" Research Paper No. 14-272, Legal Studies Research Paper Series, Emory University School of Law, Atlanta, 2014. http://ssrn.com.

Priest, Patricia C., Lance C. Jennings, Alasdair R. Duncan, Cheryl R. Brunton, and Michael G. Baker. "Effectiveness of Border Screening for Detecting Influenza in Arriving Airline Travelers." *American Journal of Public Health* 103, no. 8 (August 2013): 1412–1418. doi: 10.2105/AJPH.2012.300761.

Prüss-Üstün, Annette, and Carlos Corvalán. *Preventing Disease through Healthy Environments: Towards an Estimate of the Environmental Burden of Disease.* Geneva: World Health Organization, 2006. http://www.who.int.

Putnam, Robert D. *Bowling Alone: The Collapse and Revival of American Community.* New York: Simon and Schuster, 2000.

———. "*E Pluribus Unum*: Diversity and Community in the Twenty-First Century." *Scandinavian Political Studies* 30, no. 2 (June 2007): 137–174. doi: 10.1111/j.1467-9477.2007.00176.x.

Pylypchuk, Yuriy, and Julie Hudson. "Immigrants and the Use of Preventive Care in the United States." *Health Economics* 18, no. 7 (July 2009): 783–806. doi: 10.1002/hec.1401.

Rabin, Roni Caryn. "Unemployment May Be Hazardous to Your Health." *New York Times,* May 8, 2009. http://www.nytimes.com.

Raghavan, Rajeev, and Ricardo Nuila. "Survivors—Dialysis, Immigration, and U.S. Law." *New England Journal of Medicine* 364, no. 23 (June 9, 2011): 2183–2185. doi: 10.1056/NEJMp1101195.

Ratha, Dilip. "Leveraging Remittances for Development." Migration Policy Institute, June 2007. http://www.migrationpolicy.org.

Ratner, Lizzy. "The Legacy of Guantanamo." *Nation*, July 14, 2003. http://www.thenation.com.

Rechel, Bernd, Philipa Mladovsky, Walter Devillé, Barbara Rijks, Roumyana Petrova-Benedict, and Martin McKee, eds. *Migration and Health in the European Union*. New York: McGraw Hill, 2011.

Rechel, Bernd, Philipa Mladovsky, David Ingleby, Johan P. Mackenbach, and Martin McKee. "Migration and Health in an Increasingly Diverse Europe." *Lancet* 381, no. 9873 (April 6, 2013): 1235–1245. doi: 10.1016/S0140-6736(12)62086-8.

Reeske, Anna, and Oliver Razum. "Maternal and Child Health—From Conception to First Birthday." In Rechel et al., *Migration and Health in the European Union*, 139–153.

Reuters. "California Senate Approves Bill Allowing Undocumented Immigrants to Buy Health Insurance." *Huffington Post*, June 2, 2015. http://www.huffingtonpost.com.

———. "Polish Opposition Warns Refugees Could Spread Infectious Diseases." October 15, 2015. http://www.reuters.com.

Reyes, Raul. "Infants Caught in Political Crossfire." *USA Today*, November 4, 2006, 19A.

Richinick, Michele. "GOP Congressman: Ebola Could Spread Across the Border." MSNBC, July 15, 2014. http://www.msnbc.com.

Ricks, Philip M., Kevin P. Cain, John E. Oeltmann, J. Steve Kammerer, and Patrick K. Moonan. "Estimating the Burden of Tuberculosis among Foreign-Born Persons Acquired Prior to Entering the U.S., 2005–2009." *PLoS ONE* 6, no. 11 (November 2011). doi: 10.1371/journal.pone.0027405.

Riosmena, Fernando. "Policy Shocks: On the Legal Auspices of Latin American Migration to the United States." *Annals of the American Academy of Political and Social Science* 630 (July 2010): 270–293. doi: 10.1177/0002716210368113.

Robbins, Liz, Michael Barbaro, and Marc Santora. "Unapologetic, Christie Frees Nurse from Ebola Quarantine." *New York Times*, October 27, 2014. http://www.nytimes.com.

Romney, Lee, Jeff Brazil, and Martin Miller. "Child Cited as Prop. 187 Casualty Had Leukemia: Immigration: Anaheim Boy Also Suffered Bacterial Infection. His Death Gains More Political Ramifications." *Los Angeles Times*, November 24, 1994, Orange County edition, A1.

Rosen, Sydney, Petan Hamazakaza, Frank Feeley, and Matthew Fox. "The Impact of AIDS on Government Service Delivery: The Case of the Zambia Wildlife Authority." *AIDS* 21, no. S3 (June 2007): S53–S59. doi: 10.1097/01.aids.0000279694.61652.e3.

Rosenquist, James N., James H. Fowler, and Nicholas A. Christakis. "Social Network Determinants of Depression." *Molecular Psychiatry* 16, no. 3 (March 2011): 273–281. doi: 10.1038/mp.2010.13.

Rosenthal, Elisabeth. "In Need of a New Hip, but Priced Out of the U.S." *New York Times*, August 3, 2013. http://www.nytimes.com.

Ruggie, John. "Guiding Principles on Business and Human Rights" (Annex to "Report of the Special Representative of the Secretary-General on the Issue of Human Rights and Transnational Corporations and Other Business Enterprises, John Ruggie"). UN Doc. A/HRC/17/31 (2011). http://www.ohchr.org.

Sack, Kevin. "Deal Reached on Dialysis for Immigrants." *New York Times*, September 9, 2011, A11.

———. "Immigrants Cling to Fragile Lifeline at Safety-Net Hospital." *New York Times*, September 24, 2009, A16.

———. "Judge Rules That Hospital Can Close Dialysis Unit." *New York Times*, September 26, 2009, A1.

Sack, Kevin, David Agren, and Catrin Einhorn. "Ailing Immigrants Find No Relief Back Home." *New York Times*, January 1, 2010, A1.

Sahara Reporters. "Ebola: Australia Suspends Humanitarian Aid, Closes Border to West Africans." October 18, 2014. http://saharareporters.com.

Sampson, Robert J., Jeffrey D. Morenoff, and Stephen Raudenbush. "Social Anatomy of Racial and Ethnic Disparities in Violence." *American Journal of Public Health* 95, no. 2 (February 2005): 224–232. doi: 10.2105/AJPH.2004.037705.

Sandgren, Andreas, Monica Sañé Schepisi, Giovanni Sotgiu, Emma Huitric, Giovanni Battista Migliori, Davide Manissero, Marieke J. van der Werf, and Enrico Girardi. "Tuberculosis Transmission between Foreign- and Native-Born Populations in the EU/EEA: A Systematic Review." *European Respiratory Journal* 43, no. 4 (April 2014): 1159–1171. doi: 10.1183/09031936.00117213.

Sargent, Greg. "Scott Brown: Anyone with Ebola Can 'Walk Across' Our 'Porous' Border." *Plum Line* (blog), *Washington Post*, October 14, 2014. http://www.washingtonpost.com.

Save the Children. "Whose Charity?: Africa's Aid to the NHS." 2005. http://www.africanchildinfo.net.

Saxenian, AnnaLee. "Brain Circulation: How High-Skill Immigration Makes Everyone Better Off." Brookings Institution, Winter 2002. http://www.brookings.edu.

———. "Silicon Valley's New Immigrant High-Growth Entrepreneurs." *Economic Development Quarterly* 16, no. 1 (February 2002): 20–31. doi: 10.1177/0891242402016001003.

Scheper-Hughes, Nancy. "Organs without Borders." *Foreign Policy* no. 146 (January–February 2005): 26–27.

Schlosser, Katherine. "Trachoma through History." Trachoma Matters, International Trachoma Initiative. 2004. http://www.nps.gov.

Schuck, Peter H., and Rogers M. Smith. *Citizenship without Consent: Illegal Aliens in the American Polity*. New Haven, CT: Yale University Press, 1985.

Schwartz, David S. "The Amorality of Consent." Review of *Citizenship without Consent: Illegal Aliens in the American Polity*, by Peter H. Schuck and Rogers M. Smith. *California Law Review* 74, no. 6 (December 1986): 2143–2171.

Seo, Jennifer Y. "Justice Not for All: Challenges to Obtaining Equal Access to Health Care for Non-Citizen Immigrants in the United States." *Georgetown Journal of Law and Modern Critical Race Perspectives* 3, no. 2 (Fall 2011): 143–170.

Sen, Amartya. *Commodities and Capabilities*. New York: Oxford University Press, 1999.

Shah, Anup. "Climate Change and Global Warming: Introduction." Global Issues Online, February 1, 2015. http://www.globalissues.org.

Shah, Nayan. *Contagious Divides: Epidemics and Race in San Francisco's Chinatown*. Berkeley: University of California Press, 2001.

Shain, Andrew. "Rep. Wilson: Ebola-Infected Terrorists Could Strike US." *The Buzz* (blog), *State* (Columbia, SC), October 17, 2014. http://www.thestate.com.

Sheikh-Hamad, David, Elian Paiuk, Andrew J. Wright, Craig Kleinmann, Uday Khosla, and Wayne X. Shandera. "Care for Immigrants with End-Stage Renal Disease in Houston: A Comparison of Two Practices." *Texas Medicine* 103, no. 4 (April 2007): 54–58.

Sheikh, Mohamud, Abhijit Pal, Shu Wang, C. Raina MacIntyre, Nicholas J. Wood, David Isaacs, Hasantha Gunasekera, Shanti Raman, Katherine Hale, and Alison Howell. "The Epidemiology of Health Conditions of Newly Arrived Refugee Children: A Review of Patients Attending a Specialist Health Clinic in Sydney." *Journal of Paediatrics and Child Health* 45, no. 9 (September 2009): 509–513. doi: 10.1111/j.1440-1754.2009.01550.x.

Shetty, Priya. "Medical Tourism Booms in India, but at What Cost?" *Lancet* 376, no. 9742 (August 28, 2010): 671–672. doi: 10.1016/S0140-6736(10)61320-7.

Shimazono, Yosuke. "The State of the International Organ Trade: A Provisional Picture Based on Integration of Available Information." *Bulletin of the World Health Organization* 85, no. 12 (December 2007): 955–962. doi: 10.2471/BLT.06.039370.

Siddiqi, Arjumand, Daniyal Zuberi, and Quynh C. Nguyen. "The Role of Health Insurance in Explaining Immigrant versus Non-Immigrant Disparities in Access to Health Care: Comparing the United States to Canada." *Social Science and Medicine* 69, no. 10 (November 2009): 1452–1459. doi: 10.1016/j.socscimed.2009.08.030.

Siegel, Jacob S. "Health and Migration." With S. Jay Olshansky. Chap. 10 in *The Demography and Epidemiology of Human Health and Aging*, 533–578. New York: Springer Science, 2012.

Sikarwar, Deepshikha. "Multinational Companies Rush to Seal Tax Pacts in Advance." *Economic Times*, March 31, 2014. http://articles.economictimes.indiatimes.com.

Simons, Marlise, and J. David Goodman. "Ex-Liberian Leader Gets 50 Years for War Crimes." *New York Times*, May 30, 2012. http://www.nytimes.com.

Singer, Peter. *The Most Good You Can Do: How Effective Altruism Is Changing Ideas about Living Ethically*. New Haven, CT: Yale University Press, 2015.

———. *One World: The Ethics of Globalization*. New Haven, CT: Yale University Press, 2002.

———. *Practical Ethics*. 2nd ed. New York: Cambridge University Press, 1993.

Singh, Gopal K., and Barry A. Miller. "Health, Life Expectancy, and Mortality Patterns among Immigrant Populations in the United States." *Canadian Journal of Public Health* 95, no. 3 (May–June 2004): I-14–I-21.

Skinner, Jessica. "7,000 People, One Clinic, No Running Water: Ebola and Health Systems." *Policy and Practice* (blog), Oxfam, April 16, 2015. http://policy-practice. oxfam.org.uk.

Smith, Alex Duval. "Fear and Xenophobia Poison Polish Polls." *Guardian* (Manchester), October 23, 2015. http://www.theguardian.com.

Solomon, Andrew. "Shameful Profiling of the Mentally Ill." *New York Times*, December 7, 2013. http://www.nytimes.com.

Sontag, Deborah. "Deported, by U.S. Hospitals: Immigrants, Spurned on Rehabilitation, Are Forced Out." *New York Times*, August 3, 2008, A-1. http://www.nytimes. com.

———. "Deported in a Coma, Saved Back in U.S." *New York Times*, November 8, 2008. http://www.nytimes.com.

Stanciole, Anderson E., and Manfred Huber. "Access to Health Care for Migrants, Ethnic Minorities and Asylum Seekers in Europe." Policy Brief, European Centre for Social Welfare, May 2009. http://www.euro.centre.org.

Steele, Sarah, David Stuckler, Martin McKee, and Allyson M. Pollock. "The Immigration Bill: Extending Charging Regimes and Scapegoating the Vulnerable Will Pose Risks to Public Health." *Journal of the Royal Society of Medicine* 107, no. 4 (April 2014): 132–133. doi: 10.1177/0141076814526132.

Stern, Ken. *With Charity for All: Why Charities Are Failing and a Better Way to Give.* New York: Doubleday, 2013.

Stilwell, Barbara, Khassoum Diallo, Pascal Zurn, Marko Vujicic, Orvill Adams, and Mario Dal Poz. "Migration of Health-Care Workers from Developing Countries: Strategic Approaches to Its Management." *Bulletin of the World Health Organization* 82, no. 8 (August 2004): 595–600. http://www.who.int.

Stimpson, Jim P., Fernando A. Wilson, Rosenda Murillo, and José A. Pagán. "Persistent Disparities in Cholesterol Screening among Immigrants to the United States." *International Journal for Equity in Health* 11 (2012). doi: 10.1186/1475-9276-11-22.

Stoddard, Ed, and Pascal Fletcher. "Surviving Ebola: Africa Cries Out for Healthcare Boost." Reuters, August 21, 2014. http://www.reuters.com.

Stojanovic, Dusan. "Thousands Stranded as EU Countries Close Borders to Economic Migrants." *Huffington Post*, November 19, 2015. http://www.huffingtonpost.com.

Stylianou, Nassos. "How World's Worst Ebola Outbreak Began with One Boy's Death." BBC News, November 27, 2014. http://www.bbc.com.

Sumner, Andy. "Where Will the World's Poor Live?: Global Poverty Projections for 2020 and 2030." In Focus Policy Briefing 26, Institute of Development Studies, University of Sussex, Brighton, UK, August 2012. http://www.ids.ac.uk.

Sunstein, Cass R. "Social Norms and Social Roles." *Columbia Law Review* 96, no. 4 (May 1996): 903–968.

Svensson, Erik, Julie Millet, Anna Lindqvist, Margareta Olsson, Malin Ridell, Nalin Rastogi, The Western Sweden Tuberculosis Study Group. "Impact of Immigration on Tuberculosis Epidemiology in a Low-Incidence Country." *Clinical Microbiology and Infection* 17, no. 6 (June 2011): 881–887. doi: 10.1111/j.1469-0691.2010.03358.x.

Tajfel, Henri, and Michael Billic. "Familiarity and Categorization in Intergroup Behavior." *Journal of Experimental Social Psychology* 10, no. 2 (March 1974): 159–170. doi: 10.1016/0022-1031(74)90064-X.

Telegraph. "Riots in China over SARS Quarantine." May 5, 2003. http://www.telegraph.co.uk.

Tencer, Daniel. "Syrian Refugees Will Boost Economy in Canada's Have-Not Regions, Experts Say." *Huffington Post*, November 26, 2015. http://www.huffingtonpost.ca.

Thaler, Richard H., and Cass R. Sunstein. *Nudge: Improving Decisions about Health, Wealth, and Happiness*. Rev. ed. New York: Penguin, 2009.

Thomas, Felicity, Peter Aggleton, and Jane Anderson. "'If I Cannot Access Services, Then There Is No Reason for Me to Test': The Impacts of Health Service Charges on HIV Testing and Treatment amongst Migrants in England." *AIDS Care* 22, no. 4 (2010): 526–531. doi: 10.1080/09540120903499170.

Thomas, Roger E., and Brian Gushulak. "Screening and Treatment of Immigrants and Refugees to Canada for Tuberculosis: Implications of the Experience of Canada and Other Industrialized Countries." *Canadian Journal of Infectious Diseases* 6, no. 5 (September–October 1995): 246–255.

Time. "The Directors: The Ebola Fighters in Their Own Words." December 10, 2014. http://time.com.

Tobey, James A. "Public Health and the Police Power." *New York University Law Review* 4, no. 2 (April 1927): 126–133.

Todrys, Katherine Wiltenburg. "Returned to Risk: Deportation of HIV-Positive Migrants." Human Rights Watch, September 2009. http://www.hrw.org.

Tomes, Nancy. "The Making of a Germ Panic, Then and Now." *American Journal of Public Health* 90, no. 2 (February 2000): 191–198. doi: 10.2105/AJPH.90.2.191.

Top 10 Companies in India. "Top 10 Multinational Companies in India." May 21, 2013. http://top10companiesinindia.co.in.

Torres-Cantero, Alberto M., A. G. Miguel, C. Gallardo, and S. Ippolito. "Health Care Provision for Illegal Migrants: May Health Policy Make a Difference?" *European Journal of Public Health* 17, no. 5 (October 2007): 483–485. doi: 10.1093/eurpub/ckl266.

Trump, Donald. "Donald J. Trump Statement on Preventing Muslim Immigration." Donald J. Trump for President, December 7, 2015. http://www.donaldjtrump.com.

Tyson, Peter. "In Her Own Words." *Nova*, PBS. August 2004. http://www.pbs.org.

Ungar, Sheldon. "Moral Panic versus the Risk Society: The Implications of the Changing Sites of Social Anxiety." *British Journal of Sociology* 52, no. 2 (June 2001): 271–291. doi: 10.1080/00071310120044980.

UK Border Agency. "Entry Clearance Guidance, Medical Issues (MED)." Accessed November 6, 2013. http://www.ukba.homeoffice.gov.uk.

United Nations. Convention on the Rights of Persons with Disabilities. Status as at: 03-06-2015, United Nations Treaty Collections. https://treaties.un.org.

———. "Millennium Development Goals." Accessed July 2015. http://www.un.org.

———. "232 Million International Migrants Living abroad Worldwide–New UN Global Migration Statistics Reveal." September 11, 2013. http://www.un.org.

United Nations Commission on Human Rights. "Siracusa Principles on the Limitation and Derogation Provisions in the International Covenant on Civil and Political Rights." September 28, 1984. http://www.umn.edu.

United Nations Development Programme. "What Will It Take to Achieve the Millennium Development Goals?: An International Assessment." June 2010. http://content.undp.org.

United Nations Framework Convention on Climate Change. "The Cancun Agreements." Accessed June 2015. http://cancun.unfccc.int.

US Council of Economic Advisers. "The US Council of Economic Advisers on Immigration's Economic Impact." *Population and Development Review* 33, no. 3 (September 2007): 641–646.

US Department of Health and Human Services. "Proposed Rules: Medical Examination of Aliens (AIDS)." 51 Fed. Reg. 15354 (April 23, 1986).

US Department of State. "2008 Human Rights Report: United Arab Emirates." Bureau of Democracy, Human Rights, and Labor. February 25, 2009. http://www.state.gov.

US General Accounting Office. "Undocumented Aliens: Questions Persist about Their Impact on Hospitals' Uncompensated Care Costs" (Report GAO-04-472). May 2004. http://www.gao.gov.

US Homeland Security Council. "National Strategy for Pandemic Influenza." November 2005. http://www.flu.gov.

US Presidential Commission for the Study of Bioethical Issues. "Ethics and Ebola: Public Health Planning and Response." February 2015. http://bioethics.gov.

US Public Health Service. *Annual Report of the Chief Medical Officer of Ellis Island, June 30, 1911*. Washington, DC: United States National Archives and Public Records Service, 1911.

———. *Book of Instructions for the Medical Inspection of Immigrants*. Washington, DC: US Government Printing Office, 1903.

Venkatapuram, Sridhar. *Health Justice: An Argument from the Capabilities Approach*. Malden, MA: Polity, 2011.

Von Drehle, David. "The Ebola Fighters: The Ones Who Answered the Call." With Aryn Baker. *Time*, December 10, 2014. http://time.com.

Vu, H. H. "Cultural Barriers between Obstetrician-Gynecologists and Vietnamese/Chinese Immigrant Women." *Texas Medicine* 92, no. 10 (October 1996): 47–52.

Wadhwa, Vivek, AnnaLee Saxenian, Ben Rissing, and Gary Gereffi. "Skilled Immigration and Economic Growth." *Applied Research in Economic Development* 5, no. 1 (May 2008): 6–14.

Wadhwa, Vivek, AnnaLee Saxenian, and F. Daniel Siciliano. "Then and Now: America's New Immigrant Entrepreneurs, Part VII." Ewing Marion Kauffman Foundation, October 2012. http://www.kauffman.org.

Wald, Priscilla. *Contagious: Cultures, Carriers, and the Outbreak Narrative*. Durham, NC: Duke University Press, 2007.

Walker, Patricia F., and Elizabeth D. Barnett, eds. *Immigrant Medicine*. Philadelphia: Saunders, 2007.

Walzer, Michael. "Citizenship." In *Political Innovation and Conceptual Change*, edited by Terence Ball, James Farr, and Russell L. Hanson, 211–219. New York: Cambridge University Press, 1989.

———. *Spheres of Justice*. New York: Basic Books, 1983.

Warner, Koko, and Frank Laczko. "Migration, Environment and Development: New Directions for Research." In *International Migration and Development: Continuing the Dialogue; Legal and Policy Perspectives*, edited by Joseph Chamie and Luca Dall'Oglio, 235–251. Geneva: International Organization for Migration, 2008. http://publications.iom.int.

Washer, Peter. *Emerging Infectious Diseases and Society*. New York: Palgrave Macmillan, 2010.

Washington, Jesse. "Immigration Foes Link Flu to Mexican Threat Claims." *Seattle Times*, May 2, 2009.

Watkins, James D., et al. *Report of the Presidential Commission on the Human Immunodeficiency Virus Epidemic*. Washington, DC: US Government Printing Office, 1988. http://archive.org.

Wenar, Leif. "Clean Trade in Natural Resources: A Policy Framework for Importing States and Multinationals in the Extractive Industries." Clean Trade, 2010. http://www.cleantrade.org.

Wheatstone, Richard. "Refugee Who Dragged Pregnant Wife and Baby Son onto Train Track Did It Because 'Death Would Be Better.'" *Mirror* (London), September 5, 2015. http://www.mirror.co.uk.

Wilkinson, Richard, and Kate Pickett. *The Spirit Level: Why Greater Equality Makes Societies Stronger*. New York: Bloomsbury, 2011.

Willrich, Michael. *Pox: An American History*. New York: Penguin, 2011.

Wilper, Andrew P., Steffie Woolhandler, Karen E. Lasser, Danny McCormick, David H. Bor, and David U. Himmelstein. "Health Insurance and Mortality in US Adults." *American Journal of Public Health* 99, no. 12 (December 2009): 2289–2295. doi: 10.2105/AJPH.2008.157685.

Wolff, Jonathan. *The Human Right to Health*. New York: Norton, 2012.

Wood, James G., Nasim Zamani, C. Raina MacIntyre, and Niels G. Becker. "Effects of Internal Border Control on Spread of Pandemic Influenza." *Emerging Infectious Diseases* 13, no. 7 (July 2007): 1038–1045. doi: 10.3201/eid1307.060740.

Woodward, David, and Richard D. Smith. "Global Public Goods and Health: Concepts and Issues." In *Global Public Goods for Health: Health Economic and Public Health Perspectives*, edited by Richard Smith, Robert Beaglehole, David Woodward, and Nick Drager, 3–29. New York: Oxford University Press, 2003.

World Bank. "The Economic Impact of the 2014 Ebola Epidemic: Short and Medium Term Estimates for West Africa." October 7, 2014. http://documents.worldbank.org.

———. "Poverty and Equity: India." Accessed July 2015. http://povertydata.worldbank.org.

———. "Remittances to Developing Countries to Stay Robust This Year, Despite Increased Deportations of Migrant Workers, Says WB." April 11, 2014. http://www.worldbank.org.

World Health Organization. *Closing the Gap in a Generation: Health Equity through Action on the Social Determinants of Health; Final Report of the Commission on Social Determinants of Health.* Geneva: World Health Organization, 2008. http://whqlibdoc.who.int.

———. "Global Health Workforce Shortage to Reach 12.9 Million in Coming Decades." November 11, 2013. http://www.who.int.

———. *Global Tuberculosis Report 2013.* Geneva: World Health Organization, 2013. http://apps.who.int.

———. *Global Tuberculosis Report 2015.* Geneva: World Health Organization, 2015. http://www.who.int.

———. "Health in the Post-2015 Development Agenda" (A66/47). 66th World Health Assembly, May 1, 2013. http://apps.who.int.

———. "Health of Migrants" (Resolution WHA 61.17). 61st World Health Assembly, May 24, 2008. http://apps.who.int.

———. "International Health Regulations." http://whqlibdoc.who.int.

———. "Nonpharmaceutical Interventions for Pandemic Influenza, International Measures." *Emerging Infectious Diseases* 12, no. 1 (January 2006): 84–85. http://www.cdc.gov.

———. "The Patients' Charter for Tuberculosis Care: Patients' Rights and Responsibilities." World Care Council. 2006. http://www.who.int.

———. "Sierra Leone: A Traditional Healer and a Funeral." Accessed June 2015. http://www.who.int.

———. "Smallpox." 2001. Accessed August 2012. http://www.who.int.

———. "Social Determinants of Health." Accessed July 2015. http://www.who.int.

———. "The WHO Global Code of Practice on the International Recruitment of Health Personnel" (WHA 63.16). 63rd World Health Assembly, May 2010. http://www.who.int.

———. "Update 42—Travel Advice for Toronto, Situation in China." April 23, 2003. http://www.who.int.

———. "What Are Social Determinants of Health?" Accessed June 2015. http://www.who.int.

———. "WHO Framework Convention on Tobacco Control." 56th World Health Assembly, May 21, 2003. http://www.who.int.

———. "WHO Guidance on Human Rights and Involuntary Detention for xdr-tb Control." January 24, 2007. http://www.who.int.

———. *The World Health Report 2006: Working Together for Health.* Geneva: World Health Organization, 2006. http://www.who.int.

World Trade Organization. "An Agreement on Trade-Related Aspects of Intellectual Property Rights." Annex 1C of "Marrakesh Agreement Establishing the World Trade Organization." April 15, 1994.

Wynia, Matthew K., Stephen R. Latham, Audiey C. Kao, Jessica W. Berg, and Linda L. Emanuel. "Medical Professionalism in Society." *New England Journal of Medicine* 341, no. 21 (November 18, 1999): 1612–1616. doi: 10.1056/NEJM199911183412112.

Yardley, Jim. "Bangladesh Pollution, Told in Colors and Smells." *New York Times*, July 14, 2013. http://www.nytimes.com.

Young, Iris Marion. "Responsibility and Global Justice: A Social Connection Model." *Social Philosophy and Policy* 23, no. 1 (January 2006): 102–130. doi: 10.1017/S0265052506060043.

———. *Responsibility for Justice*. New York: Oxford University Press, 2011.

Zallman, Leah, Steffie Woolhandler, David Himmelstein, David Bor, and Danny McCormick. "Immigrants Contributed an Estimated $115.2 Billion More to the Medicare Trust Fund Than They Took Out in 2002–09." *Health Affairs* 32, no. 6 (June 2013): 1153–1160. doi: 10.1377/hlthaff.2012.1223.

Zilio, Michelle. "Liberals Restore Refugee Health Benefits Cut by Previous Government." *Globe and Mail* (Toronto), February 18, 2016. http://www.theglobeandmail.com.

Zuckerman, Stephen, Timothy A. Waidmann, and Emily Lawton. "Undocumented Immigrants, Left Out of Health Reform, Likely to Continue to Grow as Share of the Uninsured." *Health Affairs* 30, no. 10 (October 2011): 1997–2004. doi: 10.1377/hlthaff.2011.0604.

LEGAL SOURCES

United States Federal and State Court Cases

Aliessa *ex rel.* Fayad v. Novello, 754 N.E.2d 1085 (N.Y. 2001).

Arellano v. Dep't of Human Servs., 402 Ill. App. 3d 665 (2010).

Arizona v. U.S., 567 U.S. ___; 132 S.Ct. 2492 (2012).

Barbier v. Connolly, 113 U.S. 27 (1885).

Chae Chan Ping v. United States, 130 U.S. 581 (1889).

Chinese Exclusion Cases, 130 U.S. 581 (1889).

City of Chicago v. Shalala, 189 F.3d 598 (7th Cir. 1999).

City of Newark v. J. S., 652 A.2d 265 (N.J. Super. Ct. Law Div. 1993).

In re City of New York v. Antoinette R., 630 N.Y.S.2d 1008 (N.Y. Sup. Ct. 1995).

Compagnie Francaise de Navigation a Vapeur v. Louisiana State Bd. of Health, 186 U.S. 380 (1902) (Brown, J., dissenting).

Cruz v. Central Iowa Hospital Corp., 826 N.W. 2d 516 (Iowa App. Dec. 12, 2012).

Diaz v. Division of Social Services, 360 N.C. 384 (2006).

Ehrlich v. Perez, 908 A.2d 1220 (2006).

Finch v. Commonwealth Health Ins. Connector Auth., 946 N.E.2d 1262 (Mass. 2011).

Finch v. Commonwealth Health Ins. Connector Auth., 959 N.E.2d 970 (Mass. 2012).

Gibbons v. Ogden, 22 U.S. 1 (1824).

Graham v. Richardson, 403 U.S. 365 (1971).

Greene v. Edwards, 263 S.E.2d 661 (W. Va. 1980).

Greenery Rehab Group, Inc. v. Hammon, 150 F.3d 226 (2d Cir. 1998).

Haitian Centers Council v. Sale, 823 F. Supp. 1028 (E.D.N.Y. 1993).

Haitian Refugee Center, Inc. v. Baker, 949 F.2d 1109 (11th Cir. 1991) (per curiam), *cert. denied*, 502 U.S. 1122 (1992).

Hill v. United States Immigration and Naturalization Serv., 714 F.2d 1470 (9th Cir. 1983).

Hong Pham v. Starkowski, 300 Conn. 412 (2011).

Jacobson v. Massachusetts, 197 U.S. 11 (1905).

Jew Ho v. Williamson, 103 F. 10 (N.D. Cal. 1900).

League of United Latin American Citizens v. Wilson, 908 F. Supp. 755 (C.D. Cal. 1995).

League of United Latin American Citizens v. Wilson, 997 F. Supp. 1244 (C.D. Cal. 1997).

Mathews v. Diaz, 426 U.S. 67 (1976).

Mayhew v. Hickox, No. CV-2014–36 (D. Me. Oct. 31, 2014) (order pending hearing). http://courts.maine.gov/news_reference/high_profile/hickox/order_pending_hearing.pdf.

Mayor of New York v. Miln, 36 U.S. 102 (1837).

Ex parte Mitchell, 256 F. 229 (D.N.Y. 1919).

Montejo v. Martin Mem'l Med. Ctr., Inc., 874 So.2d 654 (Fla. Dist. Ct. App. 2004).

Montejo v. Martin Mem'l Med. Ctr., Inc., 935 So.2d 1266 (Fla. Dist. Ct. App. 2006).

Nat'l Fed'n of Indep. Bus. v. Sebelius, 132 S.Ct. 2566 (2012).

Passenger Cases, Smith v. Turner, 48 U.S. 283 (1849).

Sale v. Haitian Centers Council, Inc., 509 U.S. 155 (1993).

Scottsdale Healthcare, Inc. v. Arizona Health Care Containment Admin., 206 Ariz. 1 (2003).

Smith v. Turner, 48 U.S. 283 (1849).

Soon Hing v. Crowley, 113 U.S. 703 (1885).

Soskin v. Reinertson, 353 F.3d 1242 (10th Cir. 2004).

Spring Creek Mgmt., L.P. v. Dep't of Pub. Welfare, 45 A.3d 474 (Pa. Commw. Ct. 2012).

Wong Wai v. Williamson, 103 F. 1 (N.D. Cal. 1900).

Yick Wo. v. Hopkins, 118 U.S. 356 (1886).

Canada

Canadian Doctors for Refugee Care v. Attorney General of Canada [2014]. F.C. 651.

Australia

Australian Government, "Response to the Joint Standing Committee on Migration Report" (2012), http://www.immi.gov.au.

Department of Immigration and Citizenship, "Inquiry into Immigration Treatment of Disability: Submission 66 to the Joint Standing Committee on Migration" (2009).

Joint Standing Committee on Migration, "Enabling Australia: Inquiry into Immigration Treatment of Disability" (2010), http://www.aph.gov.au

United Kingdom

MM (Zimbabwe) v. Sec'y of State for the Home Dept. [2012] EWCA (Civ) 279.

N. v. United Kingdom, App. No. 26565/05, Eur. Ct. H.R. (2008).

R (on the application of) SQ (Pakistan) & Anor v. The Upper Tribunal Immigration and Asylum Chamber & Anor [2013] EWCA (Civ) 1251.

Sec'y of State for the Home Dept. v. Roseline Onoshoagbe Akhalu [2013] UKUT 400 (IAC).

"Tax in Developing Countries: Increasing Resources for Development," Fourth Report of Session 2012–13, International Development Committee, House of Commons, July 16, 2012, http://www.publications.parliament.uk.

INDEX

access goods, 121, 126

acculturation, 14, 24–25, 89

affidavit of support, 81

Affordable Care Act (ACA), 5, 11, 73–74, 77, 81–83, 96

Afghanistan, 18, 146

Africa: case study, 134; climate change, 144; disease in, 30, 153; economy, 196; HIV/AIDS, 122; medical brain drain, 154, 158; migrant health workers, 8; taxation, 141; tuberculosis, 62–63; Western narratives, 193–194. *See also* North Africa; sub-Saharan Africa; West Africa; *specific countries*

African Americans, 24–25, 32, 60, 170, 172

Alagha, Karim, 166, 179, 181, 213

alcohol, 24, 47, 66, 123, 129

American Civil Liberties Union (ACLU), 61

American Convention on Human Rights, 100

American Medical Association (AMA), 93

Americans with Disabilities Act, 49

Antoinette R., In re City of New York v., 68

apartheid (South Africa), 26, 172

Apple Inc., 131

Arellano v. Department of Homeland Security, 229n86

Arendt, Hannah, 169

Aristide, Jean-Bertrand, 27, 39

Arizona, 21, 59, 61–62, 73, 86, 88

Arizona Health Care Cost Containment System Administration, Scottsdale Healthcare v., 86

Arizona v. United States, 59

Arpaio, Joe, 61–62

ascriptive theory of citizenship, 170–171

Asia, 18, 23, 30, 40, 41, 129. *See also specific countries*

Asian Americans, 32, 33, 58–59, 81. *See also* Chinese Americans

Assal, Kareem El-, 203

assimilation. *See* acculturation

asylum and asylees: case studies, 11, 27, 39; claims to, 174, 187; definition, 20; Europe, 106–108; global migrant crisis (2011–2015), 18, 187; health of, 24, 111, 209; Personal Responsibility and Work Opportunity Reconciliation Act of 1996 (PRWORA), 78, 79; right of, 170; right to health, 99

Asylum Seekers' Benefits Law (Germany), 107–108

Attorney General of Canada, Canadian Doctors for Refugee Care v., 103–104

Australia: Department of Immigration and Citizenship, 48; disabilities, 49; Ebola outbreak (2014), 43, 191; economic impact of migration, 48; entry restrictions, 47–48, 191, 208; influenza, 43; healthy immigrant effect, 24; migrant health workers, 154, 158, 180; migrants from China, 70; migrants in, 18, 70; quarantine and isolation, 43, 70; tax burden of newcomers, 15; transplant tourism, 162; tuberculosis, 63, 66, 70

Austria, 106, 109

Aziga, Johnson, 11, 14

ABOUT THE AUTHORS

Patricia Illingworth is Professor in the Department of Philosophy and in the College of Business Administration at Northeastern University, where she is also Lecturer in Law. Professor Illingworth has held fellowships at Harvard Law School and at Harvard Medical School. She is the author of *AIDS and the Good Society*, *Trusting Medicine: The Moral Costs of Managed Care*, and *Us before Me: Ethics and Social Capital for Global Well-Being*. She is a co-editor, with Thomas Pogge and Leif Wenar, of *Giving Well: The Ethics of Philanthropy*. Her blog posts can be found on the Huffington Post.

Wendy E. Parmet is George J. and Kathleen Waters Matthews Distinguished Professor of Law and Professor of Public Policy and Urban Affairs at Northeastern University, where she directs the Center on Health Policy & Law. Professor Parmet has published widely on issues related to health law policy, and ethics and has served as lead counsel in *Finch v. Commonwealth Health Insurance Connector Authority*, which established the right of legal immigrants in Massachusetts to receive state-subsidized health insurance.